JOURNAL FOR THE STUDY OF THE NEW TESTAMENT
SUPPLEMENT SERIES

46

Executive Editor, Supplement Series
David Hill

Publishing Editor
David E Orton

JSOT Press
Sheffield

THE LAST
SHALL BE FIRST

The Rhetoric of Reversal in Luke

John O. York

Journal for the Study of the New Testament
Supplement Series 46

To
Anne,
Matt and Brad

Thanks for helping me never lose heart.

Copyright © 1991 Sheffield Academic Press

Published by JSOT Press
JSOT Press is an imprint of
Sheffield Academic Press Ltd
The University of Sheffield
343 Fulwood Road
Sheffield S10 3BP
England

Printed on acid-free paper in Great Britain
by Billing & Sons Ltd
Worcester

British Library Cataloguing in Publication Data

York, John O.
    The last shall be first.
    1. Bible. N.T. Luke—Critical Studies
    I. Title   II. Series
    226.406

    ISBN 1-85075-278-8
    ISSN 0143-5108

CONTENTS

Chapter 4
BI-POLAR REVERSAL AND AUDIENCE EXPECTATIONS:
THE FORM CONTEXTUALIZED IN THE

PREFACE

The completion and publication of this work would not have been possible without the help and support of a number of people. I am indebted to Vernon K. Robbins for his patient support of this project from its inception. Without his constructive help, the project would have floundered from the beginning. I also wish to thank Carl Holladay and Hendrikus Boers for their suggestions along the way, and Bob Detweiler for his enthusiastic response to the finished product.

I am indebted to my colleagues and the administration at Columbia Christian College for the time granted away from classroom and committee duties to complete the work. I also want to recognize the contributions made by members of the Hillcrest Church of Christ in Temple, Texas, all of whom listened to far too many sermons and classes on this subject!

The publication of this book owes much to Dr David Orton and Dr David Hill of Sheffield Academic Press. I am especially appreciative of the editorial contributions by Professor David Clines. These people saved the author from not a few embarrassing glitches in the finished product.

Finally, I wish to thank my family—my wife Anne and my sons, Matt and Brad—for their lasting love and longsuffering in living without a father and husband for too long, even when I was in the same room!

Chapter 1

INTRODUCTION

Long before modern literary criticism became a popular
method for approaching the Gospels the literary plot device of
reversal—Aristotle's περιπέτεια—was associated with particular texts in Luke–Acts. For over a century the parable of
the rich man and Lazarus has been described as presenting an
eschatological reversal of roles.[1] Likewise, Dodd and others
have noted that the beatitudes and woes reflect a reversal of
fortunes which the poor and the rich are to experience in the
new Kingdom.[2] However, the use of 'reversal' as a technical
term for a literary pattern or theme is a recent development.
The impetus for such usage has come primarily from literary
and structural studies of the parables and sayings of Jesus. In
studies of Luke–Acts, interest in the rich/poor motif has
prompted an extension of the use of reversal to other Lukan
passages. A recent dissertation by Larry Drake has even

1. See, e.g., the discussions of J.M. Creed, *The Gospel according to
St. Luke* (London: Macmillan, 1957), 208-14; F. Godet, *A Commentary
on the Gospel of St. Luke*, trans. from second French edition by E.W.
Shalders and M.D. Cusin (New York: I.K. Funk, 1881), 392-95.
2. C.H. Dodd, 'The Beatitudes: A Form-critical Study', *More New
Testament Studies* (Grand Rapids: Eerdmans, 1968), 1-10 (see esp.
pp. 4-6). This article was first published in 1955. Also see David
Seccombe, *Possessions and the Poor in Luke–Acts* (Studien zum
Neuen Testament und seiner Umwelt; Linz: Fuchs, 1982), 71, 173.
Seccombe notes that, as early as de Wette's *Exegetisches Handbuch
zum Neuen Testament* (1839), scholars grouped the beatitudes and
woes with the parable of the rich man and Lazarus as evidence for a
doctrine of eschatological reversal.

attempted to catalogue 'all of the reversals in Luke' in an effort to demonstrate reversal as a theme in this Gospel.[1] However, as the following history of research will demonstrate, no attempt has been made to define precisely what is meant by the term 'reversal' in the Lukan context and then to ascertain the purpose or function reversal has in the Gospel as a whole. A great deal of scholarly effort has focused on isolated sayings or parables, often removed from the Lukan context, in order to pursue the elusive historical Jesus, but no effort has been made to determine what purpose the author might have had for incorporating this pattern in his Gospel.

Previous Research

Although the style and literary artistry of Luke–Acts have long been noted and discussed,[2] and efforts have been made to compare Luke's vocabulary with that of other first-century writers, none of these discussions has included attempts to delineate particular literary themes or structures. This development occurred in Gospel studies with the rebirth of literary criticism, particularly through the impulse of Amos Wilder.[3] The literary interests were in some ways a reaction to form-critical approaches that dissected the text into small isolated units. Literary criticism renewed the task of seeing the text as a whole. In the case of Luke–Acts, this meant a renewed interest in viewing the two-volume work as a whole, as story in some sense. Attempts still were made to study independent units within the Gospels, such as parables and proverbs, but the focus was on the literary function of these units rather than peeling back the layers of historical devel-

1. Larry Drake, 'The Reversal Theme in Luke' (Ph.D. dissertation, St Louis University, 1985), 1.

2. See S.C. Carpenter, *Christianity according to St. Luke* (New York: Macmillan, 1919), 189ff.; H.J. Cadbury, *The Style and Literary Method of Luke–Acts* (Harvard Theological Studies, 6; Cambridge, MA: Harvard University Press, 1920); *idem*, 'Four Features of Lukan Style', in *Studies in Luke–Acts*, ed. Leander E. Keck and J. Louis Martyn (Philadelphia: Fortress, 1980), 87-102. The works of Cadbury were the standard for many years.

3. Amos Wilder, *Early Christian Rhetoric: The Language of the Gospel* (2nd edn; Cambridge, MA: Harvard University Press, 1971).

opment in a particular unit. As will be seen, these studies began to use the term 'reversal' in a technical sense to describe a motif found especially in many sayings and stories in the Gospel of Luke.

The second area in Luke–Acts studies in which the term 'reversal' is found repeatedly is the analysis of Luke's interest in special groups, particularly the rich and the poor. Efforts to explore special interest groups in Luke–Acts have been numerous since the development of redaction criticism and the rehabilitation of Luke as theologian.[1] Since Conzelmann, every scholar dealing with Luke–Acts has had to address the author's theological interests as well as historical and literary concerns. When combined with a modern (Western) societal interest in the socio-economic status of the oppressed, Luke–Acts has been fertile ground for trying to discover the teaching of Jesus and the early community on such matters.

The rich/poor motif generally has been studied in combination with—or in reaction to—studies in Lukan eschatology, since several passages dealing with the rich and the poor in Luke indicate that the two groups will experience a reversal of fortunes in the coming age. As suggested above, it is in connection with two texts in particular—the beatitudes and woes (6.20-26) and the rich man and Lazarus (16.19-31)—that the term 'reversal' has been applied most often. It is with these two texts, and the work of C.H. Dodd, that the survey of individual works begins. In his study of the beatitudes and woes in Luke, Dodd argued that the eschatological reversal was evidence of the common plot device mentioned by Aristotle in the *Poetics* and known as περιπέτεια.[2] The surprise reversal of fortunes was a common plot device in Greek tragedy and Dodd claimed that this was the literary background for the impending eschatological reversal to which Jesus referred in Luke 6.20-26 and 16.19-31. The latter, in fact, illustrated the reality of the reversal. There was no effort on Dodd's part, however, to expand the theme of reversal outside these texts, nor to elabo-

---

1. The pioneering work in Luke–Acts was Hans Conzelmann's *Die Mitte der Zeit*, first published in 1955 and later translated into English and entitled *The Theology of St. Luke*, trans. Geo. Buswell (New York: Harper and Row, 1961).
2. 'The Beatitudes', p. 7.

rate on the impact of these texts for the broader issue of eschatology in Luke–Acts.

Several scholars more recently have argued that reversal is a key ingredient in the self-understanding of an apocalyptic community.[1] George Nickelsburg has attempted, more specifically, to demonstrate its importance by exploring the relationship between *1 Enoch* 92–105 and the Gospel of Luke.[2] Seeking to build upon parallels between Luke and *1 Enoch* already pointed out by Aalen,[3] particularly the 'common conception of rich and poor, mighty and lowly',[4] Nickelsburg first analyzes the materials in *1 Enoch* 92–105 that depict the fate of the rich and the poor, the sinners and the righteous.[5] He concludes that a consistent pattern of denunciation of the rich runs throughout these texts. The rich, who have often obtained their wealth through falsehood and oppression of the poor and lowly, will be condemned in God's judgment and delivered to eternal punishment.[6] The righteous who have endured will then be rewarded.[7]

Nickelsburg then turns to Luke and looks at a series of passages, some of which have parallels in Mark and Matthew, in order to ascertain whether this is a common conception in

1. E.g. Paul D. Hanson, *The Dawn of Apocalyptic* (Philadelphia: Fortress, 1979), 434; Walter Pilgrim, *Good News to the Poor: Wealth and Poverty in Luke–Acts* (Minneapolis: Augsburg, 1981), 34.

2. G.W.E. Nickelsburg, 'Riches, the Rich, and God's Judgment in *1 Enoch* 92–105 and the Gospel According to Luke', *New Testament Studies* 25 (1978), 324-44. The foundation for this study is laid in 'The Apocalyptic Message of *1 Enoch* 92–105', *Catholic Biblical Quarterly* 39 (1977), 309-28. Here Nickelsburg describes the world-view of the author of *1 Enoch* as 'a world out of kilter, a world of unresolved tensions and polarities' (p. 311). Through a series of woes, exhortations, and predictions of the future, the author indicates that there will be a great reversal in which the righteous will be vindicated and the wicked rich will be brought down in the world to come (pp. 313-21).

3. S. Aalen, 'St. Luke's Gospel and the Last Chapters of *1 Enoch*', *New Testament Studies* 13 (1966), 1-13.

4. Nickelsburg, 'Riches', 326.

5. *Ibid.*, 326-32.

6. *Ibid.*, 332.

7. *Ibid.*, 331.

Luke only.[1] Nickelsburg concludes that 'The accumulation and holding of riches and possessions are inversely related to the possibility of salvation. In every passage that we have studied, riches or possessions are mentioned in the context of judgment or salvation.'[2] Particularly in the parable of the rich man and Lazarus, Nickelsburg notes that this judgment comes in the form of reversal after death, which is a common element in the judgment of *1 Enoch*.[3]

While concluding that the similarities between Luke and *1 Enoch* are sufficient to posit some sort of contact between them, Nickelsburg also suggests certain differences between the two. Luke's Gospel presents a greater opportunity for the rich to repent and be saved, and there is more attention paid to the physical circumstances of the poor.[4] The link between the apocalyptic eschatology of *1 Enoch* and Luke, and the fact that the entire discussion of Nickelsburg focuses on passages dealing with the rich and poor in Luke, are important for this study. There are certain questions that Nickelsburg does not address. If some contact between Luke and *1 Enoch* exists, does that indicate that Luke himself believes there will soon be some kind of eschatological reversal? Are there reversals in Luke that are not apocalyptic reversals of judgment? In terms of Lukan vocabulary, is the term 'rich' always to be equated with the term 'sinner', and 'poor' equated with 'righteous?' These parallels do not, in fact, always work in Luke,[5] suggesting other differences as well between *1 Enoch* and Luke.[6]

1. These are 1.46-55 (esp. vv. 51-53); 3.10-14; 6.20-26; 12.13-34; 14.12-14; 16.1-13, 16, 19-31; 18.1-8, 18, 18-30; 19.1-10.
2. *Ibid.*, 340.
3. *Ibid.*, 338 n. 60.
4. *Ibid.*, 341-42.
5. The term 'sinner' (ἁμαρτωλός) functions as a technical term for outcasts of society who, in fact, are 'righteous' because they receive the testimony of John and Jesus.
6. Philip Esler's socio-redaction critical study, *Community and Gospel in Luke–Acts* (Cambridge: Cambridge University Press, 1987), raises related questions about the comparison by Nickelsburg. Esler argues that, given the Jewish origins and audience of *1 Enoch*, it is doubtful that Luke's audience—which he assumes is primarily Gentile Christian—would have had prior contact with the writing. Esler also believes the purely eschatological nature of *1 Enoch* is different

The close connection between the rich/poor motif and apocalyptic or eschatological reversal is also seen in the work of
Richard Batey.[1] His study includes a section called 'Theology
of Reversal', in which he attributes the theme in the Gospels to
the apocalyptic thrust of Jesus' message. The new era would
be accompanied by a reversal of the existing social order.

> The respected in society would reject and in turn be excluded
> from the kingdom, while the poor and sinners would be admit-
> ted into membership. The apocalyptic theology of reversal car-
> ried with it the understanding that the economic structure
> would be subjected to reform, to be brought about by God's
> power. The ministry of Jesus itself was a sign of this turning of
> the tables, when the poor would be privileged and the rich
> excluded.[2]

Batey states that while the theology of reversal is present in
all three Synoptics, it is especially apparent in Luke. He discusses a variety of passages in Luke that exhibit reversal:
13.26-30 (cf. Mt. 8.11-12), 'outsiders' would sit at table in the
Kingdom, while Jews who were heirs would be thrust out;
14.16-24 (cf. Mt. 22.1-10), the original guests at the banquet
would be excluded and the common people would be brought
in off the streets; 15.11-32, the prodigal son and self-righteous
brother; 16.19-31, the rich man and Lazarus; the numerous
sayings about the 'first being last and the last first' (Mt. 19.30;
20.16; Mk 10.31; Lk. 13.30). The reversal in the Kingdom
would be most obvious in the economic order, as indicated by
the beatitudes and woes (Lk. 6.20-26).[3]

Several common assumptions surface in Batey's work with
regard to the reversal motif in the Gospels. First, while the
motif is present throughout the Synoptics, it is most prominent
in Luke. Second, the motif encompasses a variety of materials,
including prophetic sayings of Jesus, proverbs, and parables,
that are diverse in form and content but contain some sort of
reversal pattern. Third, the rich/poor motif is the most strik-

from Luke's broader concern for actual life situations. See his discussion on pp. 189-91.
1. R. Batey, *Jesus and the Poor* (New York: Harper and Row, 1972).
2. *Ibid.*, 18.
3. *Ibid.*, 20.

ing instance of reversal, as seen in the beatitudes and woes, and the rich man and Lazarus.

However, Batey is interested not in the Lukan use and understanding of reversal but in the apocalyptic thrust of Jesus' preaching. He is interested neither in demonstrating that reversal is necessarily limited to the mind-set of apocalyptic, nor in providing more than general assumptions about the definition of reversal. He assumes both of these, leaving such tasks to others.

In the work of Schottroff and Stegemann, a clearer definition of reversal in terms of the rich/poor motif in Luke begins to emerge.[1] They argue that there are two themes in Luke that are part of the oldest Jesus tradition: the reversal of the destitute situation of the poor in the coming kingdom of God, and the friendship of Jesus with tax collectors and sinners.[2] The earliest traceable traditions about Jesus' followers suggest these were poor, often sick and socially outcast Palestinians who believed there would soon be an eschatological reversal of situations in the coming kingdom of God. There the rich of this life would be poor, and the poor rich; the last socially, politically, and economically in this life would be first in the Kingdom. Schottroff and Stegemann believe this oldest tradition can be discovered through examination of the beatitudes in Lk. 6.20-22, the saying of Jesus about the difficulty of the rich entering the Kingdom (Mk 10.25 and par.), the proverb 'the first shall be last and the last first' (Mt. 20.16 and par.), the story of the rich man and Lazarus (Lk. 16.19-31), and the Magnificat (Lk. 1.46-54).[3] The authors note that the apocalyptic eschatology found in these texts is foreign and even offensive to a modern world-view[4] and to modern schol-

1. Luise Schottroff and Wolfgang Stegemann, *Jesus von Nazareth: Hoffnung der Armen* (Stuttgart: Kohlhammer, 1978).
2. *Ibid.*, 30. The themes of reversal and tax collectors/sinners are more thoroughly treated on pp. 30-47 and 47-53, respectively.
3. The Gospels themselves represent a stage in the tradition well-removed from this 'oldest tradition of Jesus'. A brief explanation of their method is given on pp. 29-30. Also see Schottroff's article, 'Das Magnificat und die älteste Tradition über Jesus von Nazareth', *Evangelische Theologie* 38 (1978), 298-313.
4. *Jesus von Nazareth*, 33-34.

arship.[1] They seek not to explain it away but rather to explain the reversal texts as the interpreter Luke later understood and used them.

Jesus' friendship with tax collectors and sinners is found in the most primitive form in Mt. 11.19Q, Mt. 21.31 and Mk 2.13-17.[2] Schottroff and Stegemann believe the numerous references in Luke to these groups indicate a particular concern and modification by the author for his purposes. Texts that reflect the contrast between tax-collectors/sinners and Pharisees/Scribes in Luke have been edited by Luke to fit the needs of his late first-century Hellenistic audience.[3] Schottroff and Stegemann argue that Luke had no interest in the actual identity of Pharisees in Jesus' time. Rather they represented the wealthy, esteemed classes of society within Luke's audience.[4] These texts are thus used in conjunction with all of the other texts in Luke dealing with the rich and the poor. The message intended through all of this is not consolation or adulation of the poor or poverty, but a severe critique of the rich Christians in Luke's audience.[5]

Thus, while Schottroff and Stegemann believe that the Gospels, particularly Luke, contain hints of a primitive belief in eschatological reversal, their interpretation focuses on how Luke reinterpreted the texts. The blessing of the poor and needy is seen as an idealization of primitive community practice. The early disciples were depicted as freely choosing poverty as a lifestyle.[6] Luke, however, understands this only as an idealization intended to cause the wealthy in his audience to renounce their need for and trust in possessions.[7] In a similar manner, the eschatological reversal serves as a warning to

1. *Ibid.*, 45-47.
2. *Ibid.*, 48.
3. Cf. *ibid.*, 47, 114-18, and their discussion of Pharisees as 'lovers of money' (Lk. 16.14), on pp. 122-24. On pp. 114-18 they discuss Lk. 5.30; 15.1f.; 18.9-14; 7.36-50; 14.1-24; 7.11-17.
4. *Ibid.*, 123.
5. *Ibid.*, 119-35. In their conclusion, Schottroff and Stegemann argue that the center of Luke's concern is neither the hope of the poor, nor an ethic of mercy which takes care of the needy, but the rich themselves (pp. 150-51).
6. *Ibid.*, 102-104.
7. *Ibid.*, 108-13.

rich Christians that wealth should be properly used and dis-
tributed within the church community so that none within the
Christian community are destitute.[1]

Two points are important for the present study. One is the
effort to separate the Lukan understanding from the primitive tradition. The fact that so many of the texts presenting an
eschatological reversal are preserved only in Luke makes it
difficult to accept the claim of Schottroff and Stegemann that
the reversal pattern—or at least the eschatological content of
the reversal pattern—has little meaning for the author of the
Gospel. Their decision to eliminate eschatological reversal
from Luke seems to be based upon modern theological tastes
and a preconceived understanding of Lukan eschatology. On
the positive side, demonstrating that the contrast of sinner/tax
collector versus Pharisee/Scribe is thematically related to the
rich/poor motif is a significant contribution.[2]

The study by Pilgrim of wealth and poverty in Luke–Acts
makes extensive use of the work of Schottroff and Stegemann,
but differs somewhat in its conclusions.[3] Indeed, Pilgrim
believes the rich/poor passages in Luke–Acts reflect actual
conditions, and a promised reversal for the downtrodden.

> With the coming of God's redemption in Christ the great rever-
> sal of status is underway and God manifests his bias for the poor
> and lowly. Thus we find anticipated already in the Magnificat
> the theme of the beatitudes and woes. Any attempt to spiritualize
> the text in such a way as to avoid its social impact will not do it
> justice. For it speaks unequivocally of the saving God who acts

---

1. *Ibid.*, 149-53. In their conclusion, they cite passages in Acts which
demonstrate this interpretation, e.g. Acts 2.41-47, 4.32-37, and the negative example of Ananias and Sapphira (5.1-11).

2. I.H. Marshall, *Luke: Historian and Theologian* (Grand Rapids:
Zondervan, 1971), in a brief treatment of reversal, also links the two
motifs, but for different reasons. Marshall argues that the reversal is
not temporal or eschatological but spiritual. The message of the
rich/poor passages is best seen in the parable of the Pharisee and publican (18.9-14), where the issue is self-justification versus justification
by God. The brevity of Marshall's comments necessitates assuming
such connections to be valid rather than demonstrating the claims.

3. Walter E. Pilgrim, *Good News to the Poor*. For his use of Schottroff
and Stegemann, see p. 181 n. 26.

with justice to bring down the proud and oppressors and to exalt the lowly and oppressed.[1]

The identity of the 'poor' in Luke is linked to the Jewish *anawim*, the pious poor first seen in the Psalms and found throughout later Jewish writings.[2] In the New Testament the *anawim* mentality can best be seen in the infancy narrative of Luke and in the piety presupposed by the first two beatitudes of the sermons in Matthew and Luke.[3] Through an examination of texts in Luke which reflect the 'oldest traditions in the Gospels',[4] Pilgrim concludes that the appearance of Jesus sounded the dawn of the reign of God. Associated with the fulfillment of that reign was a coming reversal that was 'God's way of making right the present social disorders and injustices'.[5]

Pilgrim then looks at the inaugural sermon of Jesus' ministry in Luke (4.16-21) and related texts that proclaim 'good news to the poor'.[6] His intent in the chapter is to demonstrate the centrality of this theme for the Lukan Jesus, and that the 'poor' are suffering from literal poverty and suffering.[7] In the chapter he also connects Jesus' message of hope to sinners and

---

1. *Ibid.*, 79.
2. *Ibid.*, 30. The *anawim* can be traced through apocalyptic literature such as *1 Enoch* 92–105, in certain Qumran texts, and other intertestamental Jewish writings. See *ibid.*, pp. 33-36.
3. *Ibid.*, 56.
4. *Ibid.*, 57-63. The texts are Lk. 6.20-21 (Mt. 5.3-9); 16.19-26; 1.52-53; 13.30 (par. Mk 10.31; Mt. 19.30; 20.16). This list corresponds to the list developed by Schottroff and Stegemann.
5. *Ibid.*, 63. David Seccombe's work, *Possessions and the Poor in Luke–Acts*, should also be noted at this point. He also analyzes 1.46-54, 6.20-26, and 16.19-31, but concludes that these passages do not reflect any reversal at all. Rather, they simply contrast the true characterization of Israel with that of the nations. The poor and the humble are the true Israel; the rich and exalted are the nations which oppress Israel, and have no part in their salvation. While Seccombe denies any reversal in these passages, he seems to be referring to economic reversals in particular, since he does indicate that the nations will have no part in the true Israel's salvation. That would seem to suggest some form of eschatological reversal. See his pp. 71-95.
6. *Ibid.*, 64-84. The other texts are 7.18-23; 14.13, 21; 6.20-23; and the first two chapters of Luke.
7. *Ibid.*, 83.

social outcasts with the message to the poor. Citing such texts as Lk. 5.31; 19.10; 18.9-14; 15.1-2; 7.18-35, Pilgrim demonstrates Jesus' acceptance of these people and, conversely, his rejection of their constant opponents, the Pharisees.[1] They become a part of the poor and needy in contrast to the rich and powerful, all of whom are promised a 'radical social reversal of their lot in the coming age'.[2]

Pilgrim then turns his attention to Jesus' message to the wealthy in Luke. He notes, in a similar fashion to Schottroff and Stegemann, the critique of wealth and the wealthy. His conclusions are similar, except for his maintenance of a Lukan interest in a final eschatological reversal.[3] It is, in fact, this expected reversal that provides the ultimate hope for the poor and the greatest warning to the rich and powerful.[4] Like Schottroff and Stegemann, however, Pilgrim is uncomfortable with the belief in an actual eschatological reversal, and in his final chapter states that the validity of such a claim lies in the way in which such a hope spurs people to action in the present. Jesus himself announced the dawn of the Kingdom even in his own life and ministry.[5] Furthermore, the hope for the poor in the present is tied, for Luke, to the fellowship of the new community, where hopes of the future are a present reality. The

1. *Ibid.*, 81-82. Speaking of the acceptance of sinners/outcasts by Jesus, Pilgrim states, 'In this sense, "the first will be last and the last first", and God's promised eschatological reversal for the poor has already become a reality in the ministry of Jesus' (p. 82).
2. *Ibid.*, 83. Pilgrim goes on to say, 'The poor also include the sick and the possessed, those living on the edge of society, who are offered healing and full acceptance within the fellowship gathered around the healer. They include as well the outcasts and sinners, those excluded socially and religiously because of despised professions and immoral lives, who are welcomed back into the Father's good graces, and offered a new status of full participation in the community gathered around Jesus and his disciples. They include even the disciples of Jesus, who have left all in his service, and who await with eager anticipation the coming deliverance, when the lowly will be exalted and the mighty brought low.'
3. See *ibid.*, pp. 90, 92, 100, for Pilgrim's agreement with Schottroff and Stegemann. For his interest in the eschatological reversal see pp. 104-107.
4. *Ibid.*, 161.
5. *Ibid.*

rich, in turn, are challenged to share their possessions in the present, with Zacchaeus as the example of the new standard.[1] The questions raised by Pilgrim's study are similar to the preceding one by Schottroff and Stegemann. Pilgrim argues in opposition to Schottroff and Stegemann that the eschatological element remains for Luke in the reversals. He also argues that the message to the poor refers to those who actually live in poverty within Luke's audience as well as the hearers of Jesus. He cannot say, as Schottroff and Stegemann, that Luke's Gospel is 'the gospel for the rich'. It is the gospel for the pious poor, the *anawim*, and also contains an admonition on the proper use of wealth.[2] In agreement with Stegemann and Schottroff, Pilgrim incorporates the sinners and outcasts into the class of the poor, and notes that some of those texts indicate reversal in the present age. A question that emerges here is whether the rich/poor motif and the sinner/outcast versus Pharisee/Scribe motif should not be incorporated into a more encompassing eschatological reversal motif.

The study by Luke Johnson serves as a bridge between treatments of the rich/poor motif and literary concerns. Building upon the suggestion of Nils Dahl that prophetic fulfillment was expanded and refined by Luke into a literary method,[3] Johnson uses 'proof from prophecy' as a means of understanding Luke–Acts as story. An examination of the characters in Luke's narrative reveals that the main characters of Luke–Acts—Jesus and his apostles[4]—fit the prophetic model of Moses, and that the narrative revolves around the pattern of acceptance and rejection of their prophetic message

---

1. *Ibid.*, 164-66.
2. Pilgrim's belief that the core group of Luke's audience were *anawim*, as were the disciples of Jesus, may be unwarranted. Schottroff and Stegemann would disagree with this, as would Robert J. Karris, who argues that many in Luke's audience were wealthy and that these passages are intended as warnings rather than consolation. See 'Poor and Rich: The Lukan Sitz im Leben', *Perspectives on Luke–Acts*, ed. Charles Talbert (Danville, PA: Association of Baptist Professors of Religion, 1978), 112-25.
3. *Ibid.*, 15. See Nils Dahl, 'The Story of Abraham in Luke–Acts', *Studies in Luke–Acts*, 152.
4. *The Literary Function of Possessions in Luke–Acts* (Missoula, MT: Scholars Press, 1977), 23.

by the masses.[1] After developing this model in Acts, Johnson turns to the Gospel to develop a model of Jesus as the rejected prophet. The prophecy of Simeon in 2.34 is seen as programmatic for the rest of the Gospel and Acts. It implicitly depicts the way in which people will be divided over the prophet and his message.[2]

In his discussion of Lk. 6.20-26 Johnson explicitly speaks of 'divine reversal' in Luke.[3]

> There is a double pattern of reversal in the beatitudes and woes: a) The present situation of the poor and rejected will be reversed by God (6.23). b) The blessings given to the poor are contrasted to the woes levelled at the rich.[4]

The reversals are prophetic oracles of judgment to those who are accepting the prophet and his message (the poor) and those who are rejecting it (the rich).[5] The Magnificat also takes up the theme of the raising of the poor (in this case ταπεινοί instead of πτωχοί) and the lowering of the rich and powerful. Johnson identifies the poor and lowly with all of those in Luke who are social outcasts.[6] The rich belong to the cast of characters identified as socially and politically acceptable and powerful, as do the Pharisees who are 'lovers of money' (16.14). He concludes that wealth and poverty are not important values in themselves but rather reflect the spiritual character of those who are accepting or rejecting the prophet like Moses.[7]

As already stated, Johnson's concerns are literary. Possessions or economic status are addressed only in terms of their relationship to the literary pattern of the prophet and the peo-

---

1. *Ibid.*, 77-78.
2. *Ibid.*, 91.
3. Johnson treats several other texts to which other scholars ascribe the term reversal, such as 4.16-30; 7.36-50; 15.1–16.31. However, his interest is solely in showing how these texts exemplify the rejection/acceptance pattern. See *ibid.*, pp. 92-110.
4. *Ibid.*, 135.
5. *Ibid.*
6. *Ibid.*, 137. He cites 3.4-6; 14.7-24; 18.14 as examples of other social outcasts who fit this category.
7. *Ibid.*, 140. He illustrates this by an analysis of the Lukan parable of the rich man and Lazarus, pp. 140-44.

ple. Reversal as an eschatological event or as a literary pattern is rarely mentioned although Johnson often refers to the same texts addressed by scholars like Pilgrim, Schottroff and Stegemann. However, in a shorter booklet summarizing the conclusions of his dissertation, Johnson devotes an entire section to 'Eschatology as Reversal'.[1] Johnson indicates that reversal is not simply a literary theme, but rather, 'it expresses the heart of the Gospel'.[2]

> God's word is a disquieting visitor. Indeed, a characteristic of Luke's Good News is that God reverses human expectations. We know it is God's kingdom when it doesn't look the way we think it should. As the Magnificat announced: 'He has put down the mighty from their thrones and exalted those of low degree; he has filled the hungry with good things and the rich he has sent empty away'. Luke's gospel narrative plays out the reversal.[3]

Johnson's comments introduce literary interests in reversal not found in previous studies of the rich and poor. He suggests that the reversal is one of human expectations, and that Luke's narrative demonstrates the reversal. He does not effectively describe how this is to be understood as eschatological reversal, nor specifically how Luke's narrative demonstrates this 'reversal of human expectations'. The audience Johnson appears to have in mind is a modern one, not Luke's auditors or those who might have heard this from Jesus.[4]

The work of Nils Dahl preceded Johnson's and, in a similar fashion, suggested the importance of a reversal theme in Luke–Acts. In an article entitled 'The Purpose of Luke–Acts', Dahl states that the theme of reversal is represented in Luke–Acts as the normal way God deals with his people.[5] Dahl understands such reversal to be a part of a proof-from-

---

1. *Luke–Acts: A Story of Prophet and People* (Chicago: Franciscan Herald Press, 1981), 59-60.

2. *Ibid.*, 60.

3. *Ibid.*, 59.

4. In fairness to Johnson, the latter two audiences are not of interest to him in this short study.

5. In *Jesus in the Memory of the Early Church* (Minneapolis: Augsburg, 1976), 91. Joseph Fitzmyer (*The Gospel according to Luke I–IX*, Anchor Bible [New York: Doubleday, 1981], 10) mentions the reversal theme in Luke–Acts and refers only to this article by Dahl for support.

prophecy motif in Luke–Acts that is evident particularly in the speeches of Acts 2–5, 10, and 13. The 'turning of the tables' is anticipated first in the Magnificat and recounted in the Gospel in stories and sayings that reflect help and salvation for the poor while the rich and mighty are being excluded.[1] The Gospel narrative also anticipates the reversals of the second volume by 'predicting that the kingdom is to be given to the apostles who had shared the trials of Jesus—in contrast to the leaders of Israel who had rejected him'.[2] In Acts, reversal is seen in the repeated way in which church leaders suffer adversity but are miraculously delivered and the gospel promoted.[3] Dahl also proposes that the reversal theme is closely linked to Old Testament fulfillment in Luke–Acts. The reversal pattern makes possible the exclusion of unbelieving Jews and the inclusion of believing Gentiles in Luke's presentation.[4] The most significant aspect of the study is Dahl's claim that reversal is central to the overall message of Luke–Acts. It is also important to note that Dahl understands this theme to have its roots completely within the context of Old Testament prophetic fulfillment.

Dahl's only support for his thesis is a reference to a dissertation by David Adams.[5] Adams's dissertation does indeed treat reversal, but only in Acts, and only within the context of his study of Luke's presentation of Paul. Adams includes a section on the 'turning of the tables' motif in which he argues this is a frequent pattern in the life of Paul.[6] It is seen most noticeably in the ironic reversal of Paul the persecutor to Paul the persecuted.[7] It is further developed in the repeated experiences of Paul of being bound, imprisoned, beaten, even shipwrecked on his journeys, but always escaping triumphant.[8] The death of Jesus and his victorious resurrection/exaltation provide the

1. 'The Purpose of Luke–Acts', 91.
2. *Ibid.*
3. *Ibid.*
4. *Ibid.*, 96.
5. 'The Suffering of Paul and the Dynamics of Luke–Acts' (Ph.D. dissertation, Yale University, 1979).
6. *Ibid.*, 22-27.
7. *Ibid.*, 23-24.
8. *Ibid.*, 35-36.

reversal pattern and theological context for Paul's repeated sufferings and deliverance and other similar reversals recorded in Acts.

> The rapid reversals of fortune Paul undergoes are anticipated in the careers of Jesus and Stephen, and also the prophets and apostles, whose own adversity culminates in vindication if not outright success. God exalts those of low degree, including those who suffer unjustly. By the time Paul enters the plot, the element of role reversal has assumed the status of *Leitmotif*, and it is in accord with it that Luke models Paul's story. Again it is not so much the fact of reversal as the fact of its persistence that is striking.[1]

Adams's work has been the only effort to trace reversal in Luke's second volume. Adams demonstrates the way in which one aspect of the double reversals often found in the Gospel is carried over into Acts, namely, that of the exaltation of the lowly. The lowly in the Gospel represent the followers of Jesus in Acts whose fortunes are repeatedly reversed, not simply in an eschatological sense, but in their physical circumstances. It seems doubtful, however, that Luke's repeated use of a double pattern in the Gospel was intended to be understood solely as a support for the motif of suffering/exaltation of the church leaders in Acts.

Paul Minear's book, *To Heal and to Reveal*, includes a section called 'The Reversal of Directions'.[2] He seeks to demonstrate how Jesus' teaching on authority reverses the 'directional flow of societal power'.[3] Those with access to this new power introduced by Jesus are not the wise and understanding, nor the rich and powerful, but the powerless poor, the blind, the lame, the weak. Jesus' own lowliness shows 'the mystery of how weakness had become the channel for God's power'.[4] Minear also speaks of the way in which such a presentation reverses normal human expectations. It is not the wise who hear and understand, but babes (Lk. 10.21-23).[5] The

1. *Ibid.*, 293.
2. Paul S. Minear, *To Heal and to Reveal: The Prophetic Vocation according to Luke* (New York: Seabury, 1976), 19-30.
3. *Ibid.*, 20.
4. *Ibid.*, 75.
5. *Ibid.*, 41-42.

direction of authority and reception of power is thus reversed in the new Kingdom. Addressing the meaning of Lk. 7.28, Minear concludes

> 'Greater than John' are the poor, the captives, the blind, the oppressed, the impotent who, baptized by the Spirit, have received forgiveness of sins, together with the other gifts of God in this new age. The paradoxical form of the saying may also indicate how the advent of the kingdom reversed all criteria of Greatness. Not only does the new age give priority to the humblest, life within that age is organized around the law that the least become the greatest.[1]

Minear's comments again suggest that reversal is a pervasive motif in Luke. However, his work is written on a popular level, and no effort is made to treat systematically the texts that demonstrate reversal, nor even to define the motif beyond the way in which all is reversed in the Kingdom. Throughout his discussion Minear is not interested in the eschatological content of these reversals, but the way in which they present a new consciousness—the mind of the disciple in the new kingdom, a kingdom experienced by the early Christian community.[2]

---

1. *Ibid.*, 119.
2. Three other works should be mentioned which briefly discuss reversal in Luke. John Drury, in his redactional study, *Tradition and Design in Luke's Gospel* (Atlanta: John Knox, 1976), 53-54, states in his discussion of the infancy narrative that the pattern of the reversal of fortunes announced in the Magnificat is the 'structure of Luke's story'. However, Drury only refers to the pattern on four other occasions (pp. 64, 77, 104, 135f.) and never actually demonstrates how reversal is the structure of the Gospel. The dissertation of James Dawsey, 'The Literary Function of Point of View in Controlling Confusion and Irony in the Gospel of Luke' (Ph.D dissertation, Emory University, 1983), esp. pp. 303-14—revised and published as *The Lukan Voice: Confusion and Irony in the Gospel of Luke* (Macon, GA: Mercer, 1986); and the article by James Resseguie, 'Point of View in the Central Section of Luke (9.51–19.44)', *Journal of the Evangelical Theological Society* 25 (1982), 41-47, both discuss the reversal motif as it relates to point of view. Dawsey links the reversal motif to Jesus' point of view—Jesus is the transformer of society; God is turning society upside down through him. Resseguie also sees this reversal of society, but speaks of it in terms of how others react to Jesus. Both seem to reject the notion that only an eschatological reversal of fortunes is proclaimed in the Gospel. Rather the motif must be seen within the

F.W. Danker's recently revised commentary on Luke in the Proclamation Commentary series contains an entirely new chapter entitled 'Reversal of Fortunes'.[1] He begins his discussion by giving examples of περιπέτεια from ancient Greek works such as Sophocles' *King Oedipus*, and then links the reversal of fortunes found in Greek literature to similar reversals found in Luke.[2] When Danker begins to explore the Gospel and Acts for examples of reversal, he finds an almost limitless supply.

> There is no end of peripeteia! Ordinary fishers and a publican named Levi become privileged partners of the New Age Deliverer (5.1-11, 27-32); a leper joins Naaman in receipt of healing (vv. 12-16); a paralytic (vv. 17-26) becomes the beneficiary of forgiveness that was announced at Nazareth; and another sufferer has his hand restored to usefulness (6.6-11). Jesus calls a halt to a widow's lamentations (7.11-17). And a notorious woman is raised to honorable status.[3]

Danker proceeds to list more than 50 references to various healings, sayings, and narratives that depict some kind of reversal in Luke–Acts.[4] Most helpful, however, is his discussion of a common Greek literary feature that would have been familiar to Luke's audience when employed by Luke, the 'then–now' motif. He demonstrates from Homer and later Hellenistic writings the technique of νῦν δέ, used to compare

---

Lukan framework in which the focus is on the age of the church and 'turning the tables' of society in the present age. The overall interests of Dawsey and Resseguie, however, are not focused on reversal as such, and their contribution to the study, like Drury's, is limited.

1. Frederick W. Danker (*Luke*, Proclamation Commentaries, 2nd edn; Philadelphia: Fortress, 1987), 47-57. Danker describes the revised version of this work as an introductory volume to his also recently revised commentary, *Jesus and the New Age* (Philadelphia: Fortress, 1988).

2. *Luke*, 47-49. Particularly important is the quotation of the Greek poet Archilochos (pp. 48-49), which Danker compares to the Magnificat (1.51-53): 'The deities are ever just. Full oft they raise those who lie prostrate on the darkened earth. Full oft the prosperous are tripped, their bellies to the sky; and miseries untold attend them. Mindless, in aimless poverty they wander.'

3. *Ibid.*, 51.

4. *Ibid.*, 51-53.

past and present circumstances.[1] Danker suggests such a pattern would readily have been seen by a Graeco-Roman audience in Lk. 6.20-26 and 16.19-31.[2] The other feature of the time period to which Danker draws attention was a social progression which he described as *koros–hybris–atē* (satiety–insolence–retribution). He finds this pattern particularly in passages such as Lk. 12.16-21 and Acts 12.20-26.[3]

Danker's work is not intended to be a detailed analysis,[4] but he does raise a very important issue, namely, the relationship between reversal texts in Luke and the understanding of a Graeco-Roman audience. While it may be true that many of the reversal images in Luke–Acts have Old Testament antecedents, Danker argues that the literary use of reversal would have been readily apparent apart from one's background in the Septuagint.[5]

Literary critical studies that analyzed particular forms within the Gospels have repeatedly described some type of reversal, most often a reversal of expectations forced upon the hearer by the saying or parable. William Beardslee's discussion of the proverbial material in the Gospels is representative of studies on proverbs and aphorisms.[6] Referring to the wis-

---

1. *Ibid.*, 53-55.

2. *Ibid.*, 54-55.

3. *Ibid.*, 55. Danker also discusses briefly the relationship between cosmic fate and the controlling actions of God (p. 55). However, he cites no ancient texts and moves on to discuss the portrayal of Jesus as the humiliated savior raised from the dead by God and the impact of that reversal on the rest of the story in Luke–Acts (pp. 56-57).

4. By finding examples of περιπέτεια literally everywhere in the Gospel and Acts, the subject becomes almost meaningless. Greater definition and clarity of structure is needed to sustain the importance of reversal as either a literary or a theological concept.

5. Danker begins this chapter (p. 47) by saying, 'The second major indicator of Luke's ability to probe Greek, as well as Jewish, experience, is his mastery of the theme of altered or reversed fortunes (*peripeteia*)'. Earlier in the book (p. 5) he states, 'It is not helpful, therefore, to think narrowly in terms of what some have called "Luke's community". Rather, his work suggests a variety of publics, among them especially Greco-Romans, some acquainted with Jewish Tradition and others not.'

6. William A. Beardslee, *Literary Criticism of the New Testament* (Philadelphia: Fortress, 1969), 30-41; 'Parable, Proverb, and Koan', *Semeia* 12 (1978), 151-78; 'Saving One's Life by Losing It', *Journal of*

dom tradition out of which the proverb arises, Beardslee states,
'It is evident in the most characteristic synoptic sayings that
wisdom is immensely concentrated and intensified. The primary means of intensification are hyperbole and paradox.'[1]
The paradoxical proverbs—such as 'The last will be first and
the first last'; 'He who humbles himself will be exalted; he who
exalts himself will be humbled'—often are labeled reversal
texts. Beardslee notes that this antithetical form has ancient
roots, historically. He states:

> Here, the reversal situation is so sharp that the imagination is
> jolted out of its vision of continuous connection between one situ-
> ation and the other... The paradox of intensified antithesis is
> putting pressure on the very presupposition in which the clus-
> ters of wisdom insights had been gathered together. This pre-
> supposition is the project of making a continuous whole out of
> one's existence. All the antithetical sayings about reversal of
> status involve some shaking up of the project, but the final one
> in the series involves such a paradox that the visible, or better,
> the conscious continuity of the project is done away.[2]

Beardslee goes on to discuss hyperbolic proverbs such as
those found in Lk. 9.56-58 ('Foxes have holes..., Leave the
dead...'). Here hyperbole is used, like paradox, to jolt the
hearer out of his/her typical understanding of life.[3] Both forms
of proverb thus serve to challenge or even shatter one's prior
form of existence, to break down the attempt to construct a
framework for living.[4] Beardslee's studies do not specifically
address the question of how Luke and his audience understood

American Academy of Religion 47 (1979), 57-72; 'Uses of the Proverb in
the Synoptic Gospels', *Interpretation* 24 (1970), 61-73.
   1. 'Uses of the Proverb', 66.
   2. *Ibid.*, 67. The 'final one' to which Beardslee refers is the proverb
'Whoever seeks to gains his life will lose it; whoever loses his life will
preserve it' (Lk. 17.33, par.).
   3. *Ibid.*, 68-70.
   4. *Ibid.*, 72. Also see Robert Tannehill's discussion of antithetic aphorisms in *The Sword of His Mouth* (Missoula: Scholars Press, 1975), 88-
102; John D. Crossan, *In Fragments: The Aphorisms of Jesus* (San
Francisco: Harper and Row, 1983); Charles E. Carlston, 'Proverbs,
Maxims, and the Historical Jesus', *Journal of Biblical Literature* 99
(1980), 87-105; James G. Williams, *Those Who Ponder Proverbs: Aphoristic Thinking and Biblical Literature* (Sheffield: Almond, 1981).

these proverbs, but rather how such sayings function inde-
pendently to call hearers to re-evaluate their present circumstances.

Perrin's study of the language of the Kingdom also treats
sayings of Jesus that contain eschatological reversal.[1] He
states that eschatological reversal 'is one of the best attested
themes of the message of Jesus. It proclaims the Kingdom as
eschatological reversal of the present and so invites, indeed
demands, judgment upon that present'.[2] These sayings are
often proverbial in form and their proclamation of the coming
Kingdom causes the hearer to be 'jolted out of the effort to
make a continuous whole of human existence'.[3] As in the case
of Beardslee, Perrin is interested in the impact of reversal on
the hearer, the way in which reversal sayings 'shake the
foundations' of one's existence. Perrin agrees with Crossan in
identifying reversal as a key ingredient in parables.[4] Like the
proverbial saying these parables proclaim the coming Kingdom 'in dramatic reversal, in the clash of worlds, in the sud-
den unexpected transection of the everyday by the incursion of
the divine'.[5]

Semeia 2 is devoted to literary and structural analyses of the
parables and many of the articles in the volume discuss to
some degree the element of reversal.[6] The most important discussion is found in the article of William Doty, where he
attempts to describe and define 'the structural element in the
parables of Jesus that causes a reversal of the auditors' expec-

---

1. Norman Perrin, *Jesus and the Language of the Kingdom: Symbol
and Metaphor in New Testament Interpretation* (Philadelphia:
Fortress, 1974).
2. *Ibid.*, 52.
3. *Ibid.*, 195.
4. See the discussion of Crossan below.
5. *Jesus and the Language of the Kingdom*, 196.
6. See G. Crespy, 'The Parable of the Good Samaritan: An Essay in
Structural Research', 49-50; J.D. Crossan, 'The Good Samaritan:
Towards a Generic Definition of Parable', 82-112; Robert W. Funk,
'Structure in the Narrative Parables of Jesus', 69-71; Amos Wilder,
'The Parable of the Sower: Naivete and Method', 139, in *Semeia* 2
(1974).

tations'.[1] Doty accepts Via's conclusion that there is an element of reversal in the tragic/comic narrative patterns of the
parables,[2] but wishes to attain greater precision in 'describing
the technique of reversal itself'.[3] He describes the jarring element in parables that disorients the hearer as the 'immoral'
factor.[4] After demonstrating this principle at work in a number of Jesus' parables,[5] Doty defines the reversal element in the
following way:

> One of the structural literary characteristics of parabolic narra-
> tive is the reversal of expectations brought by the auditors/read-
> ers to the parabolic encounter; the reversal happens toward the
> end of the narrative, in such a way as to shatter 'normal' or
> 'moral' expectations, and to open up further expectations by
> casting out a line to the future, which may or may not
> sufficiently attract the auditors/readers so as to structure a
> renewed perception of the pre-parabolic universe.[6]

1. 'The Parables of Jesus, Kafka, Borges, and Others, with Structural
Observations', 171.
2. See Dan O. Via, *The Parables: Their Literary and Existential
Dimension* (Philadelphia: Fortress, 1967), and *Kerygma and Comedy
in the New Testament* (Philadelphia: Fortress, 1971).
3. 'The Parables', 171.
4. 'By this I refer to the way the contemporary audience's social,
legal, and moral expectations were not only not met, but reversed in
the course of the story. There is an "immoral" reversal which cannot
be anticipated: no pious father could have been expected to have welcomed openly a profligate son whose religious purity had been seriously compromised (Prodigal Son); an unclean foreigner (Good
Samaritan) rather than the anticipated pious layman, tends the trav-
eler's wounds' (pp. 172-73).
5. Doty describes the following parables as 'immoral': Mustard Seed
(Mt., Mk); Weeds in Wheat (Mt.); Leaven (Mt., Lk.); Treasure, Pearl
(Mt.); Lost Sheep (Mt., Lk.); Laborers in Vineyard (Mt.); Marriage
Feast (Mt., Lk.); Ten Maidens (Mt.); Talents (Mt., Lk.); Good Samaritan (Lk.); Prodigal Son (Lk.); Unjust Judge and Unjust Steward (Lk.).
On the other hand, 'moral' parables, which come out just as one
expects, are: the Unmerciful Servant, the Seed Growing Secretly, and
the Last Judgment, in Matthew; the Sower in Matthew, Mark, and
Luke; the Tower Builder, the Rich Man and Lazarus, and the Pharisee
and the Publican in Luke; and the House Builder in Matthew and
Luke (p. 178).
6. *Ibid.*, 176.

Doty's definition is not concerned with eschatological reversal, or with terminology or form that suggests reversal, but with the way in which hearer expectations are reversed. Such a definition assumes one can determine accurately what the first-century audience—of Jesus, or one of the Gospel writers—actually heard and thought, which is a presumptive task. Doty does not attempt to explore the nature of such audiences but assumes the reversals would function then as they seem to now, since the factors he describes seem 'immoral' to a modern audience.

The most important description of parables of reversal has been given by Crossan. In *The Dark Interval: Towards a Theology of Story*, he says:

> The parables of Jesus are not historical allegories telling us how God acts with mankind; neither are they moral example stories telling us how to act before God and towards one another. They are stories which shatter the deep structure of our accepted world and thereby render clear and evident to us the relativity of story itself. They make us vulnerable to God. It is only in such experiences that God can touch us, and only in such moments does the Kingdom of God arrive. My own term for this relationship is transcendence.[1]

His work *In Parables: The Challenge of the Historical Jesus* includes a chapter entitled 'Parables of Reversal'.[2] All of the parables discussed in this chapter are found in the travel narrative of Luke, and only one (The Great Supper, 14.15-24) is paralleled in other Gospel accounts.[3] In defining his use of the term reversal, Crossan writes:

> Jesus' parables of reversal are not single reversals and not even double or parallel reversals. They are what might best be termed polar reversals. If the last becomes first, we have the story of Joseph. If the first becomes last, we have the story of Job. But if

1. J.D. Crossan, *The Dark Interval: Towards a Theology of Story* (Allen, TX: Argus Communications, 1975), 121-22.
2. *In Parables: The Challenge of the Historical Jesus* (New York: Harper and Row, 1973), 53-57.
3. The other parables discussed are: The Good Samaritan, 10.25-37; The Rich Man and Lazarus, 16.19-31; The Pharisee and the Publican, 18.9-14; The Wedding Guests, 14.7-11; The Proper Guests, 14.12-14; The Prodigal Son, 15.11-32; also the narrative of the banquet in 14.1-6.

the last becomes first *and* the first becomes last we have a polar reversal, a reversal of the world as such. When the north pole becomes the south pole, and the south the north, a world is reversed and overturned and we find ourselves standing firmly on utter uncertainty. The parables of reversal intend to do precisely this to our security because such is the advent of the kingdom.[1]

With this understanding in mind Crossan attempts to extract the historical parable from the example stories of the Lukan redaction and demonstrate how each reflects this polar reversal.[2] He constructs the following chart, using the terms 'good' and 'bad' in an ontological rather than ethical sense,[3] in order to illustrate how the two 'expected' sides reverse roles in the parables.

GOOD	BAD
Priest and Levite	Samaritan
Rich Man	Lazarus
Pharisee	Publican
First-Seated	Last-Seated
Invited Guests	Uninvited Guests
Dutiful Son	Prodigal Son

He concludes, 'Such double and opposite reversal is the challenge the Kingdom brings to the complacent normalcy of one's accepted world'.[4]

An important aspect of this polar reversal is the auditor's expectations. The reversal is so jolting precisely because of the unexpected qualities in the actors whose fortunes are reversed. For example, the reversal in the parable of the Good Samaritan is shocking because the hero (the one who aided the victim) is an outcast of Judaism, as opposed to what one normally would have expected. Beneath the literal level of meaning, the hearer also is confronted by the metaphorical meaning.

> The literal point confronted the hearers with the necessity of saying the impossible and having their world turned upside

1. *Ibid.*, 55.
2. *Ibid.*, 56ff. Crossan states, 'In this chapter we are interested in the historical Jesus and not in the creative genius of Luke' (p. 56).
3. *Ibid.*, 75.
4. *Ibid.*

down and radically questioned in its presuppositions. The metaphorical point is that 'just so' does the Kingdom of God break abruptly into human consciousness and demand the overturn of prior values, closed options, set judgments, and established conclusions.[1]

This is all helpful in demonstrating and defining polar reversal in these particular parables. However, Crossan's methodology involves extracting the 'historical' parable from the example story found in Luke. He thus assumes that Luke's handling of the material will detract from the thesis. In addition, his literary interests supersede concerns for the possible eschatological meaning of the reversals as they are found in the Gospel. He is interested instead in the advent of the Kingdom upon the hearer through the jolting of world-view that occurs in the reversal. As with others who speak of hearers' expectations, the model hearer is assumed rather than explained, and often seems to be more modern than ancient. Crossan assumes everyone knows what a late-first-century audience thought about the situations described and the function of the reversal pattern itself. That assumption needs further exploration.

Robert Tannehill discusses reversal in a number of different studies related to the Gospels. In a discussion of pronouncement stories, he suggests that they have traits in common with many of the parables identified by Crossan as reversal parables.[2] These stories frequently exhibit a 'reversal of expectations and values'.[3] In fact one of the characteristics of a pronouncement story is the use of reversal.

> Jesus commends those who appear not commendable and announces the success of questors who seem to have disqualifying characteristics, thereby reversing the expectations which arise from the unusual judgments about such people. This suggests that parabolic and non-parabolic stories, especially the

1. *Ibid.*, 65. Also see Crossan's article, 'The Good Samaritan: Towards a Generic Definition', *Semeia* 2 (1974), 105.
2. 'Attitudinal Shift in Synoptic Pronouncements Stories', *Orientation by Disorientation*, ed. R.A. Spencer (Pittsburgh: Pickwick, 1980), 183-97.
3. *Ibid.*, 194.

pronouncement stories most clearly concerned with attitudinal shift, may share some common features.[1]

Tannehill suggests such reversals do not reflect an eschatological perspective, but rather have parenetic impact, causing a person to re-evaluate one's lifestyle. However, in his study of the reversal elements in the Magnificat, he states that the reversals presented in Lk. 1.51-53 do include eschatological dimensions.[2] In his recent study of the narrative unity of Luke, he further develops the reversal motif found in the Magnificat, briefly outlining its role in the rest of the Gospel.[3] Since he is not interested primarily in the motif itself, his assertions await a more detailed analysis in order to be fully demonstrated.

The dissertation by Larry Drake attempts to weave all of the material together in order to demonstrate that reversal is a theme in Luke.[4] He claims the results of his study will provide 'an organized approach to reversal in Luke's whole Gospel', and 'a substantiation of the proposal that reversal is in fact a

---

1. *Ibid.*
2. 'The Magnificat as Poem', *Journal of Biblical Literature* 93 (1974), 263-75. Two other works specifically dealing with the Magnificat should be mentioned because of their emphasis on the programmatic nature of the reversals in vv. 51-53: Edouard Hamel, 'Le Magnificat et le renversement des situations', *Gregorianum* 60 (1979), 55-84; Paul Bemile, *The Magnificat within the Context and Framework of Lukan Theology* (Frankfurt: Peter Lang, 1986).
3. *The Narrative Unity of Luke–Acts: A Literary Interpretation*, vol. 1 (Philadelphia: Fortress, 1986). 'Mary's hymn suggests a set of expectations about God's character and purpose which guide the reader in understanding what is most important in the subsequent story... At this point I will focus on the description of God as one who puts down the mighty and rich, exalting the lowly and poor in their place. Variations on this reversal motif have an important place in Luke' (pp. 29-30). Tannehill then lists a series of passages in which this motif surfaces, and also points out other authorial interests in reversals in the plot of Luke's Gospel and Acts (pp. 30-31).
4. Larry K. Drake, 'The Reversal Theme in Luke's Gospel'. Drake states in his introduction that the primary task of his work is to identify 'all passages in Luke's Gospel which contain explicit and implicit statements of reversal' (p. 1). He does not examine reversal in Acts because of the work already done by Adams.

theme in Luke'.[1] Drake is not interested in determining any
particular use, either literary or theological, for the reversals
in Luke. He seeks to compile the examples of reversal that
heretofore have been studied randomly and to provide sys-
tematization so that the thematic nature of reversal may be
seen.

Drake deals with the problem of defining the term reversal
in the opening chapter by demonstrating the variety of ways
in which scholars have used the term in Old and New Testament studies.[2] Following a survey of literature on reversal in
Luke–Acts,[3] Drake surveys the Graeco-Roman and Semitic
literature in order to discover possible backgrounds for Luke's
understanding and use of reversal.[4] From his study of the
Graeco-Roman literature, he concludes that Luke uses common cultural and literary patterns of the Hellenistic world, but
his specific patterns of reversal are unlike those found in
Greek comedy and tragedy.[5] On the other hand, his study of
Old Testament and intertestamental literature produces a
number of similarities to reversals previously labeled in
Luke–Acts, and leads him to agree with Dahl and others that

1. *Ibid.*, 1-2. By the term 'theme', Drake means that reversal is 'a
recurrent thought presented throughout a work of literature', in this
case the Gospel of Luke (p. 268).
2. *Ibid.*, 1-8. The organization of this section is confusing because
Drake interweaves examples from Lukan scholarship with other
Gospels studies, Old Testament, and intertestamental studies. He
makes no effort to distinguish between methodological approaches, for
example, literary versus redaction or form criticism.
3. *Ibid.*, 9-43.
4. Chapters 2 (pp. 44-74) and 3 (pp. 75-117), respectively.
5. Drake's study focuses almost exclusively on the Aristotelian plot
device of περιπέτεια, since so many scholars have previously linked Biblical reversal to περιπέτεια. He correctly shows that the modern application of Aristotle's plot device to a 'reversal of expectations' by the
audience was not what Aristotle and other ancient writers meant by
the term περιπέτεια (see pp. 56-58). However, limiting his pursuit of
parallels to Greek drama, he does not look at Graeco-Roman historiog-
raphy or biography, either of which is closer in form and genre to
Luke–Acts. Nor does he look at such concepts as Chance (τύχη) or Fortune (Latin *Fortuna*) for possible parallels.

the Old Testament provides the clearest source for Luke's understanding of reversal.[1]

In the fourth chapter Drake moves to the text of Luke and begins identifying and classifying the reversals in Luke. The chapter is entitled 'Explicit Bi-Polar Reversal'. He defines bi-polar reversal as 'a statement which contains two parts. The first part presents an idea and the second part, utilizing the same key terms, negates the first.'[2] With that definition, Drake analyzes the following texts: 1.46-55; 2.34; 4.16-30;[3] 6.20-26; 9.24 (par. 17.33); 13.30; 14.11 (par. 18.14).[4] The Magnificat (1.46-55) and the beatitudes and woes (6.20-26) are given significantly more space than the other texts. In the case of the proverbial statements, Drake seems to assume that the reversals are rather self-evident and require little explanation.[5] Perhaps a bigger problem is his decision not to place the parable of the rich man and Lazarus in this chapter, especially after he notes the parallels between the parable and the beatitudes and woes.[6]

1. See his conclusions, pp. 106-107, 113. One of the most helpful sections of this chapter is the concluding one on rabbinic literature. Here Drake demonstrates the peculiarities in the style of Luke over against the other Gospels and rabbinic literature.

2. *Ibid.*, 118.

3. The inaugural sermon of Jesus at Nazareth is treated here only in terms of its programmatic nature for the rest of the narrative. The aspect of reversal is saved until the following chapter.

4. There are a number of irregularities in Drake's discussion of bi-polar reversal. Aside from the rather enigmatic definition, the chapter includes a lengthy discussion of the authenticity of the entire birth narrative, and a discussion of the barrenness of Elizabeth as an example of reversal. Drake admits that this is 'polar' rather than 'bi-polar' reversal (pp. 120-21).

5. For example, in discussing 13.30, Drake notes that Matthew and Mark both include this saying following Jesus' discussion with the rich young ruler, while Luke omits it there and places it instead in an eschatological context in ch. 13. This raises some questions about Luke's handling of the proverb which Drake fails to address. If Luke is so fond of reversal—and for that matter the principle of balance—why did he remove the saying he surely found in the tradition at the end of the rich young ruler pericope? If he wanted to use the proverb in ch. 13, why not just double the use, as he doubles the other two proverbs?

6. *Ibid.*, 159.

Chapter 5 contains examples of explicit polar reversal—
'passages where there is an explicit statement of reversal from
one position to another'.[1] Included here are discussions of
Luke's use of Isa. 40.3-5 in the preaching of John the Baptist
(3.4-6),[2] and the inaugural sermon in Nazareth (4.16-30).[3]
The latter is followed by a series of short analyses of sayings
(8.17//12.2; 10.15; 9.48//22.25-27). Drake then examines a
series of parables (14.7-24; 15.3-7, 8-10, 11-32; 16.14-31; 20.9-
18). One striking omission from either this chapter or the
previous one is the parable of the Pharisee and the Publican
(18.9-13). Drake includes the aphorism (v. 14) in ch. 4 and
devotes one paragraph to the parable. However, his treatment
of the parallel aphorism in Lk. 14.11 and the parables surrounding it suggests a more detailed analysis of 18.9-13 is in
order somewhere.
The final chapter is entitled 'Implicit Reversal', and the
chapter functions as a 'catch-all' for three more categories:
'(1) parables and stories built upon reversed expectations;
(2) healing stories in Luke; and (3) the resurrection'.[4] In the
first group, Drake discusses two narratives (7.36-50 and 19.1-
10) and two parables (10.25-37 and 16.1-13). Drake is interested in the 'reversal of expectations' that occurs for the
hearer.[5] An obvious question that arises is that which accom-

1. *Ibid.*, 187.
2. Drake makes two fundamental errors in his analysis of the text.
First, he quotes Fokkelman's discussion of the Hebrew text of Isa. 40.4
as a basis for arguing that Lk. 3.5 is a clear case of reversal (p. 188;
also see J.P. Fokkelman, 'Stylistic Analysis of Isaiah 40.1-11',
Oudtestamentische Studiën 21 [1981], 77). However, the Hebrew text
contains wording which is more clearly in opposition than that of the
Greek text which Luke used. Second, if this is indeed reversal—in the
Greek text, the action seems to be more of a 'leveling' than a reversal—
then why is it not double or bi-polar reversal, since two 'parts' are
reversing positions?
3. Drake follows the lead of Luke Johnson in noting the reversed uses
of the term δεκτόν in vv. 19 and 24 (p. 194). See Luke Johnson, *Literary
Function*, 94.
4. *Ibid.*, 240.
5. For example, in the story of Jesus' anointing, Drake notes that
other reversals occur in the narrative itself (p. 244), but his main concern is the way in which the story reverses the expectations of the
hearer. Likewise, in the parable of the Good Samaritan, Drake is pri-

panies all discussions of hearer/reader expectations. Who is this reader/hearer? Is the reference to Jesus and his audience or to Luke and his reader/hearer? If the latter, how have the expectations of such readers been shaped by what has already been read/heard in the Gospel, or for that matter, by reversals in other literature?

Conclusion

Drake's dissertation demonstrates the difficulties inherent in any attempt to collect other scholars' references to reversal in Luke or Luke–Acts under a single umbrella. However, there are three areas that the history of research suggests may be addressed in a positive manner. First, it is clear both from studies of the rich/poor motif and the literary studies of Crossan that Luke exhibits a pattern of double or 'bi-polar' reversal which is not as prevalent in the other Gospels. There is a need to demonstrate that pattern and elucidate the texts that either explicitly or implicitly repeat the pattern in the narrative. Second, there is divided opinion over the eschatological content of these reversals for Luke. When one focuses on the narrative and the ways in which these texts exhibit common characteristics, it is hoped that some clarity can be gained with respect to their impact on Lukan eschatology. Third, there is a need for further investigation not simply of the reversal background of the author, but of his audience. Only recently have there been attempts to understand the socio-economic status of the Lukan audience in any detail. If one is to ask how the reversal motif functions in the narrative, the question must be asked in terms of the author and the audience, rather than of the author alone. The following study will analyze these three areas in an attempt to understand better Luke's use of double or 'bi-polar' reversal, the impact of these passages on our overall perspective of Lukan eschatology, and the message a first-century audience would have 'heard' in the combined reading of these reversals.

---

marily interested in showing how 'The Samaritan's actions present a reversal of the reader's expectations concerning who would be the hero of the story' (p. 250).

Chapter 2

EXPLICIT BI-POLAR REVERSAL IN LUKE

Methodological Considerations

As the history of research has demonstrated, attempts to analyze reversal in the Gospels have often focused on the literary
parallels to περιπέτεια, using Aristotle's *Poetics* as the source
for definition and comparison. Drake has shown that Aristotle's definition of περιπέτεια is inadequate for describing the use
of reversal in Luke.[1] Recent literary, rhetorical, and social
analyses of the Gospels suggest an alternative approach for
understanding the function of reversal in Luke. Rather than
viewing the reversal pattern as a form solely in the traditional
sense of *Gattungen*, this study will appropriate a rhetorical
definition of form suggested by Kenneth Burke. According to
Burke, 'Form in literature is an arousing and fulfillment of
desires. A work has form in so far as one part of it leads a
reader to anticipate another part, to be gratified by the
sequence.'[2] Burke further delineates several different aspects
of form: progressive (either syllogistic or qualitative), repeti-

1. Drake, 'Reversal Theme', 44-74. Especially note pp. 56-58, where
Drake, following earlier studies of Lock and Lucas on περιπέτεια in
Aristotle, argues that the modern focus on audience expectations
misses the original meaning understood by Aristotle, viz. the reversal
of intentions.
2. Kenneth Burke, *Counter-Statement* (Berkeley: University of California Press, 1968), 124. Vernon K. Robbins, *Jesus the Teacher* (Philadelphia: Fortress, 1984), adopts Burke's definition as a part of his
'socio-rhetorical' approach to Mark. Robbins is interested in determining the various forms and formal structure of Mark. The present study
is not interested in discovering the variety of forms or even the pre-
dominant formal structures of Luke, but in analyzing a particular
double reversal pattern to determine its function as a rhetorical form
in the Gospel.

tive, conventional, and minor or incidental forms.[1] These different aspects of form are often interrelated, and at times may be in conflict with one another to produce the desired effect on the reader. Of particular importance for this study is Burke's discussion of minor and incidental forms and the way forms such as paradox or reversal may function within larger formal patterns. By carrying an argument forward, a minor form may function as progressive form; by continuing a certain theme, it may have importance as repetitive form. At the same time it may be so complete within itself that the reader memorizes it apart from its setting.[2] As the history of research already has shown, the reversal pattern in Luke repeatedly has been demonstrated in isolated minor forms, but no attempt has been made to determine how the different examples of reversal function either in the progression of Luke's message, or as the repetition of a particular theme or themes.

On isolated texts, Tannehill has demonstrated the importance of repetitive patterns ranging from individual words or short phrases to parallel sentences or more elaborate parallel structures.[3] Parallelism often involves what he calls 'coupl-

1. *Counterstatement*, 124-28. 'Syllogistic progression is the form of a perfectly conducted argument, advancing step by step . . . To go from A to E through stages B, C, and D is to obtain such form' (p. 124). Burke suggests περιπέτεια is a classic example of the way in which, in a logical sequence of events, audience expectations are reversed. Qualitative progression lacks the 'pronounced anticipatory nature of the syllogistic progression'. Rather, 'the presence of one quality prepares us for the introduction of another' (p. 125). 'Repetitive form is the consistent maintaining of a principle under new guises. It is restatement of the same thing in different ways' (p. 125). Conventional forms are those which the reader recognizes as form and whose appeal is as form. Any form can become conventional form whenever the expectations of the reader are anterior to the reading due to the recognition of the form itself (see pp. 126-27). In defining what is meant by minor or incidental form, Burke states, 'When analyzing a work of any length, we may find it bristling with minor or incidental forms—such as metaphor, paradox, disclosure, reversal, contraction, expansion, pathos, apostrophe, series, chiasmus, which can be discussed as formal events in themselves' (p. 127).

2. *Ibid.*, 127. This is an important point, particularly in light of research already done by Beardslee, Tannehill and others on antithetic aphorisms, and the work of Crossan on the parables.

3. Tannehill, *Sword*, 39-57.

ing', in which words are no longer heard separately but in interaction with each other. Words that are not completely synonymous in and of themselves blend and modify each other. Even synonyms are no longer simply synonyms. 'They differ in subtle ways, and the parallel lines contain significant variations, thereby bringing out different aspects of a thought, helping it to grow in importance and richness of meaning'.[1] Such patterns of repetition 'retard the forward movement of thought, the common tendency to pass on quickly from one thought to another. By doubling back on what has already been said and expressing it in a new way the text gains in intensity and depth'.[2] Repetition, and the variations that interact with each other, may also point beyond the specific words or ideas to situations unnamed but implied by the pattern. 'When various elements are set within a repetitive pattern, we also experience an expansion of meaning within the pattern. We find it connected not only to this but also to that, which leads us to expect it capable of more expansion.'[3]

The importance of this for the present study is that the reversal texts in Luke exhibit these repetitive patterns, both as isolated texts and texts related to one another. Their function within immediate contexts and their collective function within the Gospel will involve Tannehill's understanding of repetition in particular texts and Burke's concept of repetitive form. One aspect of this will be the way in which related words or oppositions overlap or change from one example to the next. How do the examples reflect the same aspects of reversal and how are they different? Or, put another way, how do they reflect either a progression of thought or the restatement of a particular theme?

Burke's discussion of the term 'polar' in literary studies is helpful in understanding the term 'bi-polar reversal'. In *Language as Symbolic Action*, Burke discusses the role of antithesis

> in what are called 'polar' terms, not just Yes-No, but such similarly constructed pairs as: true-false, order-disorder, cosmos-

---

1. *Ibid.*, 42.
2. Tannehill, 'The Magnificat as Poem', 264.
3. Tannehill, *Sword*, 42-43.

chaos, life-death, love-hate. These are to be distinguished from
sheerly positive terms. The word 'table', for instance, involves
no thought of counter-table, anti-table, non-table, or un-table...
We can settle for the indubitable fact that all moral terms are of
this polar sort. And we can settle merely for the fact that such
positives and negatives imply each other.[1]

The term 'polar' thus denotes opposites: words or concepts
that are antithetical to one another. Bi-polar reversal refers to
oppositions whose 'poles' are reversed—for example *good*
becomes *bad* and *bad* becomes *good*.[2] An important question to
be addressed concerns the exactness of the oppositions found in
the reversal texts of Luke. While 'rich' and 'poor' are true
opposites (6.20, 24), 'rich' and 'hungry' (1.53) are better
described as contraries—words that logically conflict with
each other but are not true opposites. By using contraries, a
tension is created that heightens the conflict already being
expressed in the reversal.[3] By the process of coupling and the

---

1. Kenneth Burke, *Language as Symbolic Action* (Berkeley: University of California Press, 1966), 11-12. Burke goes on to state that such
antithesis is endemic to the formation of religion itself. 'Our tendency
to write works on such topics as 'The Spirit of Christianity', or 'The
Soul of Islam', or 'The Meaning of Metempsychosis', leads us to over-
look a strongly negativistic aspect of religions. I refer here not just to
the principle of moral negativity already discussed, but also to the fact
that religions are so often built antithetically to other persuasions'
(p. 12). Tannehill also discusses the function of antithesis in challenging prevailing perspectives and 'worlds'. In antithesis the prevailing
perspective is allowed expression so that it can be challenged and the
new perspective appears over against it. Thus the hearer is prevented
from subsuming the new perspective under the old. It is this clash of
perspectives which is revelatory' (*Sword*, 54). With regard to antithetical patterns in Luke, this perspective seems important on two fronts:
Luke's portrait of Christianity in relation to Judaism—in particular
Pharisaic Judaism of the late first century—and the pagan religions of
the Graeco-Roman world. What do the reversals and/or antitheses
attack, and what alternative is being put forth?

2. The term 'bi-polar' is used in place of Crossan's term 'polar' reversal to indicate the double reversal of opposites. The term 'polar reversal' is reserved for instances in which only one reversal of opposites
takes place, i.e. *good* becomes *bad* but there is no explicit reference to
bad becoming *good*.

3. On the use of 'tensive language' in paradox and antithetic aphorisms, see Tannehill, *Sword*, 11, 89. Tannehill attributes the phrase

chiastic structure of the verse, 'rich' and 'hungry' function as oppositions and in turn expand the meaning of each other to create a larger opposition than either of the words implies by itself. This interrelation and expansion of meaning will be important in determining the function of the pattern as a whole in Luke.

The definitions of three other words need to be mentioned before proceeding to the analysis of texts. The terms *Leitwort*, 'motif', and 'theme' are all used in various discussions of reversal in Luke. In this study they will carry the meanings they have in the work of Robert Alter:[1]

> 1. *Leitwort*. Through abundant repetition, the semantic range of the word-root is explored, different forms of the root are deployed, branching off at times into phonetic relatives (that is, word-play), synonymity, and antonymity; by virtue of its verbal status, the *Leitwort* refers immediately to meaning and thus to theme as well... 2. Motif. A concrete image, sensory quality, action, or object recurs through a particular narrative; it may be intermittently associated with a *Leitwort*; it has no meaning in itself without the defining context of the narrative; it may be incipiently symbolic or instead primarily a means of giving formal coherence to a narrative... 3. Theme. An idea which is part of the value-system of the narrative—it may be moral, moral-psychological, legal, political, historiosophical, theological—is made evident in some recurring pattern. It is often associated with one or more *Leitwörter* but it is not co-extensive with them; it may also be associated with a motif.[2]

The interrelationship of these terms will be important in demonstrating the function of the various bi-polar reversal texts in Luke's narrative as a whole.

'tensive language' to Philip Wheelwright, *The Burning Foundation* (Bloomington: Indiana University Press, 1968).

1. Robert Alter, *The Art of Biblical Narrative* (New York: Basic Books, 1981).

2. *Ibid.*, 95. See the chapter entitled 'The Techniques of Repetition', 88-113.

Explicit Bi-Polar Reversals in the Lukan Context

The Magnificat (1.53-55)

The thematic importance of the first two chapters of Luke—
the infancy narrative—has been noted by a number of scholars.[1] As an overture or prologue to the rest of Luke–Acts, certain motifs and themes first presented in the infancy narrative
recur repeatedly in the following chapters.[2] Drury suggests
that the songs, especially, express themes that are found
throughout the author's work. The first theme he lists is 'God's
classical action of raising the low and bringing down the
lofty'.[3] Only the Magnificat expresses such a reversal pattern.

---

1. See D.S. Tam, 'The Literary and Theological Unity between Lk. 1–2
and Lk. 3–Acts 28' (Ph.D. dissertation, Duke University, 1978); C.H.
Talbert, *Literary Patterns, Theological Themes and the Genre of
Luke–Acts* (Missoula, MT: Scholars Press), 1974; Raymond E. Brown,
The Birth of the Messiah (Garden City, NY: Doubleday, 1977), 239-53;
H.H. Oliver, 'The Lucan Birth Stories and the Purpose of Luke–Acts',
New Testament Studies 10 (1963/64), 202-36; P.S. Minear, 'Luke's Use
of the Birth Stories', in *Studies in Luke–Acts*, 111-30; W.B. Tatum,
'The Epoch of Israel: Luke i–ii and the Theological Plan of Luke–
Acts', *New Testament Studies* 13 (1966/67), 184-95.
   2. Cf. David L. Tiede, *Prophecy and History in Luke–Acts* (Philadel-
phia: Fortress, 1980), 24; Fitzmyer, *Gospel*, 306; Brown, *Birth*, 232.
F.W. Danker notes the importance of the narrative in preparing the
auditors for later thematic developments 'concerning the cooperative
work of God and Jesus in the rescue of humanity. The auditors of
course know the basic story, but they are interested in knowing what
Luke will do with it' ('Graeco-Roman Cultural Accommodation in the
Christology of Luke–Acts', *SBL 1983 Seminar Papers* [Chico, CA:
Scholars Press, 1983], 394). While Danker's thematic pursuits are dif-
ferent from this study, the role of bi-polar reversal in the Magnificat in
preparing the auditors for later repetitions is a parallel concern.
   3. Drury, *Tradition*, 50. Speaking about possessions in Luke–Acts,
Donald Juel expresses a similar concept of the thematic nature of the
Magnificat: 'Jesus' story is one of striking reversals. The one born to
sit on the throne of his father David and to reign over the house of
Jacob forever spends most of his career with the poor and the outcast.
His call, lifted from Isaiah, is to "preach good news to the poor" and to
"set at liberty those who are oppressed" (Luke 4.18). Eating with sinners and healing the sick, Jesus fulfills his commission. His overturning of established values in the name of the kingdom of God aptly mir-
rors the will of God as Mary expresses it in her Magnificat' (*Luke–
Acts: The Promise of History* [Atlanta: John Knox, 1983], 90-91).

The setting of the Magnificat within the infancy narrative is the scene in which the two prospective mothers, Mary and Elizabeth, are brought together (1.39-45).[1] Elizabeth and Mary are identified as relatives (v. 36), and Mary travels from Nazareth to the hill country of Judah to visit Zechariah and Elizabeth. Following Mary's greeting, Elizabeth, filled with the Holy Spirit (v. 41), expresses surprise that 'the mother of my Lord' should come to her. In the midst of her own divinely given pregnancy, she sets the stage for the response of Mary by calling attention to the primacy of Mary's child over her own.[2] Similarities between Hannah's Song in 1 Samuel 2 and the Magnificat, and parallels between the situation of Elizabeth and Hannah, have led numerous scholars to opt for the variant reading in v. 46 that suggests Elizabeth is also the singer of the Song.[3] However, the parallel use of δούλη in vv. 38 and 48, the inappropriateness of v. 48b on the lips of Elizabeth, and lack of reference to prior barrenness (cf. 1 Sam. 2.5) support the external evidence for assuming the singer is intended to be Mary.[4]

1. This scene, sandwiched between the annunciations and the births, also serves as the climax of the annunciation stories. Cf. Seccombe, *Possessions*, 72.
2. C.T. Davis ('The Literary Structure of Luke 1–2', in *Art and Meaning: Rhetoric in Biblical Literature*, ed. David J.A. Clines, D.M. Gunn, and A.J. Hauser [Sheffield: JSOT Press, 1982], 217), suggests that v. 43 is the center of this scene, since it reflects a departure from convention. Normally a servant visits the king; here the mother of the servant has visited the mother of the servant—the forerunner. 'Why this surprising departure from convention? The Magnificat forms Mary's answer. God's king, like God himself, reverses the expected pattern of power. Those of low degree are raised up.'
3. For a history of the debate, see S. Benko, 'The Magnificat: A History of the Controversy', *Journal of Biblical Literature* 86 (1967), 263-75; Bemile, *Magnificat*, 5-19; Seccombe, *Possessions*, 72-73 n. 282.
4. Cf. Seccombe, *Possessions*, 72-73 n. 282. Brown, *Birth*, 340, 361, suggests that the only reason the hymn is ascribed to Mary is because she fits the description of the poor and outcast of Israel in whom Luke is otherwise interested. Also see Bemile, *Magnificat*, 5-19. Of course, no assumption is being made with regard to Mary or Elizabeth being the actual originator of the hymn. Just as Luke often supplies speeches in Acts, the hymns have been included in the narrative at points he deems appropriate.

Tannehill has identified the repetitive patterns that occur in the Magnificat and the function of those patterns in focusing the reader's attention. The poem contains different kinds of parallelism, repetitive rhythm and rhyme patterns, and recurring words or word roots[1] that provoke comparison and retard the forward progress of thought.[2] 'By doubling back on what has already been said and expressing it in a new way the text gains in intensity and depth.'[3] The repetitive patterns also unite contrasting ideas, creating a tension in which opposites are placed in some sort of relationship. While the text is unified by these patterns, the patterns contain elements that are normally at odds with each other. This tension forces the reader to meditate on the particular event being described and to seek ways of understanding the unity and tension that the described event evokes.

An important feature of the Magnificat is that almost every line contains allusions to the Greek Old Testament. Along with the obvious similarity to the song of Hannah, scholars such as Bailey have focused on the language of the Exodus, particularly the song of Moses (Exod. 15).[4] Verses 52-53 are paralleled closely, but not identically, in Sir. 10.14, Ezek. 21.31, and Job 12.19.[5] It seems difficult to imagine that the images of the Old Testament are not to be understood at every point in the text by the reader.[6] The task is to determine precisely what the

1. μεγαλύνει–μεγάλα, γενεαί–γενεάς, ἔλεος–ἐλέους, ταπείνωσιν–ταπεινούς, δυνατός–δυνάστας, ἐποίησεν–ἐποίησεν.
2. 'The Magnificat as Poem', 264.
3. *Ibid.*
4. 'Song of Mary', 33.
5. Also see 1 Sam. 2.7-8. The chiastic structure of vv. 52-53 adds force to the reversals and creates a stronger sense that the two sides have exchanged places, rather than being levelled. For a concordant view of the LXX and intertestamental literature parallels to the Magnificat, see Bemile, *Magnificat*, 116-32. Also see Brown, *Birth*, 358-60.
6. Such an assumption presumes an audience which is also quite familiar with the Septuagint. Otherwise there is no transmission of such allusions. The general consensus regarding the Lukan audience has been that it was composed primarily of Gentile Christians in a predominantly Gentile setting. Cf. Fitzmyer, *Gospel*, 57-59. Philip Esler has recently argued that the abundance of Old Testament allusions in Luke–Acts suggests that, while the Lukan audience was pre-

author is trying to convey by the allusions. It is also important to note where the literary structure of the Magnificat may emphasize ideas which, though present in their antecedents, now are stated more forcefully.

The poem begins with two lines in synonymous parallelism that establish the celebrative character of the song. The primary actor of the song, God, is praised by the recipient of God's action. The switch in tenses between μεγαλύνει and ἠγαλλίασεν is sometimes thought to be evidence of a Hebrew original.[1] The effect of this tense change within two synonymous lines is to create a link between the past event which is the cause of her rejoicing and the present.[2] God (θεός) is understood as κύριος and σωτήρ, and the following lines unfold the nature of God's actions that have produced the celebration. Verses 48a and 49a give the cause for celebration. God has 'looked upon the low estate of his handmaiden'.[3] The contrast is between the

dominantly Gentile, the majority were already proselytes or God-fearers before becoming converts. See *Community and Gospel*, 24-45.

1. Cf. R. Buth, 'Hebrew Poetic Tenses and the Magnificat', *Journal for the Study of the New Testament* 21 (1984), 67-83. Fitzmyer (*Gospel*, 366) notes this possibility, but emphasizes the lack of any external evidence for a Hebrew original. The use of the aorist tense becomes a bigger issue in vv. 51-53.

2. Tannehill ('The Magnificat as Poem', 266) notes that the two lines are synonymous parallelism, but assimilates the aorist tense to the present without comment. Fitzmyer (*Gospel*, 366) believes the aorist tense is 'timeless', and invokes the discussion of the gnomic aorist in F. Blass, A. Debrunner, R.W. Funk, *A Greek Grammar of the New Testament and Other Early Christian Literature* (Chicago: University of Chicago Press, 1961), §333. Bemile (*Magnificat*, 48) notes that the use of the aorist active form of ἀγαλλιάω is rare (the other three uses in Luke–Acts are aorist deponents—10.21, Acts 2.26, 16.34), and regardless of the explanation must be seen in relationship to the noun ἀγαλλίασις in Lk. 1.14 and 1.44.

3. Cf. 1 Sam. 1.11: 'O Lord of Hosts, if you will look upon the low estate of your handmaid' (ταπείνωσιν τῆς δούλης σου). The parallel to Hannah's barrenness contributed greatly to the theory that Elizabeth was the intended Psalmist. Bemile (*Magnificat*, 50) suggests 1 Sam. 9.16 (ὅτι ἐπέβλεψα ἐπὶ τὴν ταπείνωσιν τοῦ λαοῦ μου) is taken up in v. 48, with δούλης ἀὑτοῦ being substituted for λαοῦ μου. W. Grundmann ('ταπεινόω', *Theological Dictionary of the New Testament*, VIII, 1-3 [hereafter cited as *TDNT*]) argued that in Graeco-Roman literature ταπεινόω and related words had only negative moral and ethical connotations. In the LXX, however, the word came to be associated with the

δυνατός and δούλη, between ταπείνωσις and μεγάλα. A slave
girl of no importance has been looked upon by ὁ δυνατός, who
in turn has done 'great things' to her.

Verse 48 often is thought to be a Lukan insertion into the
original because it includes the only personal reference to
Mary, and the second half of the verse, especially, fits awk-
wardly into the structure of the poem.[1] Whether it is original
or not, it describes a particular result of God's actions. 'From
now on all generations will call me blessed'.[2] The effect of this
line is to take the past-present tension already created and
extend it into the future. The past acts of God will now have
ongoing impact on 'all generations'.[3] Verses 49b-50, in contrast to the previous lines, contain no finite verbs, and the
thought shifts to the timeless nature of the one who has acted.
Attention also shifts from the single individual, Mary, and the
activity of God in her life, to the recognition that God's mercies

ani, the pious, humble poor of God. There is general agreement that
the LXX usage forms the background here, but Leivestad is correct in
asserting that one should be careful not to argue too much for the positive meaning of the term in New Testament texts. He suggests that the
word ταπεινός should be understood in the ethically neutral sense of
'needy, powerless, weak' rather than loading the term with religious
overtones. See R. Leivestad, 'ΤΑΠΕΙΝΟΣ–ΤΑΠΕΙΝΟΦΡΩΝ', *Novum
Testamentum* 8 (1966), 45. The parallel between the use of ταπεινός in
v. 52 and ταπείνωσις in v. 48 suggests the same caution should be used
with regard to Mary. Cf. Bemile, *Magnificat*, 50 n. 172; Fitzmyer,
Gospel, 367. On the use of δούλη, cf. v. 38. On the LXX heritage of the
term, see J.T. Forestell, 'Old Testament Background of the
Magnificat', *Marian Studies* 12 (1961), 209ff.

    1. Cf. Brown, *Birth*, 356; Fitzmyer, *Gospel*, 358. Tannehill, 'The
Magnificat as Poem', 268, suggests v. 48b should seen as a parenthesis
in the poem rather than as a redactional addition. See also the discussion of Dupont, 'Le Magnificat comme discours sur Dieu', *Nouvelle
Revue Théologique* 102 (1980), 326.

    2. The verb μακαρίζω is found only here and in Jas 5.11. However, the
noun μακάριος is used often and the link to 1.45 should be noted. The
numerous parallels between these verses and 6.20-26 will be noted
below.

    3. If v. 48 is a Lukan addition, the meaning of v. 48b becomes impor-
tant in an added sense: 'all generations', while clearly having Old Testament antecedents, seems discordant in the midst of what are often
described as eschatological events. The verse by itself implies an
extended time frame, rather than looking toward an imminent end.

have been and always will be extended to 'those who fear him'. Mary's own situation, and its impact as described in v. 48b, now affect the way in which God's mercies are to be understood.[1]

Verses 49b and 50 are also linked to vv. 54 and 55 by the use of ἔλεος. Furthermore, both passages relate God's mercy to past and future generations. While τοῖς φοβουμένοις is not specific, vv. 54-55 specifically refer to 'his servant Israel' and to 'our fathers, to Abraham and to his seed'. Just as v. 50 suggests the timeless nature of God's activity by the lack of a finite verb and the phrase εἰς γενεὰς καὶ γενεάς, v. 55 ends with εἰς τὸν αἰῶνα. In both passages there is also definite variation in the length of lines from those preceding, thus interrupting the patterns established in previous verses. The abrupt shift in tone and the return to a description of the acts of God in v. 51 suggests that vv. 49b-50 and 54-55 are parallel conclusions to a two-strophe structure.[2] The first strophe presents the salvific act of God for one woman whose low estate is exalted. The second strophe expands the horizon from the individual to the community. God's act of salvation becomes a dual act of salvation–judgment: the lowly are exalted and the exalted are brought down.[3]

In vv. 51-52, the verbs again appear in initial position, as they were in vv. 46-47, 48a, and 49a. Verse 51a, linked to v. 49a by the repeated use of ἐποίησεν, also emphasizes the power of God by the use of imagery taken from the Old Testament.[4]

---

1. This is suggested by the word link, γενεαί–γενεάς.
2. Cf. Tannehill, 'The Magnificat as Poem', 269. Tannehill further supports this structure on the basis of the rhythm which he finds in the poetic lines. D. Jones, however, argues that no such rhythm can be determined in the poem. See 'The Background and Character of the Lukan Psalms', *Journal of Theological Studies* n.s. 19 (1968), 21.
3. Bailey, 'Song of Mary', 32. Cf. Charles H. Talbert, *Reading Luke: A Literary and Theological Commentary on the Third Gospel* (New York: Crossroad, 1982), 24-25.
4. The closest parallel is Psalm 88.11: σὺ ἐταπείνωσας ὡς τραυματίαν ὑπερήφανον καὶ ἐν τῷ βραχίονι τῆς δυνάμεώς σου διεσκόρπισας τοὺς ἐχθρούς σου. J.M. Ford, *My Enemy is My Guest* (Maryknoll, NY: Orbis, 1984), finds echoes of strong military language in the Magnificat and notes that the phrase 'arm of the Lord' emphasizes the Exodus as a paradigm for salvation. She points to the use of the phrase in Isa.

The line is in synthetic parallelism with v. 51b, which provides greater specificity and identifies a new character set that is in contrast both to those who receive God's mercy in v. 50 and to the recipient of 'great things' in v. 49.[1] The words used in v. 51 are harsher in tone[2] and more graphic in their description of God's actions.[3] Whereas God has 'done great things' to Mary (v. 49), 'he has scattered (διεσκόρπισεν) the proud (ὑπερηφά-νους) in the imagination of their hearts' (v. 51). The strong language of the verse points toward the very forceful, carefully constructed climax of the poem found in vv. 52-53.[4] Both verses contain antithetic parallelism and the repetition of the antithetic pattern results in synonymous parallelism between the two verses. The verses are further welded together by a chiasmus which, along with rhyming patterns at the end of the lines, makes the two verses the rhetorical center of the poem.

40.10; 51.5, 9; 53.1 as illustrative of the phrase as a symbol for the New Exodus. See her discussion, pp. 21-22.

1. Tannehill, 'The Magnificat as Poem', 266. Bailey, 'The Song of Mary', 31, believes the original poem included an additional line in v. 51 ('He aided his servant Israel') which more naturally completed a chiastic structure. If, however, an opposition is needed to complete the thought of v. 51, it seems more appropriate to consider 'those who fear him' (v. 50b) as the opposite term rather than hypothetically interjecting another line.

2. Georg Bertram ('ὑπερήφανος', *TDNT*, VIII, 525) has shown that in secular use ὑπερήφανος referred to one who with pride and arrogance bragged about his position, power, and wealth, and despised others. In the LXX the word had similar negative connotations. Particularly noteworthy is the repeated use of the term in Sirach 10—v. 14 is a close parallel to v. 52—where the word refers to an attitude hated by God and humans alike (v. 7) which consistently brings about separation from God (vv. 12-13). For a more complete treatment of the Old Testament background of ὑπερήφανος, see P.L. Schoonheim, 'Der alttestamentliche Boden der Vokabel ὑπερήφανος Lukas 1,51', *Novum Testamentum* 8 (1966), 235-46.

3. Tannehill, 'The Magnificat as Poem', 273.

4. Cf. K. Bailey, 'The Song of Mary: Vision of a New Exodus', *Theological Review* 2 (1979), 29; Tannehill, 'The Magnificat as Poem', 267; E. Hamel, 'Le Magnificat et le renversement des situations', *Gregorianum* 60 (1979), 58; L. Schottroff, 'Das Magnificat und die älteste Tradition über Jesus von Nazareth', *Evangelische Theologie* 38 (1978), 298.

A	καθεῖλεν	δυνάστας ἀπὸ θρό<u>νων</u>
B	καὶ ὕψωσεν	ταπειν<u>ούς</u>
B′	πεινῶντας	ἐνέπλησεν ἀγα<u>θῶν</u>
A′	καὶ πλουτοῦντας	ἐξαπέστειλεν κεν<u>ούς</u>

In the context of this chiasmus, two opposite sets of characters experience a reversal of positions.[1] This is a double reversal, for which we are using the phrase 'bi-polar reversal'. The parallelism in the two verses suggests that the powerful (δυνάστας)[2] and the rich (πλουτοῦντας)[3] are to be understood as one group;[4] likewise those of low estate (ταπεινούς)[5] and the hungry (πεινῶντας)[6] represent another group. In each case, the emphasis of the wording indicates a set of physical conditions that are reversed. The powerful and rich are 'brought down from their thrones' and 'sent away empty'; the lowly and hungry are 'exalted' and 'filled with good things'.[7] The shift in structure in v. 53 from the finite verb to the substantival par-

1. It is true that neither δυνάστας–ταπεινούς nor πεινῶντας–πλουτοῦντας are true opposites, but they are contraries in Luke's Gospel. Each set is made functionally opposite by the reversed action taken toward them by God: 'brought down'—'exalted' or 'raised up'; 'filled with good things'—'sent away empty'. The powerful are thus contrasted with the powerless, the 'have-nots' are contrasted with the 'haves'.
2. The word occurs two other times in the New Testament (Acts 8.27, referring to the Ethiopian eunuch, and 1 Tim. 6.15, referring to God). Here it is used for earthly rulers in contrast to ὁ δυνατός, the ultimate power (v. 49). In LXX, cf. Job 12.19.
3. The verb form πλουτέω occurs only one other time in Luke (12.21). The adjective πλούσιος is a Lukan favorite, found 11 times (6.24; 12.16; 14.12; 16.1, 19, 21, 22; 18.23, 25; 19.2; 21.1). In contrast Matthew uses the adjective three times, Mark twice; neither uses the verb πλουτέω.
4. To this group should be added the 'proud' of v. 51.
5. ταπεινός is found only here in Luke. The verb ταπεινόω, however, is found in 3.5 (quotation of Isa. 40.4), 14.11, and 18.14. The verb ὑψόω (1.52) is also found in 14.11 and 18.14 (also 10.15).
6. In Luke πεινάω is used of Jesus' hunger for food following the wilderness experience (4.2), in reference to David and his men (6.3), in the beatitudes and woes (6.21, 25), and here in v. 53.
7. ἐμπίπλημι ('fill') is found only here and in 6.25 in Luke. Here it is used to describe the positive reversal experienced by the hungry. In 6.25, the opposite reversal takes place: the 'full now' will hunger (πεινάσετε).

ticiple in initial position arrests the reader's attention, with the noun forms carrying the antithesis.

The use of the aorist tense for the six finite verbs in vv. 51-53 has been the subject of much debate. A common suggestion has been that these are all gnomic aorists, reflecting how God habitually acts.[1] Others have argued that they are prophetic aorists, referring to the eschatological reversal of fortunes coming at the end of the age.[2] A third option is to posit an original post-resurrection community setting for the hymn, in which case the aorist refers in some way to the crucifixion.[3] The problem with the latter suggestion is that it fails to address the use of the hymn in the gospel narrative. Whether one opts for a gnomic or prophetic use, the verbs in these verses cannot be isolated from the rest of the hymn.[4] The word links between the first strophe and the second suggest not two different referents for the verbs but some relationship between the actions

1. Bemile, *Magnificat*, 217; Blass–Debrunner–Funk, *Grammar*, §333; Nigel Turner, *Syntax*, vol. 3 of *Grammar of New Testament Greek* by J.R. Moulton, W.F. Howard, and N. Turner (Edinburgh: T. & T. Clark, 1963), 74. Cf. the discussion of Dupont, 'Le Magnificat', 333, where he rejects this position—which he previously held (cf. *Les Beatitudes,* III, 189-93). Brown, *Birth*, 362-63, also rejects this conclusion, on the basis of the use of the present tense in 1 Sam. 2, and his assumption that the Magnificat is too closely modeled on Hannah's song for such a tense change if the concern is to express the habitual acts of God.

2. For example, see Alfred Plummer, *The Gospel according to St. Luke* (New York: Scribner's, 1902), 33; M.D. Goulder and M.A. Sanders, 'St. Luke's Genesis', *Journal of Theological Studies* n.s. 8 (1957), 25; Talbert, *Reading Luke*, 25.

3. Brown, *Birth*, 363; Fitzmyer, *Gospel*, 361. P. Winter argued on the basis of these verses that the original hymn was written to celebrate a Maccabean victory. However, such a view does not fit the rest of the hymn nor does it explain the Lukan use. See his 'Magnificat and Benedictus—Maccabean Psalms?', *Bulletin of the John Rylands Library* 37 (1954), 328-47.

4. Once the verses are placed in the larger context of the repetitive bipolar reversal form, it would appear that the gnomic sense best describes the Lukan understanding.

of God toward Mary and the reversals of vv. 51-53.[1] Tannehill
is correct in stating:

> The poem presents God's choice of the lowly mother and his
> overturning of society as one act. It suggests an underlying
> qualitative unity between what appear to be separate events; for
> in both, God's surprising concern for the lowly is manifest.
> Thus the mighty God's regard for a humble woman is the sign
> of God's eschatological act for the world.[2]

Following the climactic language of vv. 51-53, the final two
verses close the song by clarifying that God's actions fulfill the
promise made to Abraham and his posterity (v. 55). Whereas
the recipients of his mercy are only vaguely identified in v. 50,
Israel is now specified.[3] Likewise Mary's cause for celebration
is not simply a personal one, but it fulfills a long-awaited
promise made by God to Israel. God's mighty act not only does
great things for a handmaiden of low estate, it reverses societal conditions, thereby demonstrating God's mercy and
faithfulness toward Israel. Throughout the poem, the emphasis is upon the action taken by God, and the poem thus
demands that primacy be given to the acts of God, not conditions of the human characters. God chooses to act in behalf of
an unimportant handmaiden. That act signals a similar concern for all those who are needy, hungry, and powerless. At
the same time God's act means judgment upon the self-suffi-

1. The verses are linked to the previous strophe by the contrast
between δυνατός (v. 49) and δυνάστας (v. 52a) and the comparison of
ταπείνωσις (v. 48) and ταπεινούς (v. 52b).

2. 'The Magnificat as Poem', 274. Tannehill also suggests that the
aorist-tense verbs of vv. 51-54a are necessitated by the internal structure of the poem and the author's desire to maintain the unity of the
two strophes (p. 274 n. 26). Cf. Dupont, 'Le Magnificat', 334.

3. The identification of Israel led Seccombe, *Possessions*, to conclude
that the poem was nationalistic throughout, and a message of salvation for Israel over against its outside oppressors. Thus, the humble
and hungry are representative of Israel; the rich and powerful are
outside oppressors. 'The only doctrine of reversal to be found is the
conviction that Israel, which at present is humbled and afflicted, will
be raised to a state of power and glory' (p. 83). However, such a view
fails to deal with the personal aspect of God's act for Mary, nor does it
adequately represent the reversal passages in Luke which suggest the
reversal is not simply between the nation of Israel and outside oppressors, but between various groups in Israel as well.

cient, the proud, the rulers, and the rich. The reversal is not generated by humans in either category. The proletariat does not rise up and overthrow the bourgeoisie. God is the one responsible, 'in remembrance of his mercies'.

Two questions remain partially unanswered. The first is the exact nature of the oppositions of vv. 51-53. Do the terms 'proud', 'powerful', 'low estate', 'hungry', and 'rich' indicate physical or spiritual conditions? It has been popular to link the humble and hungry of the song with the *anawim*, the pious poor of late Judaism which Dibelius so successfully connected with the poor in the epistle of James.[1] A Jewish-Christian *anawim* group thus is posited as those from whom the hymns came and to whom passages such as the beatitudes and woes were most meaningful.[2] It also has been common to argue, as Brown does, that the conditions of the poor and hungry 'are primarily spiritual, but we should not forget the physical realities faced by early Christians'.[3] However, it is not clear that one should consider the spiritual aspect ahead of the physical. Furthermore, it is not altogether certain that a connection should be made between the *anawim* and those positively acted upon by God in the Magnificat.[4] It seems better to allow the Lukan text to establish its own meaning for the terms as the narrative proceeds.

A second unanswered question involves the eschatological content of the Magnificat, particularly vv. 51-53. The bi-polar reversal presented in these verses is almost universally described as eschatological reversal. Such an identification, however, does not solve the problem of the function of these verses in the narrative as a whole.[5] Whatever one claims for

---

1. Martin Dibelius, *The Epistle of James* (Hermeneia NT Commentaries; Philadelphia: Fortress, 1976), 39-43.

2. For this identification, see Brown, *Birth*, 350-55; Pilgrim, *Good News*, 60-61; Fitzmyer, *Gospel*, 361-62.

3. *Birth*, 363. Brown does go on to delineate the physical poverty probably experienced by early Christians.

4. Seccombe (*Possessions*, 24-28), rejects this identification entirely, on the basis that such a Jewish-Christian community is only hypothetical in the first place.

5. Schottroff, 'Das Magnificat', 305-306, believes that these verses represent the 'oldest traditions of Jesus', but she is convinced that the

the eschatological nature of the reversals in these verses must also take into consideration the relationship of the second strophe to the prior one, in which Mary states, 'From now on all generations will call me blessed' (v. 48). Regardless of one's decisions about the authenticity of v. 48b, it projects an extended period of time before the Last Day.[1] The suggestion by Schottroff that God's action toward Mary is an eschatological event signaling the beginning of the end still may be appropriate for the Gospel as a whole if one does not demand that the 'end' be imminent.[2] If by eschatology one is referring to the broader concept of the break-up of existing order,[3] then it is possible to understand God's acts toward Mary as eschatological and to see the reversals of vv. 51-53 as indicative of the new order that has already been inaugurated.[4] While Luke never rules out the apocalyptic notions of a new age, it is clear that, in the person of Jesus, the future has broken into the present.[5] It is therefore appropriate that the bi-polar reversal found in the Magnificat should be linked to God's actions toward his lowly handmaiden. In her the new order has begun.

The Beatitudes and Woes (6.20-26)
The next appearance of explicit bi-polar reversal in the sequence of Luke occurs in the beatitudes and woes in ch. 6. A number of recent literary studies dealing with New Testament Wisdom discuss the beatitudes and woes as examples of proverbs or aphorisms.[6] Most helpful is the discussion of

---

author of the Gospel has completely misappropriated them since he has no use for eschatology otherwise.
    1. Cf. Esler, *Community and Gospel*, p. 64.
    2. Schottroff, 'Das Magnificat', 305-306. Cf. the discussion of Lukan eschatology in Fitzmyer, *Gospel*, 18-22 and 231-35, and Earle Ellis, *Eschatology in Luke* (Facet Books; Philadelphia: Fortress, 1972), for the way in which the future breaks into the present in Luke.
    3. Cf. the definition given by Beardslee, *Literary Criticism*, 84.
    4. However, one must be careful not to read a modern perspective into the first century. This view is appropriate only as it fits within the 'now/not yet' eschatology of Luke's Gospel.
    5. Cf. the conclusions of Hamel, 'Le Magnificat', 83-84.
    6. For example, see Beardslee, *Literary Criticism*, 36-39; Crossan, *In Fragments*, 168-73; Williams, *Those Who Ponder Proverbs*, 26; Leo G. Perdue, 'Wisdom Sayings of Jesus', *Forum* 2 (1986), 30; Vernon K.

Beardslee, who points out two important features of the beatitudes and woes. Referring to the beatitudes of Q, which he understands to be the source behind the formulations in Matthew and Luke, Beardslee notes the power of the macarism to 'not only bring a fortunate situation to expression but to work on the situation; the word has power'.[1] He goes on to discuss the eschatological nature of the macarisms in the Gospels which distinguishes them from wisdom beatitudes. The beatitudes of the Gospels put the future in tension with the present.

> The apocalyptic commonplace of reversal, the view that at the end there will be a sharp reversal of roles ('the last shall be first and the first shall be last') has become a paradoxical reversal of roles in the present. Those who are really fortunate are the ones who are judged unhappy by ordinary standards, and this is asserted not merely as a future hope but as a paradoxical reality.[2]

This paradoxical reversal presented in the combination of beatitudes and woes serves as the exordium for Luke's sermon on the plain and repeats the form of bi-polar reversal encountered in the Magnificat.

The sermon in Luke follows the selection of the twelve (6.12-16) and a healing and teaching episode among 'a great crowd of disciples' and a 'great multitude of the people' from Jerusalem, Judea, and the seacoast region of Tyre and Sidon.[3] In the midst of Jesus' healing of people and the crowd's seeking to touch him (v. 19), Jesus looks at his disciples and begins

---

Robbins, 'Pragmatic Relations as a Criterion for Authentic Sayings', *Forum* 1/3 (1985), 35-61.

1. *Literary Criticism*, 36.

2. *Ibid.*, 37-38. Beardslee describes the way in which the present tense of the first clause in each beatitude is transformed by the future tense of the second clause in each. He also notes the way in which wisdom and eschatological traditions are welded together in the Q beatitudes. See the rest of his discussion, pp. 38-39.

3. Although Luke is following Mk 3.7-19 at this point, he has reversed the sequence of the call of the twelve and Jesus' preaching to the multitude in order to set the scene for the larger teaching discourse. The mention of members of the λαός being from Tyre and Sidon is not unimportant since it continues Luke's interest in Gentiles, already stated in 2.31-32; 3.6; 4.24-27.

to speak (v. 20). Although the address is directed specifically at
the larger group of disciples, it is clear that the multitude of
people, some of whom may not be sympathetic hearers, are
also part of the audience.[1] The statement in v. 27, Ἀλλὰ ὑμῖν
λέγω τοῖς ἀκούουσιν, might imply that the intended recipients
of the woes are absent.[2] However, the repeated use of ὑμῖν in
the woes suggests the opposite.[3] In conjunction with vv. 47 and
49, it is best to understand 'those who hear' in v. 27 not as the
entire audience of the sermon, but specifically as those who
accept Jesus' teaching. The woes are thus also intended to be

---

1. Cf. George E. Kennedy, *New Testament Interpretation through
Rhetorical Criticism* (Chapel Hill, NC: University of North Carolina
Press, 1984), 64-65. Kennedy notes that the 'distinction between the
crowd of disciples and the multitude of people suggests a greater
diversity and less initial sympathy than is found in the rhetorical situation as described by Matthew'. He goes on to argue that the beatitudes
and woes indicate a mixed audience, some more sympathetic, some
more hostile to the message. Against such a view, see E. Schweizer,
The Good News according to Luke (Atlanta: John Knox, 1984), 120,
who claims that the μαθηταί of v. 20 are limited to the smaller group of
the twelve rather than the ὄχλος μαθητῶν (v. 17), basing his argument
on the distinction made in ch. 12 between disciples and crowds.
Tannehill (*Narrative Unity*, 208) also seems to assume that the 12 are
recipients of the beatitudes, since they are the ones who have left everything and therefore are 'the poor'.
2. Cf. Creed, *Gospel*, 92. Referring to vv. 24-26, he states, 'They are
not addressed to the disciples then present, but to the rich and successful who are absent. The disciples are again addressed at v. 27 Ἀλλὰ
ὑμῖν λέγω τοῖς ἀκούουσιν.'
3. Cf. Marshall, *Gospel*, 255-56. The word ἀκούω occurs four times in
the chapter (vv. 18, 27, 47, 49). In the first instance the crowds are coming to listen to Jesus. In the second, third, and fourth uses Jesus is
challenging his audience to listen to his teaching. Drake ('Reversal
Theme', 141), perhaps following Fitzmyer (*Gospel*, 629), identifies only
three occurrences, vv. 18, 27, 47. The use in v. 49 seems particularly
important in validating the presence of actual hearers for the woes—
or rather the implication of such hearers, who hear but do not act.
This is not intended to be an argument for or against the historicity of
the scene or the sermon. Nor does it affirm or deny that the woes—or
the beatitudes—are intended for rich or poor Christians in Luke's
audience (cf. J. Dupont, *Les Béatitudes*, III [Paris: Gabalda, 1973], 24;
Pilgrim, *Good News*, 163-66). The question of Luke's audience is subsequent to the presentation of the sermon in a given context established
by the writer.

seen as relevant to part of the audience, perhaps those who 'hear but do not do' (v. 49).[1]

The repetitive patterns first seen in the Magnificat are amplified in the beatitudes and woes, and this amplification links the two texts together. In the beatitudes, the ones called μακάριοι (cf. μακαριοῦσιν, 1.48) are the poor (πτωχοί), the hungry (πεινῶντες; cf. πεινῶντας, 1.53), the ones weeping (κλαίοντες) and the hated (μισήσωσιν ὑμᾶς). The first three woes repeat the form of the first three beatitudes,[2] as those upon whom οὐαί is pronounced are the rich (πλούσιοι; cf. πλουτοῦντας, 1.53), the filled (ἐμπεπλησμένοι; cf. ἐνέπλησεν, 1.53), the laughing (γελῶντες), and those spoken of well (ὑμᾶς καλῶς εἴπωσιν). The step parallelism used in each set suggests that the poor and the rich are the two primary characters, with the subsequent lines adding particular nuances to the terms 'poor' and 'rich' and their respective reversals.[3] The fourth beatitude and fourth woe serve as closing statements for each group.

It is in the reversal experienced by each group that the use of repetitive words decisively links the beatitudes and woes together and exhibits the bi-polar structure. This is emphasized in the second and third members of each group where

1. From the perspective of ancient rhetoric, Kennedy (*New Testament Interpretation*, 65-67) states that the sermon on the whole is deliberative rhetoric, but he admits that only vv. 27-38 actually give advice for the future. The rest of the sermon, including the beatitudes and woes—the antithetical proem of the sermon—is epideictic, dealing with praise and blame. It is thus noteworthy that the sermon closes in the same way it begins, praising those who hear and do, and criticizing those who do not keep Jesus' words (vv. 46-49).

2. The first three beatitudes are composed of μακάριοι + definite article + adjective/participle + νῦν (second and third beatitudes) + ὅτι + promise of present/future reversal addressed to second person plural audience. The woes are composed of οὐαί + ὑμῖν (first and second woes) + definite article + adjective/participle + νῦν (second and third woes) + ὅτι + present/future promise addressed to second person plural audience. Fitzmyer (*Gospel*, 636) notes that the interjection οὐαί is not perfectly parallel to the beatitudes in form. This does not detract from the functional opposition created between the forms, however.

3. Cf. K.E. Bailey, *Poet and Peasant: A Literary-Cultural Approach to the Parables in Luke* (Grand Rapids: Eerdmans, 1976), 64; Drake, 'Reversal Theme', 161.

νῦν is also repeated. Whereas the kingdom of God belongs to the πτωχοί, the πλούσιοι already have their consolation (παράκλησιν). Those who are hungry (πεινῶντες) now will be filled (χορτασθήσεσθε);[1] those filled now will hunger (πεινάσετε).[2] Those weeping (κλαίοντες) now will laugh (γελάσετε); those laughing (γελῶντες)[3] now will mourn (πενθήσετε; cf. Mt. 5.4) and weep (κλαύσετε). The fourth beatitude and the fourth woe, though structured differently,[4] maintain the opposite fates of the two groups. Those hated now are told to rejoice, 'for your reward is great in heaven; for their fathers did the same things to the prophets' (κατὰ τὰ αὐτὰ γὰρ ἐποίουν τοῖς προφήταις οἱ πατέρες αὐτῶν). Woe is pronounced upon those spoken of well, 'for their fathers did the same things to the false prophets' (κατὰ τὰ αὐτὰ γὰρ ἐποίουν τοῖς ψευδοπροφήταις οἱ πατέρες αὐτῶν).[5]

Using the terms employed by Robert Alter, the beatitudes and woes establish word-roots first found in the Magnificat—such as μακάριος, πλούσιος, πτωχός, and πεινάω—as *Leitwörter* that branch off into synonyms and antonyms which

1. χορτάζω is used three other times in Luke: 9.17, where the 5000 are 'filled'; 15.16, in which the prodigal 'wished to be filled'; and 16.21, where Lazarus also 'wished to be filled'.
2. The construction of the phrase οἱ ἐμπεπλησμένοι νῦν, ὅτι πεινάσετε is a reversal of the wording in 1.53a—πεινῶντας ἐνέπλησεν ἀγαθῶν.
3. γελάω is found only in 6.21 and 6.25 in the New Testament.
4. Bailey points out that the fourth beatitude has its own special structure: three negatives, followed by a reference to the Son of man, balanced by three positives (*Poet and Peasant*, 64 n. 46).
5. The bi-polar structure can be seen in the following synopsis:

The Beatitudes	*The Woes*

Blessed are you poor
    for yours is the kingdom of God.
	Woe to you that are rich
	    for you have in full your
	    consolation.

Blessed are you that hunger now
    for you shall be satisfied.
	Woe to you that are full now
	    for you shall hunger.

Blessed are you that weep now
    for you shall laugh.
	Woe to you that laugh now
	    for you shall mourn and
	    weep.

Blessed are you when men
        hate and revile you
    for so their fathers did to
        the prophets.
	Woe to you when men speak
	        well of you
	    for so their fathers did to the
	        false prophets.

expand the oppositions of hungry, weeping, hated, filled, laughing, and well spoken of. As these *Leitwörter* establish a recurring pattern, the theme of bi-polar reversal emerges as part of the value-system of the narrative.

That the reversal is not simply a reversal of economic conditions is seen in the nature of the reversal which is to come about.[1] The poor are blessed because 'yours is the kingdom of God'.[2] Likewise, in the fourth beatitude, the victims of hatred and exclusion are told to 'rejoice in that day, and leap for joy, for behold, your reward is great in heaven'. The promised reversals focus not on socio-economic ideas but on a religious concept that has its roots in apocalyptic eschatology—this life will be overturned in the age to come.[3] Rather than trying to create some priority system between physical and spiritual conditions, however, Luke welds the two conditions together. Unlike Matthew, who clearly is more interested in the spiritual conditions of the individual, Luke equates them: physical conditions equal spiritual conditions. The socio-economically deprived are those spiritually blessed, those who are recipients of the Kingdom.[4] Those physically well off in this age already have their reward.

This leads into the question of eschatology. When does such a reversal take place? The first beatitude and the first woe have their promise in the present tense, but the ensuing use of the future tense gives a future orientation to both groups.[5] The inclusion of νῦν in the second and third beatitudes and woes

---

1. Cf. Marshall (*Commentary*, 250) who argues, 'The thought is undoubtedly spiritual—not that the poor will become rich instead of poor; a simple reversal of worldly position is not envisaged, although it is true that the deprived will enjoy plenty in the kingdom of God (16.19-31). Human need will be met by the fullness of divine salvation.'

2. R.B. Sloan (*The Favorable Year of the Lord* [Austin, TX: Schola Press, 1977], 126) argues that the 'kingdom of God' means the 'realm of God', with the reference being to the restoration of lands to occur in the Jubilee (cf. Isa. 61). Tannehill (*Narrative Unity*) consistently translates the phrase 'reign of God'. For a detailed discussion of the problem of translating the phrase and the history of interpretation, see Perrin, *Jesus and the Language of the Kingdom*, 15-82.

3. Cf. Beardslee, *Literary Criticism*, 37-38.

4. See the discussion of πτωχός in Chapter 3 below.

5. Fitzmyer, *Gospel*, 633.

shifts the focus from the imminence of the end to the present condition. Those who are hungry and weeping 'now' are contrasted with those who are full and laughing 'now'. The implied agent of the reversal for both groups is God.

The kingdom of God is presented as both a future and present reality in Luke, where God's reign has been manifested in the life and deeds of Jesus.[1] Although a future consummative reversal will take place, the end has already arrived.[2] Thus Jesus announces 'good news to the poor' and 'good news of the kingdom of God' (4.18, 43), and then says 'Blessed are the poor for yours is the kingdom of God'.[3] The rich, 'sent away empty' in the Magnificat, now are told, 'you have in full your consolation'.[4] Present and future are held in eschatological tension here, just as time elements were held in tension in the Magnificat. In both instances, the reversals are not yet, but now; there is the sense that the end has broken into the present. In both texts the reversals are to be meted out by God, not by some sort of human initiative. In the beatitudes and woes there is greater explanation of the types of people involved and the statements address physical circumstances.

As one proceeds through the rest of the Gospel, the repetition of terms found in the beatitudes and woes also suggests the breaking in of the Kingdom in the person of Jesus. On three different occasions in the two chapters following the sermon, Jesus responds to the tears of those who are weeping (κλαίω),[5]

1. On present and future in Luke, and the Lukan understanding of the end time arriving at the death of the individual, see Dupont, *Les Béatitudes*, III, 100-47.

2. Schweizer, *Good News*, 122.

3. Tannehill (*Narrative Unity*, 207) states: 'Jesus is fulfilling an important part of his commission as he says, "Happy are the poor, for God's reign is yours", for he was sent to "preach good news to the poor" and "preach good news of God's reign"' (4.18, 43).

4. παράκλησις is used only by Luke among the Gospel writers (2.25; 6.24; Acts 4.36; 9.31; 13.15; 15.31). The other use in the Gospel is noteworthy, since it is in the infancy narrative and refers to the not-yet-realized future longed for by Simeon. The text implies that the future has arrived in the presence of Jesus. The use in 6.24 clearly refers to that which is already present in the world apart from and prior to Jesus' arrival.

5. κλαίω is found 12 times in Luke–Acts (cf. 2 in Mt., 2 in Mk): 6.21, 25; 7.13, 32, 33; 8.52; 19.41; 22.62; 23.28 (2); Acts 9.39; 21.13.

first by raising a dead child back to life, then offering forgiveness of sins and salvation to a 'sinful woman'.[1] In ch. 9, Jesus feeds the 5000 and they are 'satisfied'.[2] Following the exaltation of Jesus, Luke depicts the church as a community in which there are no poor, hungry, or weeping people because the community's lifestyle overcomes such needs.[3] Whatever is said about the eschatological nature of these verses must therefore include the breaking in of the end upon the present in the person of Jesus. For the reader of Luke's Gospel, the bipolar reversal seen in the Magnificat, and initially tied to Mary and birth of the child, now becomes a cornerstone in the preaching of Jesus. The two sides subject to these opposite reversals have been further defined. Two opposite sets of physical circumstances are acted upon by God. Present conditions are reversed with the arrival of the kingdom of God in the person of Jesus. But as Luke's continued use of the terminology—especially πλούσιος and πτωχός—will show, it is the attitude behind those circumstances, toward God and toward Jesus and his message, that brings about the reversal of conditions.

The Rich Man and Lazarus (16.19-31)
In the parable of the rich man and Lazarus (16.19-31), which is located in the midst of the travel narrative and is unique to

---

1. Cf. 7.13, 38; 8.52. The last example is distinctive in Luke. In the parallel Markan account (5.35-43), Jesus asks the crowd outside why they are weeping (v. 39). When he tells them the girl is only sleeping, they laugh (καταγελάω) at him (v. 40). Matthew does not mention the crowd weeping, but does record the crowd laughing at Jesus (9.24). Luke, the only writer to have the earlier statements made to 'the disciples' (6.20) about laughing (γελάω, 6.21, 25), presents Jesus going inside the house with only Peter, James, John, and the girl's parents. *Inside* the house, 'all were weeping'—that is, Peter, James, John, and the parents. When Jesus tells them not to weep (μὴ κλαίετε, v. 52; cf. 7.13, μὴ κλαίετε), it is those close to him and the child who laugh in scorn (καταγελάω). There is thus an ironic twist to the weeping/laughter reversal, as weeping first turns to scornful laughter, then to astonishment (ἐξέστησαν, v. 56) when the child's life is restored.
2. 9.17. It is true that this is traditional material paralleled in both Matthew and Mark, but that does not erase its function in the narrative of Luke.
3. Acts 2.44-46; 4.32-37; 6.1-2; 11.27-30.

Luke's Gospel,[1] the *Leitwörter* and theme featured in the Magnificat, beatitudes, and woes become explicit in a narrative. This story is often cited as an example of the message conveyed in the beatitudes and woes. It is common to understand the context of the parable, ch. 16, as a unit composed primarily of the parable of the unjust steward (and interpretation, vv. 1-13) and that of the rich man and Lazarus (vv. 19-31). The first half of the chapter is directed specifically at the disciples; in v. 14 the audience becomes the Pharisees. There is a sense in which the two parables are presented in antithetical parallelism.[2] The first parable, regardless of the difficulties in determining the morality of its details, presents a positive message regarding the use of wealth. The steward 'makes friends for himself' by reducing the debts owed to his master. His 'prudence' is commended, and vv. 9-13 are instructions to the disciples on the proper use of wealth. 'Unrighteous mammon' is to be used to the benefit of others. In so doing, one demonstrates a faithful use of wealth and faithfulness toward God.

Verses 14-18 fit loosely together and form the introduction to the second parable.[3] In v. 14 the attention shifts to the Phar-

1. Although unique to the Lukan account, the story generally is not attributed to Lukan composition. Cf. Bultmann, *History*, 178. Fitzmyer (*Gospel*, 1125-26) notes the sparse Lukan vocabulary and suggests that the story is taken from the 'L' source with few changes. Cf. J. Jeremias, *Die Sprache des Lukasevangeliums* (Göttingen: Vandenhoeck & Ruprecht, 1980), 260-62. The story is usually divided into two parts, vv. 19-26 and vv. 27-31. Jeremias labels this a 'double-edged' parable: there are two main points, the second of which is most important. (J. Jeremias, *The Parables of Jesus* [New York: Charles Scribner's, 1963], 37-38, 186). Those who divide the parable into two parts include A. Jülicher (*Die Gleichnisreden Jesu*, II [Tübingen: Mohr, 1910], 634); Creed (*Gospel*, 208); Bultmann (*History*, 203); Crossan (*In Parables*, 66-67); Ellis (*Gospel*, 205); Degenhardt (*Lukas*, 133-34); Marshall (*Commentary*, 632); Stegemann and Schottroff (*Jesus von Nazareth*, 38); Pilgrim (*Good News*, 113-19); Fitzmyer (*Gospel*, 1126-28).

2. Cf. A. Feuillet, 'La parabole du mauvais riche et du pauvre Lazare', *La nouvelle revue théologique* 101 (1979), 222-23; Dupont, *Les Béatitudes*, III, 162-72; Bemile, *Magnificat*, 190.

3. On the difficulty of understanding the relationship of these verses, see Dupont, *Les Béatitudes*, III, 164-67, esp. 164 n. 1. Ellis perhaps has the best solution, if one accepts the standard two-part structure of the parable. He suggests that vv. 14-18 represent a two-pronged saying

isees, whom Luke describes as 'lovers of money' (φιλάργυροι). Their response is to scoff at Jesus' words.[1] In turn Jesus says, 'You are those who justify yourselves (οἱ δικαιοῦντες ἑαυτούς)[2] before men, but God knows your hearts; for what is exalted among men is an abomination in the sight of God'.[3] These two verses set the Pharisees at odds with the preceding verses and Jesus himself. Verses 16-18 appear to continue the attack on the Pharisees and their understanding of the Law. Verses 16-17 indicate that the era of the Pharisees, 'the Law and the Prophets', has come to an end although the Law itself is not nullified. Rather, it is transcended by the preaching of the kingdom.[4] Verse 18 then gives greater precision to the way in which the Law not only is not done away with, but its original intent is restored. The link of vv. 16-18 to vv. 19-31 appears to be the use of the phrase 'Law and Prophets' (v. 16) and 'Moses and the Prophets' (vv. 29, 31).[5] The indictment of the

which parallels the two-pronged parable. Verses 14-15 parallel vv. 19-26; vv. 16-18 parallel vv. 27-31 (*Gospel*, 201). Cf. Talbert, *Reading Luke*, 156.

1. Dupont (*Les Béatitudes*, III, 167, 172) suggests this verse is a redactional addition of Luke intended to introduce the parable of the rich man and Lazarus. He bases his conclusion on what to him is a discrepancy between the accusation of v. 14 and Jesus' response in v. 15.

2. Cf. 10.29; 18.9-14; 20.20. The Pharisees are repeatedly presented in Luke as grumblers who are disenchanted with the decision of Jesus to associate with tax collectors and sinners, and who are opposed to Jesus and his message (5.21, 30; 6.1-11; 7.30, 39ff.; 11.37-54; 14.1ff.; 15.2). Although a Pharisee invites Jesus to dine on three occasions, in each case a confrontation occurs in which the self-interest of the Pharisees is censured by Jesus. This self-interest, and Luke's description of them as ἱλάργυροι, places them in the same group as the πλούσιοι in the double-reversal pattern. Cf. the discussion of Schottroff and Stegemann, *Jesus von Nazareth*, 114-24. Also see Johnson, *Literary Function*, 110.

3. τὸ ἐν ἀνθρώποις ὑψηλόν recalls 14.11 (par. 18.14) and perhaps also 1.51-52, and 6.26.

4. Seccombe, *Possessions*, 178-79. Cf. Fitzmyer, *Gospel*, 1116-17.

5. Bailey (*Poet*, 117-18) suggests that, in the source behind ch. 16, vv. 9-15 originally came immediately prior to vv. 19-31. Verses 9-13 should be understood as the introduction to the Rich Man and Lazarus rather than as the concluding commentary to the Unjust Steward. Bailey's argument that Luke changed the structure because he knew Theophilus would be confused about the first parable seems far-

Pharisees in vv. 14-15 links them with the rich man of the parable, and perhaps more importantly to the disbelieving brothers who would not hear even if one was raised from the dead (v. 31).

Thus, when the exemplary story of the rich man and Lazarus is placed in this context, Jesus' immediate audience is Pharisaic, and certain physical and spiritual values are already attached to the two main characters in the story.[1] It begins with a comparison of two lifestyles—the rich (πλούσιος) man's luxurious living and sumptuous dining habits are compared to the beggarly qualities of the poor (πτωχός) man Lazarus. The rich (πλούσιος; cf. 1.52; 6.24) man's living conditions, described in v. 19, are a clear display of his wealth.[2] He customarily dresses (ἐνεδιδύσκετο)[3] in purple

---

fetched. The structure that Bailey posits for the chapter is also problematic since on reading this vv. 17-18 have no function at all.

1. Derrett sees strong parallels between the two parables of ch. 16, calling the second parable the reverse of the first parable: 'it summarizes pictorially the message of the earlier portions, supplies the answers to questions which they have raised, and adds, with an intriguing touch of irony, the reference to the current notion of individual retribution after death' (J.D.M. Derrett, 'Fresh Light on Luke XVI, II: Dives and Lazarus and the Preceding Sayings', *New Testament Studies* 7 [1960/61], 371).

2. It is common to treat the parable (vv. 19-26) as *amoral*, thus not assigning blame to the rich man, or to wealth itself, but simply reflecting the reversed conditions of each person. Crossan, *In Parables*, 68, says, 'Jesus was not interested in moral admonition on the dangers of riches—the folktale had already done this quite admirably—but in the reversal of human situation in which the Kingdom's disruptive advent could be metaphorically portrayed and linguistically made present'. For a similar judgment, see Johnson, *Literary Function*, 142, and Batey, *Jesus and the Poor*, 219. Schweizer, *Good News*, 260, speaks of the 'innocence' in which the rich man leads his life of ease. Such conclusions are reached on the basis of interpreting the parable outside the context of Luke, and apart from vv. 27-31. The question of this study is, what is the meaning and function of the double reversal of the two characters within the Lukan narrative as a whole? Within that framework, the moral character of 'a certain rich man' (τις πλούσιος ἄνθρωπος) and 'a certain poor man named Lazarus' (πτωχὸς δέ τις ὀνόματι Λάζαρος) has been developed since the Magnificat and the beatitudes and woes. Derrett, 'Fresh Light on Luke XVI', 373, goes so far as to argue that the rich man may have been a usurer and robber.

(πορφύραν)[1] and fine linen (βύσσον), and he feasts sumptu-
ously each day (εὐφραινόμενος καθ᾽ ἡμέραν λαμπρῶς).[2] At the
opposite extreme is poor (πτωχός; cf. 6.20) Lazarus. He lies
(sick) at the rich man's gate,[3] 'desiring to be fed' (ἐπιθυμῶν
χορτασθῆναι; cf. the references to the hungry, πεινῶντες, 1.53,
6.21)[4] from what fell from the rich man's table. Furthermore,
he is 'full of sores' (εἰλκωμένος)—a condition apparently like
leprosy but in some sense different since Lazarus still begs in
public[5]—and dogs come and lick the sores.[6] He clearly is
described as the beggar, which the term πτωχός implies. A final

Also see Nickelsburg, 'Riches', 338, where he compares Lk. 16.19-31
and *1 Enoch* 96.4-8; 98.2.
    3. On this use of the imperfect, cf. Marshall, *Commentary*, 635.
    1. Cf. Mk 15.17, 20; Rev. 18.12. The terms πορφύρα and βύσσος are
also linked together in Prov. 31.21 and 1QapGen 20.31.
    2. Luke uses εὐφραίνω six times in the Gospel. The link between its
use in 12.19 and 16.19 will be discussed below. The four other uses are
found in ch. 15 in the parable of the two sons. There it refers to the
special feast and merriment enjoyed when the lost brother is found.
The older brother is angered because the father never was given the
chance to 'make merry' with his friends. The fact that the rich man in
ch. 16 practices daily what was reserved for the lost son in ch. 15 again
points out the magnitude of his wealth, and perhaps his self-interested
use of it (12.19).
    3. The passive of βάλλω is often used of sick people who are bed-
ridden, e.g. Mt. 8.6, 14; Josephus, *Ant.* 9.209. Also see Rev. 2.22; Mk
7.30; Mt. 9.2; Josephus, *Bell.* 1.629. Cf. Walter Bauer, *A Greek–
English Lexicon of the New Testament and Other Early Christian Literature*, 131 (cited hereafter as BAGD).
    4. Cf. 6.21; 15.16. ἐπιθυμέω refers to unfulfilled desire in this instance,
since the beggar Lazarus is at the gate, not at the table. Cf. Marshall,
Commentary, 635. Ironically the dogs who lick his sores may be the
recipients of such crumbs (cf. Mk 7.28), if they are the rich man's dogs
as Derrett suggests. Cf. 'Fresh Light on Luke XVI', 372.
    5. Manson (*Sayings*, 298) suggests his condition is leprosy, which
would make him 'unclean' to the rich man, and to Jesus' Pharisaic
audience. Marshall (*Commentary*, 635) and Fitzmyer (*Gospel*, 1131)
reject the connection to leprosy because Lazarus begs in public.
    6. The construction ἀλλὰ καί suggests that the dogs intensify
Lazarus' suffering rather than mitigate it as Pax suggests in 'Der
Reiche und der arme Lazarus: Eine Milieustudie' (*Studii biblici franciscani liber annuus* 25 [1975], 260). Cf. the discussion on the identity of
the dogs in Hock, 'Lazarus and Micyllus: Greco-Roman Backgrounds
to Luke 19.19-31' (*Journal of Biblical Literature* 106 [1987], 458 n. 41).

distinctive feature of the poor man is that he is given the name Lazarus, meaning 'He whom God helps'.[1]

There can be no doubt from the descriptions given that the two men experience opposite fortunes in this life. At each man's death, however, their fortunes are reversed.[2] The one who had no one to care for him on earth is now given divine care ('carried by the angels to Abraham's bosom', v. 22).[3] The use of κόλπος suggests that Lazarus is now the honored guest at the eschatological banquet.[4] The rich man, on the other

1. Cf. Marshall, *Commentary*, 635.
2. It should be noted that the descriptions of the life and death of the rich man and Lazarus are presented chiastically:

    A   Life of rich man
    B   Life of poor man
    B´   Death of poor man—angels carry to Abraham's bosom
    A´   Death of rich man—buried, in Hades in torment

3. Fitzmyer, *Gospel*, 1132, notes that the imagery of angels carrying away the dead is not found in Jewish thought before AD 150 There is no agreement among scholars regarding what 'Abraham's bosom' represents. Marshall (*Commentary*, 636), notes three possibilities: 1. a child lying on its parent's lap (Jn 1.18; cf. Manson, *Sayings*, 299); 2. the closeness of a guest at a banquet (Jn 13.23; cf. R. Meyer, 'κόλπος', *TDNT*, III, 824-26; 3. a developed form of the idea of being gathered to one's fathers (Gen. 15.15). Hock ('Lazarus and Micyllus', 456), notes that the use of κόλπος has many parallels in sepulchral epigrams of the *Greek Anthology*, as well as on actual graves (see p. 456 n. 34 and n. 36).

4. Meyer, 'κόλπος', 824; cf. Jeremias, *Parables*, 184; Drake, 'Reversal Theme', 226; D. Smith, 'Table Fellowship', 625-26. There is no consensus among scholars on the nature of the eschatological scene. Do Hades and Abraham's bosom represent temporary waiting places before the final judgment or are they to be equated with Hell and Heaven, or are they simply two parts of Sheol? While Ellis's reminder that this is simply the setting of the story may be correct (*Gospel*, 206), the permanence of the reversal, seen in vv. 25-26, suggests more than a temporary abode for each. Likewise, the note that the rich man 'lifted up his eyes' suggests that Abraham's bosom is in the heavens. As already noted, Dupont links this text with others in Luke to demonstrate a Lukan understanding of the eschatological end coming at the death of the individual. This end, however, establishes what he calls a *Zwischenzustand*, not intended to replace the collective and final eschatological End. Such a view does not simply dismiss texts such as 12.13-21, 23.43, and 16.19-31, but explains their use in the larger picture of Luke's dealing with the delay of the parousia. Dupont's view

hand, is buried,[1] and the scene shifts to Hades where, being in torment (ὑπάρχων ἐν βασάνοις), he lifts up his eyes[2] and sees 'Abraham far off and Lazarus in his bosom' (v. 23). In the new setting it is the rich man who finds himself begging for mercy[3] and relief from his anguish in the fire.[4]

At three different times in the story the rich man refers to Abraham as 'father' (vv. 24, 27, 30), but kinship is of no value in changing his condition (cf. 3.8; 13.28ff.). Moreover, his recognition of Lazarus removes all doubt that Lazarus was known to him when they both were alive on earth, implying again his failure to do good to the poor (Deut. 15.4-8). Abraham's response (v. 25) also leaves no doubt about the reversal of fortunes each experienced at death. In life the rich man received good things (τὰ ἀγαθά)[5] and the poor man evil (τὰ

---

thus merits serious consideration. Cf. *Les Béatitudes*, III, 99-147; 'Die individuelle Eschatologie im Lukasevangelium und in der Apostelgeschichte', 37-47. On the use of βάσανος as eternal torment and the use of Abraham in the judgment scene, cf. *4 Macc.* 13.15-17: 'Great is the ordeal and peril of the soul that lies in wait in eternal torment for those who transgress the commandment of God. Let us then arm ourselves with the control over the passions which comes from divine reason. After our death in this fashion Abraham and Isaac and Jacob will receive us, and all our forefathers will praise us.' Also see *2 Clem.* 10.4; 17.7b.

1. Unlike Lazarus, who evidently is left unburied, the rich man enjoys his position on earth through the process of death and burial itself (cf. *1 Enoch* 103.5-8).

2. It is perhaps mere coincidence that the exact phrasing, ἐπάρας τοὺς ὀφθαλμούς, is found in 6.20.

3. All four uses of ἐλεέω in Luke reflect a situation of one desperate for help. Cf. 17.13; 18.38, 39.

4. ὀδυνάομαι is found only in Luke–Acts in the New Testament. It is used of Jesus' parents when they could not find him (2.48); of the Ephesian church leaders upon Paul's departure (Acts 20.38); and twice in the present context (vv. 24, 25).

5. Cf. 1.53, 'He has filled the hungry with good things' (τὰ ἀγαθά). Just as 6.24 reversed the wording of 1.53 as a variation of the form, so too τὰ ἀγαθά is now applied to the rich man's former condition. Seccombe attempts to downplay v. 25 as the 'basis' of the reversal of fortunes, arguing that the main point of vv. 19-31 is the failure of the rich man to act charitably. Reversal of fortunes after death is not the point of the story, the warning to those in danger of repeating the rich man's mistake is. Seccombe therefore denies that any reversal doctrine is present *(Possessions*, 177, 180-81). While Seccombe's point about a

κακά); now Lazarus is comforted (παρακαλεῖται)[1] and the rich man is in anguish. The permanence of each condition, the finality of the double reversal of fortunes, 'has been fixed' (ἐστήρικται)[2] by the great chasm separating the two realms; no one may pass in either direction (v. 26).[3]

The scene and the conversation continue in v. 27,[4] but the

warning to act charitably is well taken, his failure to find any reversal doctrine in the text ignores the obvious for the sake of his own agenda.

1. The verb παρακαλέω recalls the related noun form παράκλησις in Lk. 6.24. Cf. Fitzmyer, *Gospel*, 1133.

2. The passive voice is again used to indicate that God is the one who has acted. As in the other two examples of bi-polar reversal noted thus far, this story presents God as the final determiner of each man's place. 'God helps' the poor; he sends the rich away empty. The verb στηρίζω is also used in 9.51 to indicate a permanent condition: Jesus 'set' (ἐστήρισεν) his face to go to Jerusalem.

3. Whereas, by implication at least, the rich man had the choice of acting benevolently toward Lazarus during their lifetimes, after death no options for contact remain.

4. Since the account as given in Luke is of primary concern, vv. 19-31 are being treated as a unit. For a survey of research on the common assumption that the parable ends in v. 26, with vv. 27-31 being a later addition, see Hock, 'Lazarus and Mycyllus', 448-55. Hock himself defends the literary unity of vv. 19-31 on the basis of comparable stories of reversal in Graeco-Roman literature, particularly those of the Cynics. He takes seriously the failure of other approaches to explain why the two participants in the story have a reversal of fortunes after death. Against the larger background of traditional culture—rather than limiting the scope of possible parallels to Jewish or Oriental literature—Hock believes the rhetorical, philosophical and literary sources of the Graeco-Roman world give clarity to the narrative as a whole. Especially noteworthy is his discussion of two school exercises (pp. 456-57), σύγκρισις ('comparison') and ἠθοποιία ('characterization') in the ancient rhetorical curriculum. Types of comparison the student learned included the praise of one person and censure of another, and the comparing of groups by taking extreme examples from each group. Hock then cites Philostratus' observation that the rich and poor were a favorite subject for advanced declamations of rhetoricians (*V. Soph.* 481). Another recent attempt to find a unified structure for vv. 19-31 is the work of F. Schnider and W. Stenger, 'Die offene Tür und die unüberschreitbare Kluft', *New Testament Studies* 25 (1978/79), 273-83. They do, however, divide the narrative into a narrated world (vv. 19-23) and a dialogical world (vv. 24-31). Tannehill (*Narrative Unity*, 131-32, 185-87), treats the narrative as a unity with different scenes, although the only specific scene mentioned is comprised of vv. 19-21.

point of the story takes on a different focus.[1] The rich man asks father Abraham to send Lazarus to warn his five brothers, lest they also end up in torment. When Abraham suggests that the rich man's brother should listen to Moses and the prophets (v. 29), the rich man already knows the suggestion will not work, implying that, although they are sons of Abraham, they have not in the past and will not in the future pay attention to Moses and the prophets. The rich man hopes that sending Lazarus back from the dead will cause them to repent.[2] Abraham responds by saying that not even someone rising from the dead will convince them (v. 31). The rich have their consolation on earth (6.24) and their self-interested use of it hinders them from serving God (16.13). Together with vv. 14-18, these last verses serve as an indictment of the Pharisees, clearly establishing their place in the Lukan understanding of the reversal theology at work in his Gospel.

The conclusion in v. 31 functions to heighten the tension between Jesus and the Pharisees and, for the Lukan audience, gives further evidence for the refusal of some Jews, at least, to be convinced by one rising from the dead. While there is an unmistakable message about the use of wealth during one's

1. Hock compares the dialogue between the rich man and Lazarus to a similar scene in Lucian's *Cataplus* in which the rich tyrant Megapenthes engages in an extended dialogue with Clotho, the ferryman in Hades. Megapenthes repeatedly tries to bargain with Clotho, but Clotho is unmoved. Noting the similarity of the dialogues between Megapenthes and Clotho, and the rich man and Abraham, Hock remarks, 'both dialogues have the same function: to reveal further the character of the rich man and to underscore his radically altered and permanent situation in Hades. These scenes, however, are still only secondary incidents in the whole narrative. The primary outcome of both *Cataplus* and parable is the reversal in status of rich and poor.' Hock's interpretation thus goes against the approach of Jeremias and others which placed the emphasis on the last five verses as the primary point of the 'double-edged parable' ('Lazarus and Micyllus', 459).

2. Again, in the Lukan presentation, there clearly is an indictment of the rich man and his brothers; otherwise there is no need to repent, no need to hear what they have previously refused to hear, i.e. Moses and the Prophets. Funk argues that the entire parable is an attempted 'reversal of reversal', since the point of these last verses is to change the views toward wealth and its use among the hearers of the story. See 'Structure in the Narrative Parables of Jesus', *Semeia* 2 (1974), 72.

life in this passage, the bi-polar reversal also has to do with attitudes accompanying one's socio-economic condition.[1] God is accessible to the helpless and will act to reverse their fortunes. The possibility of using wealth properly is extended in the first half of ch. 16, but the self-interest of the wealthy and enjoyment of life's pleasures precludes them from hearing either Moses and the prophets, or one rising from the dead.

In the three texts examined thus far, God has been the initiator of the reversals. This last text introduces the possibility of human action changing the outcome of the reversal, but in the story no actual changes occur. The human initiative is pushed further in the parable of the Pharisee and publican and the antithetic aphorisms. God is still the ultimate determiner of reversal, but the reversal one experiences is based on human attitudes toward self and toward God. The eschatological aspect of reversal, clearly present in the three previous examples, is found in the aphorisms as well, but a greater emphasis at times is placed on the temporal side of the present/future tension.

The Pharisee and the Publican (18.9-14)
In ch. 18, the *Leitwörter* ὑψόω and ταπεινός (1.52) are taken up at the conclusion of the parable of the Pharisee and the Publican (18.9-14). The parable is the last of the exemplary stories peculiar to the third Gospel.[2] It is the second of two parables in ch. 18 which are linked on the surface, at least, by the subject of prayer.[3] The first (vv. 1-8) deals with the issue of persistence in prayer. God's vindication of the elect who persist in prayer in the face of adversity is compared to an unrighteous judge who relents to the persistent complaint of a

---

1. Johnson is correct in seeing the way in which the rich/poor motif functions to denote those who can accept and reject Jesus. Cf. *Literary Function*. Also see B.C. Aymer, 'A Socioreligious Revolution: A Sociological Exegesis of "Poor" and "Rich" in Luke–Acts', Ph.D. dissertation, Boston University, 1987.
2. Cf. Bultmann, *History*, 178-79.
3. Creed, *Gospel*, 222. The second parable clearly has more than one's manner of praying in mind, however. Cf. Fitzmyer's comments, *Gospel*, 1194.

widow.[1] Just as an uninterested judge[2] ultimately acts to vindicate the widow, surely God will speedily vindicate his elect
who cry out to him (vv. 7-8). In spite of God's faithfulness,
however, the question of human faithfulness remains in doubt.
'Nevertheless, when the Son of man comes, will he find faith
on earth?'

The question with which the first parable ends prepares
Luke's audience for a series of teachings concerning proper
and improper attitudes toward God.[3] The second parable of the
chapter (vv. 10-14a) is introduced by Luke.[4] 'He also told this
parable to some who trusted in themselves (τινας τοὺς
πεποιθότας ἐφ' ἑαυτοῖς)[5] that they were righteous (δίκαιοι)[6] and
despised others (ἐξουθενοῦντας τοὺς λοιπούς)' (v. 9). That
Luke has in mind the Pharisaic attitudes previously portrayed
in chs. 15 and 16 immediately becomes clear as Jesus tells the
story of a Pharisee and a tax collector coming to the temple to
pray who clearly represent opposite ends of the social and
religious spectrum.[7] The Pharisee's attitude as he prays[8] and

---

1. The concept of God as the ultimate patron or benefactor for his
people is central to this parable, and the following one as well. Cf.
Bruce J. Malina, *The New Testament World: Insights from Cultural
Anthropology* (Atlanta: John Knox, 1981), 86-87; Danker, *Luke*, 2nd
edn, 20.

2. Danker (*Jesus and the New Age*, 2nd rev. edn, 294-95) states that
the judge's self-description, 'I neither fear God nor regard man' (v. 4),
was a piece of stock rhetoric, probably intended to show his complete
impartiality.

3. 18.9-30. Cf. Talbert, *Reading Luke*, 170-71.

4. Jeremias, *Die Sprache*, 272. Cf. 18.1; 14.7.

5. Jeremias (*Parables*, 140) translates the phrase 'who trusted in
themselves (instead of God) because (ὅτι) they were righteous'. Cf.
2 Cor. 1.9.

6. Cf. the description of the Pharisees in 16.5, 'You are those who justify yourselves (δικαιοῦντες ἑαυτούς) before men'. Also see 10.29.

7. This opposition is implied throughout the Lukan account, but
nowhere as sharply drawn as here. Cf. 5.27-30; 7.29-30; 15.1-2.

8. The wording of v. 11a (σταθεὶς πρὸς ἑαυτὸν ταῦτα προσηύχετο) is
awkward, as the textual variants demonstrate. The two most likely
readings are 'he stood and prayed thus with himself' or 'he stood by
himself and prayed thus'. Manson (*Sayings*, 31) Creed and *Gospel*,
224, opt for the latter, believing it contributes more to the story.
Fitzmyer (*Gospel*, 1186), suggests πρὸς ἑαυτόν should be translated
'about himself'.

the prayer itself express his obvious distaste for 'other people' (οἱ λοιποὶ τῶν ἀνθρώπων; cf. v. 9) and his reliance upon his own acts of piety (v. 12). The Pharisee makes no requests, but thanks God (ὁ θεός, εὐχαριστῶ σοι) that he is not like the extortioners (ἅρπαγες), unjust (ἄδικοι; cf. δίκαιοι in v. 9), adulterers (μοιχοί), or for that matter, the tax collector standing nearby. Moreover, his fasting and tithing far exceed the requirements of the Law.[1] He obviously understands himself as 'just' compared to the 'unjust' tax collector.

In contrast to the self-confident Pharisee, the tax collector comes to the temple and, 'standing at a distance' (μακρόθεν ἑστώς),[2] dares not even look to heaven (ἤθελεν οὐδὲ τοὺς ὀφθαλμοὺς ἐπᾶραι εἰς τὸν οὐρανόν)[3] but contritely beats his breast (ἔτυπτεν τὸ στῆθος αὐτοῦ)[4] as he speaks (λέγων).[5] Unlike the boasts of the Pharisee, the publican says, 'God be merciful to me a sinner' (ἱλάσθητί μοι τῷ ἁμαρτωλῷ).[6] Jesus then declares that the tax collector went to his house justified (δεδικαιωμένος) rather than the Pharisee (παρ' ἐκεῖνον). God heard his plea for mercy and acquitted him.[7] On the other

---

1. See the discussions of this point in Jeremias, *Parables*, 140-41; Fitzmyer, *Gospel*, 1187-88; Marshall, *Commentary*, 679-80.
2. Marshall (*Commentary*, 680) suggests the meaning is that the tax collector was standing in the outer temple court. Cf. H.L. Strack and P. Billerbeck, *Kommentar zum Neuen Testament aus Talmud und Midrasch*, II (Munich: C.H. Beck, 1924), 246 (hereafter cited as Strack–Billerbeck). Whether or not that is true, the contrast between the Pharisee and the tax collector is to be seen even in their placement and posture at the temple.
3. Cf. *1 Enoch* 13.5. Fitzmyer (*Gospel*, 1188) notes the phrase ἐπαίρειν τοὺς ὀφθαλμούς is a Septuagintalism in Luke. Note that the same phrase is used, only in a positive sense, in two other reversal texts: 6.20 and 16.23.
4. Cf. 23.48. G. Stählin notes the contrast between the humble self-beating of the publican and the humiliation of being struck by another, as in Lk. 6.29. See 'τύπτω', *TDNT*, VIII, 264; also see p. 262 n. 18.
5. The words of the publican are not even identified as 'prayer', in contrast to the Pharisee's προσηύχετο (v. 11).
6. Cf. 5.8, 30-32; 7.34, 37, 39; 15.1-2, 7, 10; 19.7. Little doubt is left in the minds of Luke's audience by this point about God's response to the ἁμαρτωλός.
7. Cf. G. Schrenk, 'δικαιόω', *TDNT*, II, 215.

hand, παρ' ἐκεῖνον[1] leaves no doubt that the prayer of the Pharisee was rejected.[2] The Pharisee thus came already secure in his self-righteousness, only to be rejected by God; the tax collector came before God as a helpless sinner and found acceptance.

In the story, the justification of the tax collector clearly is a present time event. The concluding aphorism (v. 14) suggests that more than the immediate response to prayer is at stake, however. 'For everyone who exalts (ὑψῶν) himself will be humbled (ταπεινωθήσεται); everyone who humbles (ταπεινῶν) himself will be exalted (ὑψωθήσεται).'[3] The aphorism goes beyond anything stated in the story with regard to the humbling of the Pharisee, and brings overtones of eschatological reversal to the parable. The future passive, or theological passive, suggests that the reversal is to be brought about ultimately by the judgment of God.[4] The saying confirms that the self-understanding of each individual is instrumental in the bi-polar reversal that takes place in God's rejection of the Pharisee's prayer and justification of the lowly publican. The motif in the story of the 'just one being unjustified'/'unjust one being justified' is reinforced by the articulation of bi-polar reversal in the aphorism. The thematic double-reversal statement establishes the cognitive framework for thinking about

1. On the meaning of the preposition and the phrase παρ' ἐκεῖνον, see Fitzmyer, *Gospel*, 1188; Jeremias, *Parables*, 141-42; Marshall, *Commentary*, 680; G. Schrenk, 'δικαιόω', *TDNT*, II, 215 n. 16. Whether one chooses 'rather than' or 'and not' the rejection of the Pharisee and acceptance of the tax collector is still clear.

2. Jeremias, *Parables*, 142. Cf. Tullio Aurelio, *Disclosures in den Gleichnissen Jesu* (Frankfurt: Peter Lang, 1986), 163; Johnson, *Literary Function*, 137-38.

3. Various conclusions have been reached in the past regarding the authenticity of the aphorism as a conclusion to the parable. Various scholars argue that the aphorism is a Lukan redaction, or a secondary addition already in Luke's source, or perhaps originally part of the parable. Cf. Jeremias, *Parables*, 107, 144; Fitzmyer, *Gospel*, 1183; Bultmann, *History*, 178. In the context of this study, however, the aphorism is crucial for understanding the bi-polar reversal framework in which the parable is to be understood by the reader.

4. In both uses of the aphorism, the now–not yet tension is presented in the juxtaposition of the present participle and the future passive indicative.

the reversals experienced by the Pharisee and publican in the story.

The parable is one more example of the characteristic opposition in Luke of tax collector/sinner and Pharisee.[1] The story comments on the previous scenes in which Jesus' acceptance of tax collectors and sinners created conflict with the Pharisees.[2] The aphorism also affects the meaning of the following verses in ch. 18.[3] Luke illustrates the nature of the humble and self-exalted with the pericope on little children (vv. 15-17—the humble who enter the Kingdom) and the narrative of the rich ruler (vv. 18-30—one who has kept the Law from his youth but is apparently excluded from the Kingdom due to his unwillingness to part with his wealth).

The Chiastic Antithetic Aphorisms
The aphorism which concluded the parable of the Pharisee and the publican, along with the remaining examples of explicit bi-polar reversal in Luke, exhibit the theme of bi-polar reversal in sayings that have been labeled reversal texts in previous studies of proverbs or aphorisms in the Gospels.[4] Unlike the previous examples which are unique to Luke's

1. Cf. 5.30; 7.29-30; 15.2.
2. 'Instead of narrating a story about Jesus encountering Pharisees and tax collectors, the narrator has Jesus narrate a story about a Pharisee and tax collector. This story, like the parables of the great supper, lost sheep, lost coin, lost son, rich man and Lazarus (Luke 14–16), should be understood in the context of the larger Lukan story as comments on the kind of people that Jesus is encountering in his mission. Specifically, the story of the Pharisee and tax collector is a comment on the Pharisees and tax collectors in previous scenes and provides further support for Jesus' acceptance of sinners' (Tannehill, *Narrative Unity*, 107).
3. Cf. Talbert, *Reading Luke*, 170-71. Talbert views 18.9-30 as a composite unit dealing with the question of 18.8b: 'Nevertheless, when the Son of man comes will he find faith on earth?' The parable presents a self-exalted man and a humble man. Verses 15-17 are thus an illustration of the same kind of humility called forth by the parable. Verses 18-30 are a second attempt to make the comparison, this time between the rich ruler and the disciples who have left everything.
4. See the discussion of Beardslee in ch. 1, pp. 25-27. It is important to remember that, in Alter's terms, a 'theme' appears in a recurring pattern that is part of the value-system of the narrative.

account, each of the aphorisms studied here is found in other synoptic accounts. However, there is variation in the number of uses in each Gospel and in the contexts within which a particular aphorism is found.[1] These aphorisms have been called 'eschatological reversal sayings' by Perrin,[2] and have been more narrowly defined as antithetic aphorisms by Tannehill.[3] As Beardslee demonstrates, these verses have their roots in the antitheses of the Wisdom tradition which are intensified by the use of paradox.[4] Specifically he suggests that the story lying behind proverbs such as Lk. 9.24, 13.30 and 14.11 is a story of a reversal of fortune.[5]

Studies that have followed Beardslee have more sharply defined the terms proverb and aphorism.[6] Williams's distinction between the two terms focuses not on form but function.[7]

1. The texts are: Lk. 14.11//18.14b (cf. Mt. 23.12); Lk. 9.24//17.33 (cf. Mt. 10.39; 16.25; Mk 8.35; Jn 12.25); Lk. 13.30 (cf. Mt. 19.30; 20.16; Mk 10.31).

2. *Jesus and the Language of the Kingdom*, 52.

3. *Sword*, 98, 101. Tannehill defines antithetic aphorisms as 'brief pointed sayings which contain a sharp contrast. The saying tends to divide into two halves, with the same key words, in negative and positive form, or with antithetical terms. Thus there are word links between the two halves' (p. 89). By this definition it is clear that other Gospel sayings are antithetical, but not necessarily bi-polar reversals.

4. 'Uses of the Proverb', 66.

5. 'The kind of antithesis which provides the background for the Synoptic paradox is the antithesis which expresses a reversal of situations. The story which lies behind the proverb is a story of reversal of fortune. This is a very ancient proverbial form. Probably its original form, and certainly a very ancient widespread usage, was the function of expressing the disastrous consequence of exceeding one's role' ('Uses of the Proverb', 66).

6. For a discussion of the uses of terms and the aphoristic genre, see Crossan, *In Fragments*, 3-36; Vernon K. Robbins, 'Picking Up the Fragments: From Crossan's Analysis to Rhetorical Analysis', *Forum* 1/2 (1985), 31-64. Especially note Robbins's definition of an aphorism (p. 36).

7. Williams, *Those Who Ponder Proverbs*, 80. 'The real distinction between them [proverb and aphorism] is not so much formal as it is a matter of purpose and function. What was the intended use, and does the saying in question pretend to speak for a populace or tradition, or for an individual? The attribution of specific authorship to aphorism, and of popular origins and appeal to proverb, are useful but not decisive characteristics.'

He believes the primary difference is between the collective voice and the individual voice. 'The proverb expresses the voice of the human subject as ancient, collective wisdom, whereas aphorism (certainly the modern literary aphorism) brings the subjectivity of the individual more to the fore'.[1] Crossan treats the differences between proverb, aphorism, and fragment as different stages on a continuum that could be formed into a circle. 'A fragment could eventually become a proverb and a proverb could be transformed into a fragment.'[2] In the case of the three sayings in question, they are each given particular, but varying, contexts by the synoptic writers, but the authoritative voice of Jesus gives them the characteristic traits of aphorisms. Yet their appearance in related forms in ancient literature, both Graeco-Roman and Jewish, indicates the proverbial background from which they have been appropriated.

A primary feature of the antithetical aphorisms in the Gospels, particularly those which employ paradox and hyperbole, is the way in which such sayings jolt the expectations of the hearer/reader.[3] Rather than confirming one's vision of the world, such aphorisms present a counter world through paradox. Such reorientation often is described as eschatological reversal, in which the present will be radically reversed in the future. This appears to be world-denying, leaving only the prospect of a new world. But as Beardslee points out, 'Though eschatological urgency may easily take the direction of abandonment of the present, this kind of eschatological hope produces a faith sharply focused on the present, and ready to make demands on the present which are beyond common sense possibility'.[4] Or, as Perrin puts it, 'It presents the Kingdom of God as eschatological reversal of the present and so

---

1. *Ibid.*
2. Crossan, In *Fragments*, 20.
3. Beardslee, 'Uses of the Proverb', 66; 'Saving One's Life by Losing It', 58. Cf. Tannehill (*Sword*, 98) who says, 'The antithetical aphorism gains much of its force through sharp attack on a prevailing perspective. The saying is arresting because it resonates against a customary viewpoint in which the hearer has invested himself, and so the hearer feels it as a challenge to him.'
4. 'Uses of the Proverb', 72.

invites, indeed, demands, judgment upon the present'.[1] The tension between future and present, seen repeatedly in the study thus far, is now expressed in these antithetical sayings which highlight the paradox confronting the reader/hearer.

Exalted / Humbled–Humbled / Exalted (14.11 / / 18.14). The aphorism already seen above (18.14b) is first found in ch. 14 (v.11). The first 24 verses of the chapter form a unit tied together by the literary motif of table-fellowship.[2] The chapter begins with Jesus being invited to dine at the house of a 'ruler of the Pharisees' (τινος τῶν ἀρχόντων τῶν Φαρισαίων). That the occasion is not a simple matter of eating together is clear at the end of the first verse: 'they (the Pharisees) were watching (παρατηρούμενοι)[3] him'. The guests at the meal include Pharisees and lawyers (v.3), who can only watch in silence as Jesus heals a man suffering from dropsy (vv.3, 6).[4] In response to Jesus' challenge that they would save a son or an ox from the well on the Sabbath, the Pharisees 'could not reply to this' (οὐκ ἴσχυσαν ἀνταποκριθῆναι πρὸς ταῦτα).[5]

The banquet scene itself becomes the focus of vv.7-14, as Jesus gives instructions on the social behavior of guests (vv.8-

---

1. *Jesus and the Language of the Kingdom*, 52.

2. On the use of the Symposium as a Hellenistic literary device, and its use in Luke's Gospel, see D. Smith, 'Table Fellowship as a Literary Motif in the Gospel of Luke', *Journal of Biblical Literature* 106 (1987), 613-38; E. Springs Steele, 'Luke 11.37-54—A Modified Hellenistic Symposium?', *Journal of Biblical Literature* 103 (1984), 379-94; Steele, 'Jesus' Table-Fellowship with Pharisees: An Editorial Analysis of Luke 7.36-50, 11.37-54, 14.1-24' (Ph.D. dissertation, Notre Dame, 1981); J. Delobel, 'L'Onction par la pécheresse: La composition littéraire de Lc., VII, 36-50', *Ephemerides theologicae lovanienses* 42 (1966), 458-64; X. de Meeus, 'Composition de Lc., XIV et genre symposiaque', *Ephemerides theologicae lovanienses* 37 (1961), 847-70.

3. παρατηρέω is used three times in Luke (6.7; 14.1; 20.20), once in Acts (9.24). The purpose of watching is to find fault (6.7; 14.1) or to find opportunity to seize (20.20; Acts 9.24). A sense of hostility is implied in each instance. On the use of the middle voice with active meaning, see Blass–Debrunner–Funk, *Grammar*, §316.

4. The term ὑδρωπικός is found only here in the New Testament. The healing narrative is otherwise quite similar to 6.6-11, par. Mk 3.1-6, Mt. 12.9-14.

5. The term ἰσχύω is also used in 13.24, for the many who 'will not be able' to enter through the narrow door.

10) and the proper attitude of a good host (vv. 12-14).[1] In v. 7 Luke introduces the scene, calling the following sayings of Jesus a parable. These instructions are motivated by the tendency Jesus notes in his fellow guests (Pharisees and lawyers, v. 3) to seek the places of honor (πρωτοκλισίας). When one attends a marriage feast, one should not sit at the place of honor, lest someone more important be invited, and the host ask him to move. Then in shame the self-exalted person will go to the last place (ἔσχατον τόπον) to sit. Rather, when invited, one should go to the last place; then the host may invite him to go higher, thus bringing him honor in the presence of all. The aphorism in v. 11 serves as confirmation and explanation of Jesus' teaching: 'Everyone who exalts (ὑψῶν) himself will be humbled (ταπεινωθήσεται); everyone who humbles (ταπεινῶν) himself will be exalted (ὑψωθήσεται)'.[2]

As already seen, the same aphorism concludes the parable of the Pharisee and the publican. It is the particular use of the aphorism on the lips of Jesus in these contexts that determines its function in Luke's Gospel. Close parallels to the saying are found in both Jewish[3] and Graeco-Roman[4] literature. In both

1. Verses 8-10 and 12-14 are each presented in antithetical parallelism, with the aphorism in v. 11 serving as climax of the sayings. Cf. Jeremias, *Parables*, 192 n. 90, who claims that v. 11 and v. 14b serve as eschatological conclusions to each group of sayings.

2. The chiastic structure—A ὑψῶν B ταπεινωθήσεται B' ταπεινῶν A' ὑψωθήσεται—intensifies the bi-polar reversal form. The saying builds upon the *Leitwörter* ὑψόω and ταπεινόω first seen in the Magnificat (1.48, 52).

3 Cf. Ezek. 21.31 (LXX). 'This shall not be: humble that which is high and exalt that which is low' (ἐταπείνωσας τὸ ὑψηλὸν καὶ τὸ ταπεινὸν ὕψωσας); Ps. 74.8 (LXX) ὅτι ὁ θεὸς κριτής ἐστιν, τοῦτον ταπεινοῖ καὶ τοῦτον ὑψοῖ; *Ep. Arist.* 363 'God destroys the proud and exalts the gentle and humble' (quoted from *The Old Testament Pseudepigrapha*, Vol. 2, ed. J.H. Charlesworth [Garden City, NY: Doubleday, 1985], 30). Also see Strack–Billerbeck, II, 402; *Erub.* 13b 'Him who humbles himself, the Holy One, blessed be He, raises up, and him who exalts himself, the Holy One, blessed be He, humbles' (English translation from Bultmann, *History*, 21). For other rabbinic parallels, see Strack–Billerbeck, I, 774, 921.

4. Cf. Diogenes Laertius, *Lives*, 1. 69 'When Chilon the Lacedaemonian asked Aesop what Zeus was doing, he got the answer, "He is humbling the proud and exalting the humble"' (τὰ μὲν ὑψηλὰ ταπεινῶν,

uses in Luke, and the single reference in Matthew (23.12), the Pharisees are the primary targets of criticism. Both uses in Luke offer parallel critiques of the self-exalting attitudes of the Pharisees, in contrast to societal outcasts (14.13, 18.13) whose exaltation comes from God. In both contexts the aphorism gives eschatological overtones to a temporal setting, bringing out the now–not yet tension characteristic of bi-polar reversal. Also, in both uses of this aphorism, the reversal is wrought by God but human attitudes are determinate for one's ultimate position. The choices are self-humiliation and self-exaltation. God reverses the human condition of both. The aphorism suggests such attitudes can be chosen and acted upon in the present.[1]

Losing by Saving–Saving by Losing (9.24 / / 17.33). The aphorism 'whoever would save his life will lose it; whoever loses his life for my sake will save it' is used twice in Luke (9.24; 17.33). The first occurrence follows the confession of Peter that Jesus is 'the Christ of God' (9.20) and the first passion prediction (vv. 21-22). The aphorism is part of a collection of five sayings that explain the manner and means of 'following' Jesus (vv. 23-27). While the account follows the Markan order closely, there are distinctive differences that shape Luke's presentation. Rather than dividing the material into three different scenes, as both Mark and Matthew do, Luke combines vv. 18-27, making a single scene. He does this primarily by omitting words and phrases that separate the scenes in Mark.[2] In so doing the tension between Peter's confession of Jesus as the Christ and Jesus' immediate

---

τὰ δὲ ταπεινὰ ὑψῶν). Also see Cicero, *De officiis*, 1.26. 90: 'The higher we are placed, the more humbly we should walk'.

1. The verses following the aphorism in 14.11 make this point. Cf. the discussion by Tannehill, *Narrative Unity*, 184-85.

2. For example, Luke omits the phrase of Mk 8.31, καὶ ἤρξατο διδάσκειν αὐτούς, and links the passion prediction directly to Jesus' command to silence (Lk. 9.21) with the participle εἰπών. Rather than calling the crowd together (Mk 8.34 προσκαλεσάμενος τὸν ὄχλον σὺν τοῖς μαθηταῖς αὐτοῦ), Luke implies an audience larger than the disciples, using πάντας (v. 23) but maintaining the sequence of the same scene by using the imperfect ἔλεγεν.

prediction of suffering is heightened. The suffering Christ then becomes the background for the call to follow Jesus.

Luke modifies v. 23 to underscore the continuing experience of discipleship for his audience. The present infinitive ἔρχεσθαι is used instead of the aorist ἐλθεῖν,[1] and καθ᾽ ἡμέραν is added following 'take up his cross'. Just as the Spirit-filled Jesus—the conqueror of this age—must suffer, so the would-be follower must share the same experience of self-denial, daily taking up a cross[2] and following Jesus.

The eschatological tension of the present versus the future, or now versus not yet,[3] dominates the series of sayings that follow. Verses 24 and 25 present the future that must be avoided by choosing self-denial in the present. 'Whoever would save (σῶσαι) his life will lose (ἀπολέσει) it; whoever loses (ἀπολέσῃ) his life for my sake will save (σώσει) it.'[4] ἀπόλλυμι and σώζω are juxtaposed as opposites, and two types of people are placed in opposition. Wishing to save one's life will bring about the opposite, destruction or loss of life.[5] On the other hand, the one who loses his life 'for my sake' (ἕνεκεν ἐμοῦ) will save it. The person who 'wishes to save' (θέλῃ σῶσαι) his life, in

---

1. Cf. Mt. 16.24; Mk 8.34. In the latter there is a textual variant, ἀκολουθεῖν, which is the chosen reading in Nestle's 26th edition/UBS 3rd edition. Nestle's 25th edition used the variant ἐλθεῖν.

2. Cf. Lk. 14.27. For a discussion of the debate over the historicity and meaning of the metaphorical demand to 'take up his cross', see Fitzmyer, *Gospel*, 784-86, 787.

3. Talbert (*Reading Luke*, 105) discusses the balance of 'now' and 'not yet' in the eschatology of first-century Christianity: 'The New Age had broken in with the resurrection of Jesus, but the Old Age continues until the parousia'. The Christian life is thus lived in the overlap. Luke presents Jesus as both 'anointed with the Spirit' and destined to suffer and die, reflecting the coming of the New Age and the limitations of the Old. The disciples are called to live in the same tension.

4. Crossan labels this structure 'inverted or chiastic antithetical parallelism. (*In Fragments*, 89). The bi-polar reversal created by these oppositions is heightened by the obvious chiastic structure:

　　A σῶσαι → B ἀπολέσει——B´ ἀπολέσῃ → A´ σώσει.

5. ἀπόλλυμι has two possible meanings, 'to lose' or 'to destroy', both of which are employed by Luke in various contexts. Cf. BAGD, 95. Either definition stands in sharp contrast to σώζω. Tannehill (*Sword*, 190 n. 39) opts for the stronger definition 'destroy' in his discussion of this aphorism. However, in relation to v. 25 where Luke adds ἀπολέσας, the translation 'lose' fits the Lukan context better.

this context, is the opposite of the one who 'wishes to come after me' (θέλει ὀπίσω μου ἔρχεσθαι, v. 23) since the latter requires self-denial, not self-preservation. Two opposite attitudes paradoxically bring about reversed conditions.

Verse 25 illuminates the error one makes by choosing to 'save' rather than 'lose' one's life. The link between vv. 24a and 25 is made clear in Luke by the addition of ἀπολέσας; there is no profit in gaining the whole world if one 'loses or forfeits himself'.[1] Verse 26 then explains this reversal in terms of one rejecting Jesus' call to discipleship ('Whoever is ashamed of me and my words') and makes explicit the relationship of the present to the future.[2] Negative response in the present means negative reception by the Son of man in the future.

The final saying of the group, in contrast to the previous two verses, suggests a positive result for some who are present: they will not die before they see the kingdom of God.[3] The reference may be to the group of disciples who witness the transfiguration, presented in the following verses (9.28-36). More likely, however, v. 27 refers to those who accept Jesus' call to discipleship as opposed to those who attempt to 'save' their lives and therefore lose them instead.

In ch. 17, the context for the aphorism in v. 33 at first appears to be considerably different from that found in ch. 9. Verse 33 is usually understood to be an independent saying in

1. This point is later demonstrated again in Luke by the parable of the rich fool (12.13-21). The structure of 9.25 also differs from the parallels in Mark and Matthew where Luke uses ἑαυτόν in place of τῆς ψυχῆς αὐτοῦ.
2. Mk 8.37 (par. Mt. 16.26b) is omitted by Luke, tightening the structure of vv. 24-26, with the three sayings beginning in a similar way: 'For whoever'; 'For what'; 'For whoever'.
3. The contrast is brought out by the use of δέ. Luke again joins the saying more closely to the previous sayings by eliminating Mark's καὶ ἔλεγεν αὐτοῖς (Mk 9.1). Since the Kingdom is sometimes presented in Luke as having already come in the presence of Jesus (11.20; 17.21), it is not surprising that the Markan phrase 'until they see that the kingdom of God has come in power (cf. Mt. 16.28 'until they see the Son of man coming in his kingdom') is shortened in Luke to 'until they see the kingdom of God'. The tension between present and future is maintained in all of the sayings.

Q (cf. Mt. 10.39) which Luke has included as a part of an eschatological discourse within the travel narrative (vv. 22-37).[1] The collection of sayings is paralleled for the most part in Matthew 24, suggesting Q as the common source.[2] The materials unique to the Lukan discourse are striking, and in some cases reflect Lukan redaction rather than Q material omitted by Matthew.

The discourse on the coming of the Kingdom is actually introduced by a short dialogue between Jesus and the Pharisees (17.20-21) in which the Pharisees ask when the Kingdom of God is coming. Jesus replies that the Kingdom is not coming with observable signs but 'is in the midst of you' (ἐντὸς ὑμῶν ἐστιν). Having established the 'now' of the Kingdom, Jesus tells his disciples of the 'not yet' day of the Son of man (vv. 22-37). Verse 22 is unique to Luke and introduces the traditional material in vv. 23ff. The meaning of the phrase 'one of the days of the Son of man' has been the subject of much debate. The most probable suggestion, especially in light of v. 21 and v. 25, is that it refers to the earthly days of the Son of man; the time is coming when the disciples will long for Jesus' presence.[3] But the final fruition of the Kingdom is not yet. The disciples are not to believe the claims of others; there will be no need for such directions in the future day of the Son of man (vv. 23-24). First, 'the Son of man must suffer many things and be rejected by this generation' (v. 25). The verse is an obvious reference to Jesus' passion (cf. 9.22) and it assumes

---

1. Cf. the discussion of Crossan, *In Fragments*, 89-92. Crossan believes that Luke adapted the participial form of Q to the Markan form, then changed the positive verbs to avoid complete repetition.

2. Cf., in the order of the Lukan narrative, Mt. 24.23, 26-27, 37-39, 17-18, 40-41, 28. Rather than combining the Q eschatological discourse with the Markan one, as Matthew did, Luke leaves them separate, with the parallels to Mk 13 found in Lk. 21.

3. Cf. C.H. Dodd, *The Parables of the Kingdom* (New York: K. Scribner's, 1961), 81 n. 3; R. Maddox, 'The Function of the Son of Man according to the Synoptic Gospels', *New Testament Studies* 15 (1968-69), 51; C. Colpe, 'ὁ υἱὸς τοῦ ἀνθρώπου', *TDNT*, VIII, 458 n. 396. The source of the entire verse is also questioned, with some scholars believing it to be part of the L source, others Q, or perhaps Lukan redaction. See the discussion of Marshall, *Commentary*, 658-59, who admits he is rather isolated in advocating the authenticity of the verse.

the identification of Jesus with the Son of man. The verse also functions to remind the reader that suffering must precede glory (24.26). Although he must suffer first, the Son of man will come in the future.[1]

The next five verses make the coming day of the Son of man analogous to the days of Noah (vv. 26-27) and of Lot (vv. 28-30).[2] In both cases, the people were occupied with enjoying the good things of this life: eating, drinking, marriage, buying and selling, planting and building. Yet in both cases divine disasters destroyed them all.[3] The same scenario will accompany the day in which the Son of man is revealed. It will be too late to make changes, either by trying to retrieve possessions, or turning back (vv. 31-32).[4] The aphorism of v. 33 presents the bi-polar reversal, again in the context of two opposing attitudes that were introduced in vv. 31-32. Verse 33a represents the fate of Lot's wife, who tried to hold on to the past and turned back, thus losing her life (Gen. 19.26). Verse 33b represents the positive result of not returning for one's possessions at the

1. This verse is instrumental in creating a parallel context for the aphorism in 9.24 and 17.33. In both instances the positive reversal in the proverb (lose → save) is parallel to Jesus losing his life, then rising triumphantly. 17.25 also serves to remind one of the now–not yet tension by stating that the Day of the Son of man cannot be now since the death of the Son of man is still not yet. The sense of the 'not yet' drawing closer is of course heightened for a post-resurrection community.

2. Matthew 24 includes only the example of Noah (vv. 37-39). However, the use of Noah and Lot together as negative examples is regularly found in other literature, e.g. 2 Pet. 2.5-7; Wisd. 10.4-8; 3 Macc. 2.4-5; Philo, *De vita Mos.* 2.10.52-56. This fact leads some to conclude that vv. 27-29 were part of Q. Cf. the discussion of Fitzmyer, *Gospel*, 1165, who concludes, however, that other links between vv. 28-29 and 30-32 indicate vv. 28-32 were a unit in Luke's L source.

3. Verses 27 and 29 both use the phrase καὶ ἀπώλεσεν πάντας. The Matthean parallel to v. 27 (24.39) has καὶ ἦρεν ἅπαντας. The repeated used of the term ἀπόλλυμι links the verses to the aphorism with its double use of ἀπόλλυμι.

4. Verse 31 closely parallels Mk 13.15, and Luke does not have the saying in the discourse of ch. 21. This has led some to conclude that Luke inserted the Markan verse here and then created v. 32 to cement the allusion to Lot's wife at the close of v. 31. Cf. Bultmann, *History*, 123; J. Zmijewski, *Die Eschatologiereden des Lukas-Evangeliums* (Bonn: Peter Hanstein, 1972), 473-78. Regardless of the origins of the sayings, v. 32 forms an inclusio with vv. 28-29, making vv. 28-32 a unit.

coming of the Son of man (v. 31).[1] 'Whoever seeks (ζητήσῃ) to preserve (or 'keep alive'—περιποιήσασθαι) his life will lose (ἀπολέσει) it, but whoever loses (ἀπολέσῃ) his life will preserve (ζῳογονήσει) it.'[2] The chiastic structure of the verse is still apparent, although not as tightly woven as 9.24 due to the variation in terms.[3] Readiness for the coming of the Son of man—or lack thereof—in terms of one's participation in and desire for the goods and pleasures of life (vv. 26-32) thus results in opposite reversals.

The question of readiness is carried forward in the last three verses of the discourse.[4] Verses 34 and 35 present two settings, the first with two male characters, the second with two female characters. In each case one 'will be taken' (παραλημφθήσεται) and the other 'will be left' (ἀφεθήσεται).[5] In the final verse Jesus responds to the disciples' inquiry as to when this will occur. Marshall's summary is appropriate.

> It is as senseless to ask for a map of what will happen as it is to ask for a timetable. Just as the location of a corpse in the wilderness is obvious from the crowd of circling vultures, so the Son of man will appear for judgment in an unmistakable manner, and there will be no need to ask where he is.[6]

Once again, the distinctive quality of the aphorism is its function as a personal address by Jesus. As in the previous

---

1. Cf. Drake, 'Reversal Theme', 169; Zmijewski, *Die Eschatologiereden*, 472. This interpretation assumes a close link between vv. 31-33, as opposed to Crossan (*In Fragments*, 92) who claims that 17.33 contravenes 17.31-32.
2. The terms περιποιέομαι and ζῳογονέω are both found only three times in the New Testament, the former in Lk. 17.33, Acts 20.28, 1 Tim. 3.13; the latter in 17.33, Acts 7.19, 1 Tim 6.13. Both terms are found in the LXX, meaning 'to save' or 'preserve alive'. Cf. 1 Sam. 2.6 (ζῳογονέω), part of Hannah's Song, which also lies behind the Magnificat; Gen. 12.12; Exod. 1.16 (περιποιέομαι).
3. Α περιποιήσασθαι → Β ἀπολέσει——Β΄ ἀπολέσῃ → Α΄ ζῳογονήσει.
4. The sayings in vv. 34-35 follow the Noah saying in Matthew (24.40-41); Lk. 17.36 is omitted by the best MSS, an obvious assimilation to Mt. 24.40. Verse 37 is paralleled by Mt. 24.18.
5. In relation to Noah and Lot 'being taken' and the other inhabitants 'left' for destruction, the likely sense here is that 'taken' refers to salvation, 'left' to judgment. The use of the future passive gives the sense of divine action. Cf. Fitzmyer, *Gospel*, 1172-73.
6. *Commentary*, 656.

aphorism, human attitudes and actions are determinative for
the reversal itself. In the context of the previous aphorism, God
was the bringer of reversal for human attitudes and actions
already established. In the case of this aphorism, divine action
is implicit in the reversal, but the indefinite relative phrase
'whoever wishes' (ὃς ἐὰν θέλῃ) indicates that human initiative
is necessary for appropriating one or the other of the models,
i.e. saving or losing.

The motif of saving one's life by losing it for a higher good is
common to both Graeco-Roman and Jewish literature. It
appears most frequently in military settings,[1] but Beardslee
has demonstrated a variety of settings in which the motif of
gaining 'life' by dying is found.[2] Certainly the chiastic structure of the aphorism found in the Gospels intensifies the saying
and makes the paradox more striking. In both contexts in
which the saying is used in Luke, the paradox of losing by
saving/saving by losing is preceded by a prediction of Jesus'
own saving by losing (9.22; 17.25). In each context, the
'reorientation by disorientation'[3] which the aphorism itself
contains is linked to a similar reorientation demanded with
regard to Jesus and the coming of the Kingdom. In ch. 9
Peter's confession is juxtaposed to the first passion prediction;
the Christ of God must suffer the shame of death on the cross
in order to live. Only then will the Son of man come in glory
with his angels (9.26). In ch. 17, although the Kingdom is 'in
your midst' (v. 21), the Son of man is yet to come. First he must
suffer and be rejected (v. 25).

Following the paradoxical presentation of Jesus, the antithetical aphorism challenges the hearer to follow the new ori-

---

1. Bauer quotes from a 7th-century BC fragment: 'The man who risks
his life in battle has the best chance of saving it; the one who flees to
save it is most likely to lose it' (BAGD, 95). A more extensive list of
such uses is found in J.B. Bauer, 'Wer sein Leben retten will... Mk
8.35 Par.', in *Neutestamentliche Aufsätze: Festschrift für Josef
Schmid zum 70. Geburtstag* (ed. J. Blinzer *et al.*; Regensburg: Pustet,
1963), 7-10.

2. 'Saving One's Life', 61-64. Beardslee includes examples from Jewish and Graeco-Roman sources.

3. This phrase was first used by Ricoeur, and quoted by Beardslee as
appropriate for the way in which the aphorism challenges one's
understanding of existence. See 'Saving One's Life', 59, 66.

entation suggested by Jesus' own life. In ch. 9, it comes as part
of a call to discipleship. As the surrounding context makes
clear, saving by losing has both present and future conse-
quences, however. The 'now–not yet' tension is part of the
entire context. In ch. 17, in an eschatological discourse, the
proverb still serves as a call to follow Jesus in the present,[1] and
again is marked by the interplay of present and future.
Although the project of losing or saving one's life is taken up in
the present, the contexts in which the aphorism is found suggest that the great reversal ultimately is linked to the future
coming of the Son of man.

Last / First–First / Last (13.30). Whereas both of the previous
forms were explicitly directed toward human initiative in the
present, the focus in the final aphorism is on God's actions. The
Lukan rendering of this aphorism (13.30) is closest in form to
the parallel in Mt. 20.16 and is generally considered to be a Q
doublet of the form found in Mk 10.31 (par. Mt. 19.30).[2] However, the location of the saying in Luke is unique, suggesting
the aphorism was an independent saying in Q which Luke
placed in a particular context.[3] In Matthew and Mark, the
aphorism is the climactic conclusion of Jesus' encounter with
the rich young man and the following dialogue between Jesus
and his disciples on the impossibility of a rich man entering the
Kingdom. In Matthew the aphorism is explained by the parable of laborers in the vineyard (20.1-15) who are paid in
reverse order of their employment. The aphorism then is

1. Such a conclusion seems apparent from the examples of vv. 26-30,
in which those oriented toward the pleasures of life are destroyed,
those relying on God are preserved. 'Looking back' to possessions or
the life of this world results in destruction; losing the things of this
world because one is awaiting the Son of man results in life.
2. The distinction is in the order of the oppositions. Luke's order is
last/first–first/last (par. Mt. 20.16). The Markan order is first/last–
last/first (10.31, par. Mt. 19.30).
3. Crossan (*In Fragments*, 44) suggests the composition of vv. 23-30 is
most likely taken up by Luke from Q. Fitzmyer (*Gospel*, 1021-22) however, believes that vv. 22-23 are of Lukan origin, vv. 24-29 derive from Q,
and v. 30 is from the L source.

repeated (v. 16).[1] In Mark, the saying forms the climactic conclusion to the second unit of material (9.30–10.31) framed by the three passion predictions.[2]

Luke, however, omits the aphorism at the conclusion of his parallel account (18.18-30),[3] and inserts it as the conclusion of

---

1. The second use of the aphorism is written in the order found in Luke: last/first–first/last. Within the parable the terms πρῶτος and ἔσχατος are juxtaposed in v. 8. The laborers are paid in the reverse order of their hiring. The aphorism therefore does not suggest exclusion vs. inclusion; rather, God's grace extends to all. Those who are first should therefore not grumble about the inclusion of those who come late. Rather than articulating reversal, Matthew's explanation represents a leveling similar to that expressed by the form of saying found in the Gospel of Thomas: 'For many who are first will be last, and they will become one and the same' (4b). Cf. Oxyrhynchus Papyrus 654: 'For many who are f[irst] will be [last and] the last will be first and they [will have eternal life]', quoted in R.W. Funk, *New Gospel Parallels*, I, 396.

2. Crossan, *In Fragments*, 43-44. Cf. Vernon K. Robbins, 'Summons and Outline to Mark: The Three Step Progression', *Novum Testamentum* 23 (1981), 102. This section repeatedly presents the disciples thinking too highly of themselves, with Jesus having to reprimand or otherwise instruct them (e.g. 9.33-36; 9.38-39; 10.13-14). Tannehill demonstrates that the dialogue in 10.28-30 addresses false expectations the disciples had with regard to their reward for having left everything (10.28). See *Sword*, 147-52; *Narrative Unity*, 121-22. Verse 31 thus not only warns against being first like the rich man, but also of having wrong expectations as a disciple (cf. 9.35).

3. Since Luke has doubled the other two bi-polar aphorisms, it is somewhat troublesome that he omits it from the narrative of ch. 18, especially if bi-polar reversal is a form in which he is particularly interested. H. Schürmann includes the omission in his discussion of Luke's aversion to doublets ('Die Dubletten im Lukasevangelium', in *Traditionsgeschichtliche Untersuchungen zu den synoptischen Evangelien* [Düsseldorf: Patmos, 1968], 279-89). However, the double use of the other two chiastic antithetic aphorisms (9.24//17.33; 14.11//18.14) indicates that something more is involved. In the case of the other two aphorisms in Luke, there are a number of similarities in the respective contexts which give the pairs similar meanings. However, such links between 13.22-29 and 18.18-30 are not as clear. The one phrase that is similar in both narratives has to do with the question of who can be saved (13.23: 'Are those being saved few?'; 18.26: 'Then who can be saved?'). Jesus' responses are quite different, however, with the emphasis in ch. 13 being on proper human understanding and effort (v. 24) and a series of negative judgments on those who fail to enter the Kingdom (vv. 25-28). In ch. 18, the emphasis rests on the ability of God

an eschatological discourse in ch. 13.[1] The six unit aphoristic cluster (13.23-30),[2] in which the first five sayings are linked together by catchwords,[3] forms the first block of material in the second section of the travel narrative (13.22–17.10). Verse 22 repeats the reference to Jesus journeying to Jerusalem (cf. 9.51; 17.11). The section begins with a question from an unidentified source (τις): 'Are those being saved few?'[4] Jesus answers the question indirectly, calling on his audience to 'strive' (ἀγωνίζεσθε) to enter through the narrow door, 'for many will seek to enter and will not be able' (v. 24). The reference is to entrance into the Kingdom through the only door available.[5] The narrowness of the door and the 'many' unable to enter answers the question. Jesus' words also emphasize the human effort required in attaining the desired salvation.

However, v. 25 shifts the emphasis to the householder who shuts the door, after which all human effort is meaningless.

to do the impossible—'What is impossible with men is possible with God' (v. 27)—followed by positive statements toward the disciples (vv. 28-30) and later Zacchaeus (19.1-10). Furthermore, in Luke, the narrative of the rich ruler functions within the larger Lukan motif of the rich and poor. In the Lukan account, the rich ruler is contrasted not only with the disciples who have left 'their own things' (τὰ ἴδια), but also with the rich tax collector Zacchaeus (19.1-10). In Luke the disciples are indeed commended for their having left everything (5.11). Thus to use the proverb at the conclusion of the narrative would indicate that the disciples were the 'last ones' who had become first. This is the effect of the first use of the aphorism in Matthew (cf. 19.28-30). But Luke avoids the use of the terms πρῶτος and ἔσχατος in the contexts of discipleship and the twelve (cf. Mk 9.35; 10.44; Mt. 20.27; Lk. 22.24-27). The reversal form is implicit in the Lukan narrative, but the word links used are πλούσιος and πτωχός, connecting this narrative with 6.20-26 rather than 13.22-30. Cf. Tannehill, *Narrative Unity*, 122; Schottroff and Stegemann, *Jesus von Nazareth*, 99-101.

1. Bultmann, *History*, 130, believes that the discourse was created by Luke. Crossan, *In Fragments*, 44, claims the entire cluster of sayings was already in Q.

2. Crossan, *In Fragments*, 44, 153ff. Crossan also uses the term for the beatitudes and woes, pp. 168-72.

3. *Ibid.*, Appendix 2.

4. The use of εἰ to introduce direct discourse is also found in Lk. 22.49; Acts 1.6; 7.1; 19.2. Septuagintal use is the background; cf. Blass–Debrunner–Funk, *Grammar*, §440.3. The present participle σωζόμενοι has a futuristic sense, referring to eschatological salvation (cf. v. 28).

5. Fitzmyer, *Gospel*, 1024.

The scene shifts from the present, where human response is called forth, to the eschatological end, when judgment will take place. The surprise is that those people shut out assumed they would be included. Thus, they knock at the door, saying 'Lord, open to us' (v. 25). When told by the householder, 'I don't know where you come from' (v. 25b), they try to remind him of their personal ties to him and the honor they bestowed upon him: 'We ate and drank in your presence, you preached in our streets' (v. 26). But table-fellowship with the Lord and listening to him teach mean nothing once the door is shut. Once again the reply is 'I don't know where you come from', followed by a quotation of Ps. 6.8: 'Depart from me, you workers of iniquity'. Verse 28 clarifies who the 'insiders-turned-outsiders' are—they are Jews, those who recognize Abraham and Isaac and Jacob and all the prophets in the Kingdom of God. The scene of the Kingdom, however, is viewed from afar since they themselves have been cast out (ὑμᾶς ἐκβαλλομένους ἔξω, v. 28). They were first, but have become last. Instead, outsiders—those from east, west, north, and south—will have table fellowship in the kingdom of God. The reference is to the Gentiles, who were last but have become first.[1]

The aphorism then forms a fitting conclusion: 'Some are last (ἔσχατοι) who will be first (πρῶτοι), some are first (πρῶτοι)who will be last (ἔσχατοι)'. The chiastic structure and use of the opposites ἔσχατοι and πρῶτοι illustrate and intensify the complete reversal of positions between Jews and Gentiles described in the pericope.[2] The sense of 'some' (rather than 'all' or 'many') created by the added uses of εἰμί[3] implies that not all

---

1. Cf. Crossan, *In Fragments*, 45.

2. Crossan (*ibid.*) suggests that the aphorism should have used the opposite order of first/last–last/first to properly match the structure of the pericope (Jew/Gentile). He believes that the construction found in Luke 'is not dictated by the context (Jews/Gentiles), which dictates the reverse or Markan chiasm'. However, the pericope following v. 30 returns to the rejection of Jesus by the Jews, and the verse immediately preceding the aphorism discusses the Gentiles. Therefore, the order found in Luke does not seem out of place, nor does the context 'dictate' the opposite order.

3. Juxtaposing the present and future tenses of εἰμί in each reversal also serves to highlight the present/future tension usually found in the reversal form.

2. *Explicit Bi-Polar Reversal in Luke* 91

Jews will be thrust out, and not all Gentiles will be included in the Kingdom. Additional insight into the identity of the Jews to be excluded is found in vv. 34ff. Jesus mourns the condition of Jerusalem, where they kill the prophets and those sent to them. Therefore their house is forsaken (v. 35). More specifically, in ch. 14 Jesus has table-fellowship with Pharisees.[1] When Jesus notes how those invited, presumably other Pharisees, chose the 'first couches' (πρωτοκλισίας),[2] he tells a parable in which a person who chooses a place of honor (πρωτοκλισίαν) is forced to take the 'lowest place' (τὸν ἔσχατον τόπον, 14.8-10).[3] In ch. 19, the chief priest and scribes and 'principal

1. Cf. 7.36-50; 11.37-52. Luke is the only writer to record instances of Jesus having table-fellowship with Pharisees. However, in every case, the Pharisees end up being at odds with Jesus and his teaching. They are depicted as those who often are present for Jesus' teaching, but who reject the purpose of God (7.30), and scoff at Jesus' teaching because they are lovers of money (16.15). Even when they apparently try to warn Jesus not to go to Jerusalem because Herod is trying to kill Jesus, they are in the way of Jesus fulfilling his mission (13.31ff.). D. Smith also draws attention to the relationship between 13.26-30 and Jesus' table-fellowship with the Pharisees. Referring to these verses he states, 'This undoubtedly correlates with the literary tendency in Luke to have Jesus dine quite often at the table of a Pharisee. Thus, the condemnation of the Pharisees is indicated here, as it is in numerous other table fellowship references' ('Table Fellowship', 627).
2. Cf. Lk. 11.43. The Pharisees love the 'first seat' (πρωτοκαθεδρίαν) in the synagogue as well.
3. Vernon K. Robbins (*Ancient Quotes & Anecdotes: From Crib to Crypt* [Sonoma, CA: Polebridge, 1989], 21-22), lists four stories from Hellenistic literature where people make retorts about the last place being a place of honor (nos. 51a-e). Most notable are 51c—from Plutarch, *Moralia*, 'Sayings of the Spartans', 3. 219E—'Damonidas, being assigned to the last place in the chorus by the director, exclaimed, "Good! You have discovered, sir, how this place which is without honor may be made a place of honor"'; and 51e—from Diogenes Laertius, *Lives of Eminent Philosophers*, 2.73—'Being once compelled by Dionysius to enunciate some doctrine of philosophy, "It would be ludicrous", he [Aristippus] said, "that you should learn from me what to say, and yet instruct me when to say it". At this, they say, Dionysius was offended and made him recline at the end of the table. And Aristippus said, "You must have wished to confer distinction on the last place"'. Each of these stories illustrates that the reversed situation was the normal understanding shared throughout the Mediterranean world.

men of the people' (οἱ πρῶτοι τοῦ λαοῦ) are seeking to kill (ἀπολέσαι) Jesus (v. 47). Thus, some Jews, particularly the Pharisees,[1] belong to the group whose position is negatively reversed in the bi-polar reversal form. The Gentiles, on the other hand, join the social outcasts, and those who seek to follow Jesus in losing their lives in order to save them, as recipients of a positive reversal.

The aphorism in 13.30 adds new terms to the bi-polar reversal form but maintains the structure previously seen. The aphorism confirms the eschatological reversals which some 'insider' Jews and 'outsider' Gentiles will experience in the future kingdom of God. The Jews, first called by God, will be excluded from the Kingdom, becoming 'last' (vv. 25-27, 28). Rather than celebrating at the messianic feast, they will 'weep and gnash their teeth' (v. 28) as they experience a reversal which excludes them. Gentiles, previously 'last', will sit at table at the eschatological banquet, becoming 'first' (v. 29).[2] The future aspects of the reversal are at the forefront of this particular pericope. However, the initial words of Jesus (v. 24) call for proper response in the present. Also, the word links to Jesus' parable in 14.7-10 suggest certain attitudes one should have in the present, and implicitly link the Pharisees in particular to the reversal to be brought about by God in his kingdom.

Conclusion

The seven different texts examined (nine, including doublets) demonstrate similarities in structure and terminology which suggest that bi-polar reversal is a repetitive form in Luke which communicates a theme in the Lukan narrative.[3]

---

1. Even with regard to the Pharisees, v. 31 suggests that 'some Pharisees' (τινες Φαρισαῖοι) were interested in Jesus' welfare, preventing a complete stereotype of Pharisees as the enemies of Jesus to be thrust out of the Kingdom.

2. Fulfillment of this is seen throughout the book of Acts, and the reversal also is given a present tense meaning as Paul repeatedly turns from the rebellious Jews to the receptive Gentiles (Acts 13.46; 18.6; 28.28).

3. Cf. Alter's definition above, p. 43.

Although found in different forms according to the traditional definition of *Gattungen*, the different bi-polar texts present a unified form rhetorically, that is, a sequence is created in which one part leads the reader to anticipate the other part. The reversal of two opposites or contraries is presented as a series of related divine principles, describing God's action towards humanity through the inauguration of the Kingdom in the presence of his son, Jesus. Repetition of the form expands the characterization of the oppositions and intensifies the importance of the divine principles. As these principles give expression to the bi-polar reversal form, they also present a value system that is integral to the person and message of Jesus. Thus, bi-polar reversal can be called a theme of Luke's Gospel.

Chiastic structure is the most succinct and most often used formulation of bi-polar reversal. Certain terms become *Leitwörter* (e.g. πλούσιος, πτωχός, ὑψόω, ταπεινόω, πεινάω, σώζω, ἀπόλλυμι), as they recur in different statements of the principle and expand in meaning through interaction with new terms in new contexts. The Magnificat creates an expectation that divine action reverses opposite human conditions, and the beatitudes and woes, the Rich Man and Lazarus, the Pharisee and the Publican, and other antithetic aphorisms echo the expectation. All the examples following the Magnificat are placed on the lips of Jesus. The narrative parables of the Rich Man and Lazarus and the Pharisee and the Publican portray the reversals in personalized form. The other examples, including the Magnificat, function as wisdom sayings that present divine principles of action. These divine principles describe God's interaction with humanity. God humbles those who exalt themselves and exalts those who humble themselves; he makes last those who are first and makes first those who are last; he saves those who lose themselves for Jesus' sake and those who seek to save themselves will be lost; he fills the hungry but sends the rich away empty; he causes those weeping to laugh and those laughing to mourn and weep. The next step in determining the function of explicit bi-polar reversal is to explore the value system shared by Luke and his audience in which these divine principles would have been operative.

Chapter 3

IMPLICIT BI-POLAR REVERSAL IN LUKE

Chapter 2 contains analyses of bi-polar reversals of various forms in which the oppositions are obvious and the double reversal of positions straightforward. In the passages discussed in this chapter, the bi-polar reversals are not as explicit. These texts function as bi-polar reversals only when they are in a context that encourages explicit bi-polar thought. Unlike the explicit examples, which often are accompanied by aphoristic statements, the implicit examples function inductively, encouraging the reader to draw conclusions that are not explicit in the story itself. The divine principles explicitly stated in the passages discussed in the preceding chapter regularly provide the thought patterns for understanding the implicit materials in an explicit bi-polar framework. Prior to the actual analyses, however, it is necessary to incorporate in the discussion an aspect of the first-century world and its value system that is crucial for understanding the thematic importance of bi-polar reversal for the Lukan audience, namely, the values of honor and shame.

Bi-Polar Reversal in an Honor/Shame Society
Since one of the claims of scholars regarding the sayings and parables of reversal is that such reversals 'overthrow one's world', the values which make up that world must be addressed. Malina's anthropological studies on the New Testament world are helpful on this point.[1] Malina argues that the two pivotal values for society in this period were honor and

---

1. Bruce J. Malina, *The New Testament World*; 'Wealth and Poverty in the New Testament and Its World', *Interpretation* 41 (1987), 354-67.

shame.[1] Power, sexual status and religious structures all come
together to determine one's honor within one's social group.[2] It
can be ascribed or acquired;[3] its purpose is to provide a kind of
rating scale by which a person knows how to interact with
one's equals, superiors and subordinates in society.[4] Due to the
perception of limited good commonly held in the first century,[5]
maintenance of honor within one's status level was more
important than seeking any change in one's status, socio-
economically or otherwise. Wealth was important not for its
own sake but for its contribution to honor.[6]

1. *New Testament World*; see all of ch. 2, 'Honor and Shame: Pivotal
Values of the first Century Mediterranean World', 25-50. Also see
David Daube, 'Shame Culture in Luke', *Paul and Paulinism: Essays
in Honour of C.K. Barrett* (ed. Morna Hooker and S.G. Wilson; London: SPCK, 1982), 355-72; David Gilmore, ed., *Honor and Shame and
the Unity of the Mediterranean* (Washington, DC: American Anthropological Association, 1987); David B. Gowler, 'Characterization in
Luke: A Socio-Narratological Approach', *Biblical Theology Bulletin* 19
(1989), 58, 60; Ramsay MacMullen, *Roman Social Relations: 50 B.C. to
A.D. 284* (New Haven: Yale, 1974), 109; Aymer, 'Socioreligious Revolution', 123.
2. *New Testament World*, 27-28. Malina defines honor as 'the value of
a person in his or her own eyes plus the value of that person in the eyes
of his or her social group. Honor is a claim to worth along with the
social acknowledgment of worth.'
3. 'Ascribed honor befalls or happens to a person passively through
birth, family connections, or endowment by notable persons of power.
Acquired honor is honor actively sought and garnered most often at
the expense of one's equals in the social contest of challenge and
response' (*ibid.*, 47).
4. *Ibid.*
5. Malina quotes Aristotle, *Politics* 3.9.1256b: 'For the amount of such
property sufficient in itself for a good life is not unlimited'. Malina
explains: 'This means that everything of value in life can be increased
only at the expense of others. The reason for this assessment is that in
the first century Mediterranean world, just as in nearly all peasant
societies, all goods are believed to be limited... The result is a zero-
sum game in which any individual or group advancement is done to
the detriment of others' ('Wealth and Poverty', 362). Also see ch. 3 of
New Testament World, 'The Perception of Limited Good', 71-93, esp.
75-76. Cf. Gowler, 'Characterization in Luke', 58, 61-62; Halvor
Moxnes, *The Economy of the Kingdom: Social Conflict and Economic
Relations in Luke's Gospel* (Philadelphia: Fortress, 1988), 76-79.
6. 'Prestige derives from the domination of persons rather than
things. Hence any concern people show for the acquisition cf goods

Shame, on the other hand, is loss of honor before one's peers. While *having* shame suggests the positive value of being sensitive to the opinion of others and one's place of honor among others, *getting* shamed denotes the denial of honor by one's peers. The latter circumstance leads to a person becoming shameless, no longer observing social boundaries.[1] In certain instances entire groups might be shamed beyond social acceptability. Thus, in the first century, certain individuals and occupations were considered shameless, without honor (e.g. actors, tavern and inn owners, prostitutes); and others were socially marginal.[2] Since many of the bi-polar reversal texts present conditions that ultimately reflect the values of honor and shame, the reversal of such conditions and the

derives from the purpose of gaining honor through generously disposing of what one has acquired among equals or socially useful lower-class clients. In other words, honor is acquired through beneficence, not through the fact of possessions and/or the keeping of what one has acquired. Thus money, goods, and any sort of wealth are really a means to honor, and any other use of wealth is considered foolish' (*New Testament World*, 34). Cf. Gowler, 'Characterization', 59.

1. 'The shameless person is one with a dishonorable reputation beyond all social doubt, one outside the boundaries of acceptable moral life, hence one who must be denied the normal social courtesies' (Malina, *New Testament World*, 44) 'people acquire honor by personally aspiring to a certain status and having that staus socially validated. On the other hand, people *get shamed* (not *have* shame) when they aspire to a certain status and this status is denied them by public opinion. At the point a person realizes he is being denied the status, he is or gets shamed, he is humiliated, stripped of honor for aspiring to an honor not socially his. Honor assessments thus move from the inside (a person's claim) to the outside (public validation). Shame assessments move from the outside (public denial) to the inside (a person's recognition of the denial). To be or get shamed, thus, is to be thwarted or obstructed in one's personal aspiration to worth or status, along with one's recognition of loss of status involved in this attempt' (p. 46). Thus, to be shameless is have lost all honor and even the sense of shame—according to public opinion first, personal recognition second—since there can be shame only when there is still the prospect, at least, of honor.

2. Malina, *New Testament World*, 46-47. Cf. MacMullen, *Roman Social Relations*, 114-16; J. Jeremias, *Jerusalem in the Time of Jesus* (Philadelphia: Fortress, 1981), 5, 6, 303ff. The socially marginal would also include the physically disabled and the poverty-stricken. Cf. Aymer, 'Socioreligious Revolution', 122-24.

means by which the reversals take place will comprise a crucial part of any insight into the function of bi-polar reversal in Luke's Gospel.

In the context of honor and shame the *Leitwörter* πτωχός and πλούσιος, seen in the beatitudes and woes and prominent throughout Luke's Gospel, are particularly important. The role of these terms in the bi-polar reversal texts necessitates further inquiry into the function of the two terms and the identity of people categorized by these terms. Who are 'the poor' and 'the rich' in Luke's Gospel, and how do these terms relate to the values of honor and shame?[1]

The term πτωχός is a favorite of Luke, used ten times.[2] It is first introduced in the inaugural sermon in Nazareth (4.16-18). Jesus quotes Isa. 61.1-2,[3] which he says 'has been fulfilled in your hearing', speaking to his home-town audience. By quoting this passage, which had taken on eschatological overtones by the first century,[4] Jesus claims the Spirit of the Lord has anointed him 'to preach good news to the poor (εὐαγγελί-

1. For a survey of the different positions that have been held among scholars on the definition of the poor, see Seccombe, *Possessions*, 24-43. Much of the confusion in the definition comes from lack of clarity with regard to audience, i.e. defining the poor in Jesus' day versus defining the poor in the Christian community or the Lukan audience.

2. Lk. 4.18 (Isa. 61.1); 6.20; 7.22; 14.13, 21; 16.20, 22; 18.22; 19.8; 21.3. The term is not used in Acts.

3. J.H. Yoder, following the lead of an earlier work by Trocmé, argues that the coming of the Kingdom in the Gospels is borrowed from Jubilary language such as is found in Isa. 61 and quoted in Lk. 4 (*The Politics of Jesus* [Grand Rapids: Eerdmans, 1972], 36-37, 41). Sloan has expanded on the idea, arguing that Isa. 61.1-2—thus also Jubilary theology—lies behind the language of the beatitudes (*Favorable Year*, 126). Pilgrim (*Good News*, 74), agrees with this conclusion, although he admits no direct connection can be made between Isa. 61 and Lk. 6. H. Frankmölle, 'Die Makarismen (Mt. 5,1-12; Lk. 6,20-23). Motiv und Umfang der redaktionellen Komposition', *Biblische Zeitschrift* 15 (1971), 64-65, and A. Finkel, *The Pharisees and the Teacher of Nazareth* (Leiden: Brill, 1964), 155-58, also see Isa. 61 as the background for the beatitudes, but they do not place the same emphasis on the language of Jubilee. Schweizer, *Good News*, 122, believes Isa. 61.1ff. provides the background for the woes of 6.24-26.

4. Pilgrim, *Good News*, 71. Pilgrim points out the importance of Jesus saying 'Today', indicating the arrival of the future in the presence of Jesus.

σασθαι πτωχοῖς), to proclaim release to captives, recovering of sight to the blind, to set at liberty the oppressed, to proclaim the acceptable year of the Lord'. The πτωχοί in this context are grouped with the captives (αἰχμαλώτοις), the blind (τυφλοῖς), and the downtrodden (τεθραυσμένους).[1] What characterizes these terms is the helpless condition of each, and it suggests that primarily physical circumstances are to be reversed.[2]

In ch. 7, the first half of which has close parallels to the Nazareth address,[3] Jesus responds to the disciples of John by telling them that 'the blind (τυφλοί) receive their sight, the lame (χωλοί)[4] walk, lepers (λεπροί) are cleansed, the deaf (κωφοί)[5] hear, the dead are raised up, the poor have good news preached to them (πτωχοὶ εὐαγγελίζονται)' (v. 22). 'Good news to the poor' recalls the quotation of Isa. 61.1, and is listed along with a series of physical maladies, many of which were cause for societal ostracism.[6] Similar lists are given in the context of the symposium in ch. 14. In v. 13, Jesus tells the host not to invite those of equal or higher social status—his friends, kinsmen, rich neighbors—but to invite those beneath his own social status—the poor (πτωχούς), the maimed (ἀναπείρους),[7] the lame (χωλούς), and the blind (τυφλούς). In v. 21, in the midst of the Lukan account of the parable of the great banquet,[8] the

---

1. 'To set at liberty the oppressed' is an insertion from Isa. 58.6, probably added on the basis of the catchword ἄφεσιν, ἐν ἀφέσει. Cf. Fitzmyer, *Gospel*, 633; J.A. Sanders, 'Isaiah in Luke', *Interpretation* 36 (1982), 151-52.

2. These words all reflect physical circumstances, not metaphorical ones. Only once does Luke use the word τυφός in a metaphorical sense (6.39); it is doubtful that such is intended in 4.18 (cf. 7.22). αἰχμάλωτος is found only here in the New Testament (αἰχμαλωτίζω, Lk. 21.24). The same is true of θραύω.

3. Cf. Johnson, *Literary Function*, 96-103, esp. 97-98.

4. χωλός is used three times in Luke, all in lists of the oppressed and outcast: 7.22; 14.13, 21.

5. κωφός is used in 1.22 and 11.14 with reference to muteness. Only here, clearly following Q (Mt. 11.5), does Luke use it to refer to deafness.

6. Cf. Aymer, 'Socioreligious Revolution', 119-23.

7. ἀνάπειρος is found only in 14.13, 21, in the New Testament.

8. Cf. the Matthean account, 22.1-10, which gives no specification on guests invited, only the implication of outcasts in the phrase 'those in the streets'.

servant is also instructed to bring in the poor (πτωχούς) and maimed (ἀναπείρους) and blind (τυφλούς) and lame (χωλούς). Both of the lists in ch. 14 thus represent the marginal people of society, those with physical conditions that make them societal outcasts. There is no suggestion that πτωχός is to be understood as spiritual poverty in 7.22, 14.13, or 14.21. The emphasis instead is upon the inclusion of those people of marginal or no status, no honor, in the community.

The other uses of πτωχός in Luke are all found in contexts that contrast the plight of the poor with the plight of the rich (πλούσιος). In ch. 16, the term is used twice as a description of Lazarus (vv. 20, 22) in contrast to the rich man (πλούσιος, vv. 19, 21, 22). In ch. 18, the rich ruler (πλούσιος ἄρχων) is told to sell what he has and distribute it to the poor (πτωχοῖς). In ch. 19, the rich (πλούσιος) tax collector Zacchaeus declares, 'half of my goods I give to the poor' (πτωχοῖς). In ch. 21, the contribution of the poor widow (χήραν πενιχράν, v. 2, χήρα πτωχή, v. 3) is contrasted with the gifts of the rich (πλουσίους). In all of these there can be little doubt that πτωχός refers to a socio-economic condition.

The use of πτωχός in the rest of Luke's account suggests that in 6.20 as well, the primary reference is to physical, or socio-economic circumstances. However, the spiritual element often is given precedence by modern commentators. Support for such an interpretation is found in the Matthean parallel πτωχοὶ τῷ πνεύματι (5.3), which some have understood to be the correct understanding of the original beatitude in Q.[1] The reason for that assumption is the Old Testament heritage of 'the poor'. Since the poor are the recipients of 'the Kingdom of God', a concept which certainly has its roots in Jewish thought, it has been common to look to Jewish backgrounds for the meaning of πτωχός as well.[2] The conclusion to draw from such

1. See, for example, Ellis, *Gospel*, 112; Creed, *Gospel*, 91; Manson, *Sayings*, 47; David Flusser, 'Blessed Are the Poor in Spirit', *Israel Exploration Journal* 10 (1960), 9; Gary T. Meaders, 'The "Poor" in the Beatitudes of Matthew and Luke', *Grace Theological Journal* 6 (1985), 310.
2. Cf. the discussion of Guelich, *Sermon*, 67-72. The πτωχοί in Luke are often associated with the pious poor of the Old Testament, the *anawim*. Guelich, for example, notes that πτωχοί always refers to the

studies is that πτωχός has both socio-economic and religious connotations.[1] In the Lukan account of the sermon, the inclusion of the poor with the hungry and weeping—two physical conditions—and the opposition to the rich, full, and laughing all suggest that the socio-economic condition cannot be ignored but has direct bearing on one's spiritual condition.[2]

economically deprived in Hellenistic literature, but states that since the key element in the first Lukan beatitude is the Kingdom of God, the beatitude must be understood against a Jewish background. He goes on to discuss the Old Testament and LXX background for the use of πτωχός in Luke (pp. 68ff.). Pilgrim (*Good News*, 19-38), devotes his first chapter to the understanding of the poor in the Old Testament and intertestamental period. He, like Guelich, concludes that the most important background for the πτωχοί in Luke is the *anawim* (cf. Isa. 61.1), those who were poor, socio-economically, but whose poverty made them dependent on Yahweh. Poverty and piety thus become synonymous, with the focus being on piety. Pilgrim develops the link between the pious poor of late Judaism and the poor of the Gospels (36, 55-56). Talbert (*Reading Luke*, 70-71) assumes that πτωχοί in the beatitudes has a primarily religious rather than socio-economic meaning. He argues that the juxtaposition of hungry/proud in 1.51-53 suggests that hungry and poor are being used figuratively rather than depicting actual conditions. He further claims that since Luke does not uphold a particular attitude toward socio-economic standards, the religious implications should take precedence. Flusser ('Blessed are the Poor in Spirit', 1-13) asserts that Matthew's form is the correct one and that Luke has abbreviated the form without changing the meaning. Flusser's conclusion is based on the conflation of Isa. 61.1 and 66.2 in the Dead Sea Scrolls (1QM 14.7). Meaders ('The "Poor" in the Beatitudes', 310ff.) follows Flusser and ties his conclusion in with others who are convinced that the πτωχοί in Luke are the *anawim*. On the other hand, Dupont concludes that the πτωχοί are indeed the indigent, those actually impoverished, hungry, weeping, and hated (*Les Béatitudes*, III, 42-43; also 'The Poor and Poverty in the Gospels and Acts', *Gospel Poverty: Essays in Biblical Theology* [Chicago: Franciscan Herald Press, 1977], 41). Also see the discussions of E. Bammel, 'πτωχός', *TDNT*, VI, 888-89; Percy, *Botschaft*, 40-81.

1. Cf. Marshall, *Commentary*, 249-50; Guelich, *Sermon*, 72; Drake, 'Reversal Theme', 161. Drake points out that in combining economic and religious interests, the beatitudes are drawing on both wisdom and apocalyptic traditions.

2. Tannehill, *Narrative Unity*, 208 n. 11. This does not mean that the beatitudes idealize poverty or that they reflect a Christian community which understands itself as 'the poor'. Keck points out that the ultimate emphasis is not on the physical conditions but the coming reversal: 'Not only are they [Luke 6.20-26] devoid of sheer proletarian protest

While there is little doubt that the use of πτωχός in the earliest tradition was influenced by the Jewish heritage of the term, that does not necessarily explain how it would have been understood by the Lukan audience. In Greek literature, Bammel claims, the term had an exclusively socio-economic meaning.[1] However, recent anthropological studies by Malina have pointed out the importance of understanding other aspects of poverty in the first century.[2] The πτωχοί, he argues, are not necessarily economically destitute but they are destitute of all social standing in society, without any means of having honor.[3] Such an understanding fits well with the lists

and of an ideological exaltation of poverty, but they are marked by the theme of the Great Reversal which the coming of the kingdom will bring to rich and poor, strong and weak, believer and unbeliever ...The material dealing with wealth and poverty does not reflect a church's calling itself "the Poor" but a church that is composed of the poor of Palestine whose low estate will be reversed by the Coming Age' ('The Poor among the Saints in the New Testament', *Zeitschrift für die Neutestamentliche Wissenschaft und die Kunde der älteren Kirche* 56 [1965], 111).

  1. 'πτωχός', 888.
  2. Malina, 'Wealth and Poverty', 358, distinguishes four basic social institutions: kinship, economics, politics, and religion. Of these, he claims that only kinship and politics had important roles in the Graeco-Roman world (pp. 358-67). He therefore concludes that 'the poor' and poverty do not represent socio-economic status in the New Testament world or the New Testament. Cf. 'Interpreting the Bible with Anthropology: The Case of the Rich and Poor', *Listening* 21 (1986), 148-59.
  3. 'In the first century Mediterranean world, if the only free-standing social institutions were politics and kinship, would not poverty refer to the inadequacy of life without honor, with the consequent social and personal inability to participate in the activities of the community, the inability to maintain self-respect as defined by community social standards?' (Malina, 'Interpreting', 156). In *New Testament World*, 85, having examined passages dealing with the poor in the Gospels, Malina concludes, 'it would seem that being classified as poor was the result of unfortunate personal history or circumstances. A poor person seems to be one who cannot maintain his inherited status due to circumstances that befall him and his family, like debt, being in a foreign land, sickness, death (widow), or some personal physical accident. Consequently, the poor would not be a permanent social class, but a sort of revolving class of people who unfortunately cannot maintain their inherited status. Thus day-laborers, landless peasants, and

in Lk. 4.18, 7.22 and 14.13, 21, where those identified alongside the poor are those whose conditions exclude them from society. While not questioning the Jewish heritage behind some of the Lukan texts, particularly 6.20, the meaning suggested by Malina must be given consideration as that which would have been understood by a Hellenistic audience. More than being the spiritually poor, or even the indigent, economically, οἱ πτωχοί are those who have no status, no means of honor in the community, but now are blessed recipients of the Kingdom of God, which means a reversal of their plight.[1]

In contrast to the πτωχοί are the πλούσιοι. As stated above, πλούσιος is often used in Luke in opposition to πτωχός. Of the eleven uses in Luke, nine are in contexts that contrast πλούσιος with πτωχός.[2] It is apparent in every use of the term in Luke that actual wealth is understood. The negative view of wealth expressed in many of the Lukan texts is often traced to Jewish roots, particularly late prophetic and apocalyptic denunciations of the rich.[3] Yet it is important to note that in Luke the rich are not denounced because they have become wealthy by defrauding the poor.[4] Instead, the rich are characterized by an attitude of self-reliance and indifference towards

beggars born into such situations are not poor persons in first-century society, and poor would not be an economic situation.'

1. Malina agrees with those who have focused on Jubilary theology for an understanding of wealth and poverty in the New Testament. 'The theme of "poverty" and "the poor" in any "socio-economic" sense was simply not focal either in New Testament times or in the New Testament. Rather, the proclamation of the Kingdom of Heaven, with God controlling his own land in terms of Torah Jubilee, entailed the redistribution of wealth and restitution on the part of the wealthy. Such redistribution and restitution, which were part of the political economy willed by God (i.e., the Kingdom), were of primary concern' ('Interpreting', 155).

2. The term is found in 12.16, the parable of the rich fool, and 16.1, describing the landowner who has a steward. The other nine instances are: 6.24; 14.12; 16.19, 21, 22; 18.23, 25; 19.2; 21.1. πλούσιος is found 3 times in Matthew, twice in Mark. Like πτωχός, the term is not used in Acts.

3. Cf. *1 Enoch* 92–105. See Nickelsburg's comparison of Luke and *1 Enoch* 92–105, 'Riches, the Rich', 325-44; also Bultmann, *History*, 126; Talbert, *Reading Luke*, 71; Guelich, *Sermon*, 69.

4. Guelich, *Sermon*, 69.

God.[1] Those who are rich, full, laughing, and esteemed by others will experience a great reversal because their present self-satisfaction prevents them from hearing and doing the will of God.[2]

This perhaps is seen best in the parable of the rich fool (12.13-21).[3] The immediate context of the exemplary story is a pronouncement story (vv. 13-15) in which a man from the crowd asks Jesus to instruct his brother to divide the inheritance with him.[4] Jesus responds, saying, 'Who made me a judge or divider over you?' (v. 14).[5] Jesus then warns against

---

1. Cf. 1.51-53; 12.15-21; 14.15-20; 16.25-31.

2. Cf. 12.13-21; 18.18-25. It is noteworthy that the two examples of the positive use of wealth in Luke (Zacchaeus [19.1-10] and the steward [16.1-9]) are in other ways societal outcasts—Zacchaeus because he is a chief tax collector; the steward because he has lost his job, is not capable of manual labor, and ashamed to beg (v. 3). The focus is therefore not so much on their wealth, but their use of it in regaining a place in the community, going from outsider to insider.

3. Bultmann (*History*, 178), includes this parable (vv. 16-20—he argues v. 21 is editorial) in the list of exemplary stories found in Luke. The parable forms part of a major discussion of possessions in ch. 12 (vv. 13-34).

4. Marshall (*Commentary*, 522) suggests the 'situation is that of a man whose elder brother refused to give him his share of their father's inheritance. It is possible, and may even have been considered desirable, for the heirs to a property to live together and so keep it intact (cf. Ps. 133.1 and the practice alluded to in Jos. *Bel.* 2.122). In this case the younger brother apparently wanted to separate off his own share of the inheritance and be independent.' Cf. Jeremias, *Parables*, 164-65. Fitzmyer (*Gospel*, 969) correctly notes that, given the response of Jesus, the details of the dispute are unimportant. The person's question only serves as an introduction to the following teaching of Jesus. Malina's comments are also instructive with regard to the brother's request and the question of honor. 'The honorable man leads a defensive existence. He avoids the appearance of presuming on others, lest such a presumption be interpreted as trying to take something that belongs to another. (Note Jesus' response to one who wants him to intervene in a family matter: "Man, who made me a judge or divider over you?" [Luke 12.14].) In other words, the honorable man, the "good" man, embodies a sort of cultural humility which indicates that he seeks nothing that might even remotely belong to another' (*New Testament World*, 78).

5. A form of vv. 13-14 is found in the *Gospel of Thomas* §72: '[A man said] to Him, "Tell my brothers to divide my father's possessions with me". He said to him, "O man, who has made Me a divider?" He turned

the vice of greediness (πλεονέξια), arguing that a person's life does not consist in the abundance of possessions (ὑπαρχόντων).[1]

Jesus tells a parable about a certain rich man (ἀνθρώπου τινὸς πλουσίου)[2] whose land produced abundantly (εὐφόρησεν).[3] The man considered what he should do (τί ποιήσω)[4] since there was no place to store his crops. He decided the solution was to tear down his old barns (ἀποθήκας),[5] build bigger ones, and store all his grain and goods (πάντα τὸν σῖτον καὶ τὰ ἀγαθά μου).[6] In a society that had a perception of limited goods, such a decision necessarily meant deprivation of others.[7] In an honor/shame society such hoarding also represented

to His disciples and said to them, "I am not a divider, am I?"' (trans. in Funk, *New Gospel Parallels*, I [Philadelphia: Fortress, 1985], 388). This form has nothing corresponding to v. 15, nor is it connected in any way to the parable of the rich fool, found in the *Gospel of Thomas* §63.

1. Verse 15 appears to be an editorial link which ties the pronouncement story of vv. 13-14 to the parable in vv. 16ff. The lack of a parallel to v. 15 in the form found in the *Gospel of Thomas* contributes to this conclusion. Cf. Fitzmyer, *Gospel*, 968. Pilgrim (*Good News*, 109-10) notes that v. 15 is the key to understanding Luke's intention, viz. a warning against greed or covetousness.

2. Cf. 16.1 ἄνθρωπος τις ἦν πλούσιος.

3. εὐφορέω is found only here in the New Testament. Cf. Philostratus, *Vit. Apoll.* 6.39; Josephus, *Bell.* 2.592.

4. Cf. 16.3. The parables in 12.16-21 and 16.1-8 both have to do with the proper use of one's wealth but differ in their outcomes. Because of their respective uses of the wealth at their disposal, the rich man in ch. 12 is labeled a fool (ἄφρων) and the steward is commended for his prudence (φρονίμως). Cf. the discussion of Tannehill, *Narrative Unity*, 247.

5. Cf. 12.24, par. Mt. 6.24.

6. Cf. the use of ἀγαθῶν in 1.53.

7. See Malina, *New Testament World*, 71-93, esp. p. 75: 'Since all good exists in limited amounts which cannot be increased or expanded, it follows that an individual, alone or with his family, can improve his social position only at the expense of others'. Also see 'Wealth and Poverty', 362ff. Stegemann and Schottroff (*Jesus von Nazareth*, 126) argue that the man was storing up grain so that, in a time of scarcity when prices had been driven up, he could sell it at an exorbitant price, thus profiting from others' needs. Such an explanation is unnecessary, since in a limited good setting, the man's greed and abuse of others is already apparent.

improper storage and use of one's goods since they were not used to bring the man honor through patron/client relationships,[1] but were to be saved for selfish ease of lifestyle. The man wished to take his ease, eat, drink and be merry (v. 19b: ἀναπαύου, φάγε, πίε, εὐφραίνου).[2]

The man's complete self-interest brings about the rebuke of God: 'Fool (ἄφρων),[3] this night your soul is required of you'.[4] The man's self-pronounced condition in v. 19 is reversed by God in v. 20.[5] Verse 21 then summarizes the problem: 'So is the one who treasures (ὁ θησαυρίζων) up for himself and is not rich (πλουτῶν) toward God'.[6] As Pilgrim says, the man was guilty of three major offenses:

> a) He was basically self-centered, separated from God and neighbor by his love of possessions; b) He falsely assumed human life could be measured and secured by the amount of his possessions; c) He regarded his life and property as his own, thereby violating God's lordship and his own role as a responsible steward.[7]

This story serves as a personalized example of the negative reversal first mentioned in the Magnificat (1.51-53). The rich man ended up empty rather than full of the good things (τὰ

---

1. Cf. Malina, *New Testament World*, 34.

2. On the use of εὐφραίνω, cf. 15.23, 24, 29, 32; 16.19.

3. Cf. Ps. 14.1.

4. Jeremias (*Parables*, 165) argues that Jesus' words refer to the impending eschatological judgment. Fitzmyer (*Gospel*, 971) argues instead that only the death of the individual and his/her individual fate is meant. Closer to Fitzmyer and most helpful on this question is J. Dupont, 'Die individuelle Eschatologie im Lukasevangelium und in der Apostelgeschichte', in *Orientierung an Jesus: Zur Theologie der Synoptiker*, ed. Paul Hoffmann (Freiburg: Herder, 1973), 37-47. Also see Dupont, *Les Béatitudes*, III, 99-147.

5. 'Soul (ψυχή), you have many goods laid up for many years (κείμενα εἰς ἔτη πολλά)' versus 'This night (ταύτῃ τῇ νυκτί) your soul (τὴν ψυχήν σου) is required of you'.

6. It is noteworthy that in Luke these verses are followed by the Q material, paralleled in Mt. 6, on the cares and anxieties of life (12.22-32), and the summation to the disciples (v. 33). 'Sell your possessions (τὰ ὑπάρχοντα) and give alms and provide for yourselves purses that do not grow old, with a treasure (θησαυρόν) in the heavens that does not fail'.

7. Pilgrim, *Good News*, 112.

ἀγαθά) which he sought for himself. He indeed 'already has
his consolation' (6.24), which was worth nothing at his death.
The story also demonstrates that the underlying problem with
the improper use of wealth is the self-centeredness attached to
it. As Malina suggests, greed is the ultimate problem.[1] Self-
centered accumulation of wealth means deprivation for
others. Failure to use wealth as a means to gain and maintain
honor makes one a fool. Thus, one's life does not consist in the
abundance of possessions (v. 15) but in selling possessions and
giving alms (v. 33), using them to obtain not just earthly honor
but heavenly treasure.

For the Lukan audience, the use of wealth for the benefit of
others would be the means to honor. The collection of sayings
on wealth in ch. 12, along with the other uses of πλούσιος, suggests that more than honor is at stake; heavenly treasure is
the ultimate reason for the proper use of possessions. Being
rich toward God means using possessions the honorable
way—in service of others.

Luke's use of πλούσιος and πτωχός is therefore rooted in economic circumstances, but these conditions are reflections of
both societal and spiritual conditions that are deeper concerns
for Luke and his audience. Honor and shame are rooted in the
proper use of wealth or the complete lack of it. In Luke's
understanding, the social conditions of honor and shamefulness are reversed through the religious experience of the
Kingdom. The physical circumstances and spiritual conditions
of people are linked together in the values of honor and shame.
The good news of the Kingdom brings honor to the poor,
shame to the self-centered rich.

When the values of honor and shame are applied to the rest
of the bi-polar reversal texts, it becomes clear that these values
are central to the theme communicated by the repetitive form.
In the immediate context in which the Magnificat has been
placed, it is noteworthy that both Mary and Elizabeth are
portrayed as women exalted or given honor by God. Both are
described as women without honor prior to the actions of
God—Elizabeth was barren, Mary was a δούλη of low estate

---

1. See 'Wealth and Poverty', 363-65.

(ταπείνωσις).[1] Within the poem Mary serves as a paradigm for God's saving work among those without honor, the humble and hungry. However, in contrast to the personal demonstration of God's saving actions, the corresponding negative reversal to be experienced by the mighty, proud, and rich is presented only in proverbial terms. Specific demonstrations of God bringing dishonor to those with earthly honor are anticipated in the Magnificat but await specific or personal expression.

In the beatitutes and woes, in addition to the honor/shame connotations within the terms πτωχός and πλούσιος, the last beatitude and corresponding woe are not awkward but fitting conclusions to the series of beatitudes and woes which begin the sermon. They summarize the status situation for the opposing groups. Those declared blessed are the hated ones, those without honor among their peers.[2] The circumstances of being poor, hungry and weeping all point to people who are of marginal status in society. This societal ostracism is made obvious in the last beatitude, but there is also cause for rejoicing. Such ostracism, such shame, was also experienced by God's true witnesses in the past.[3] The last woe summarizes the status of the rich, full, and laughing. These are the ones who have honor among their peers. Such honor, however, was also given to the false prophets—those opposed to God in the past. Receiving such honor leaves one, by implication, opposed to God in the present with an impending loss of honor through God's great reversal. God acts favorably toward the shamed of society—the poor, hungry, weeping and hated of this world. The rich, full, laughing, and well-regarded are denounced and can only look forward to a future negative reversal of fortune.

1. The honor given Mary has an ironic twist in it, however. Although being the mother of the Messiah through miraculous conception of the Spirit meant that future generations would call her blessed, in the present, bearing a child out of wedlock necessarily meant shame in the community. Such honor was not altogether welcome. She must endure societal shame for the sake of the greater honor given by God.

2. It is important to remember Malina's definition of honor: 'honor means a person's (or group's) feeling of self-worth and the public, social acknowledgment of that worth' (*New Testament World*, 44).

3. For a similar conclusion on the function of the fourth beatitude, see Aymer, 'Socioreligious Revolution', 120-21.

The challenge to deny self and take up a cross in the aphorism of saving and losing (9.24//17.33) is ultimately a call to take shame and dishonor upon oneself. Certainly Luke's audience understands the demand in the context of Jesus' cross— the cross of shame (cf. Heb. 12.2). The demand to follow is thus a decision to shame oneself through self-denial rather than the societal norm of seeking honor. This reversal focuses not only upon up/down societal movement of honor/shame but incorporates as well the question of who is inside/outside the Kingdom.[1] The two different groups seen in the previous reversals are, in this context, defined not so much by physical circumstances—although the context of ch. 17 may suggest similar negative conditions—but by attitudes about self and the identity of Jesus. Those willing to follow Jesus in accepting shame for themselves by losing life will ultimately have life. The person desirous of preserving self and circumstances of the present—thus acquiring and maintaining societal honor—will ultimately lose all.

In ch. 13, those who consider themselves honored guests of the Kingdom because they have experienced table-fellowship with Jesus and listened to his preaching in their streets find themselves thrust outside the Kingdom. The attempt to ascribe honor to Jesus through 'speaking well of him' in this case was the wrong response (cf. 6.26). In their place sit the shameful Gentiles—those from east and west, north and south. The proximity of these verses to the discussion of the Pharisees (ch. 14) who eat with Jesus but love the 'first couches', and who otherwise are noted for 'justifying themselves' (18.9) further suggests that the self-honored are to be identified with the 'first who will be last'.

Jesus' instruction on the proper attitude of a guest at a marriage feast (14.7-10) focuses on the quest for honor and the threat of being shamed. In the midst of an honor/shame society in which honor among peers was vital and such challenges normal, Jesus reproves such self-centered thinking. Honor should not be sought but given. It is better to assume less

---

1. Saving and losing are inside/outside terms, but the decision required of the individual who would follow Jesus demands an honor/shame response.

honor for oneself—to the point of being humbled. Such a self-deprecating attitude will be rewarded. The aphorism 'Everyone who exalts himself will be humbled, everyone who humbles himself will be exalted' is therefore the logical summation of Jesus' teaching on self-seeking honor and honor given by a greater source.

In the verses that precede the parable of the rich man and Lazarus in ch. 16 (vv. 14-15), an honor/shame contest is created between Jesus and the Pharisees.[1] By scoffing at Jesus' words (v. 14), the Pharisees seek to dishonor him by rejecting his authority.[2] In response (v. 15) Jesus discredits them by referring to their shameless condition before God. The parable continues the critique of the money-loving attitudes of Pharisees—they are like the rich man whose honor in this world is turned to shamefulness in the afterlife. On the other hand, even the definition of the name Lazarus, 'He whom God helps', coincides with the established form of bi-polar reversal in which God is on the side of the shameful, the helpless outcast.[3] The physical circumstances of the two men and the proximity of Lazarus to the rich man implies that the rich man had some responsibility to act benevolently toward Lazarus, but failed to do so, thereby demonstrating an improper use of the rich man's wealth.[4] With startling finality, the reversal of

---

1. Cf. the discussion of how honor is acquired through challenge and response in B. Malina, *New Testament World*, 30-33.
2. Gowler notes that when the Pharisees are labeled 'lovers of money' in this verse, 'The status-maintenance orientation in a closed system of a limited good society brands such persons as thieves' ('Characterization', 59).
3. Talbert (*Reading Luke*, 157) states that the name Lazarus is a signal of the beggar's piety. Marshall (*Commentary*, 635) makes a similar point. Both assume the piety of Lazarus on the basis of his being described as πτωχός, to which they give a religious content. As already stated, however, the religious content of πτωχός is secondary to the actual condition of poverty. Furthermore, in the Gospel of Luke, it is not the pious who are the recipients of God's favor but the sinners, outcasts, and helpless (cf. 5.32; 19.10; 15.7). It is therefore best to understand that 'God helps' poor Lazarus not because he is pious, but because he is helpless.
4. Once again Malina's perspective (*New Testament World*, 34) on the purpose of wealth in an honor/shame society is instructive: 'any concern for the acquisition of goods derives from the purpose of gain-

their conditions that takes place in the afterlife reverses the social conditions of honor and shame each previously experienced.

In the parable of the Pharisee and publican, the Pharisee sees himself as a man of honor while those he mentions in his prayer are the shameful ones of society.[1] Contrary to the Pharisee's self-assuredness before God, the tax collector contritely asks for God's mercy to be upon him, a sinner (ἁμαρτωλῷ, v. 13).[2] The bi-polar reversal invoked as a rationale for the story places the tax collector and the Pharisee on respective sides of the two poles found in all of the bi-polar reversal examples. Honor and shame are reversed once again. Beyond the specific characterizations, two attitudes toward Jesus and God are placed in opposition—self-humbling and self-exalting. Poor and rich (Lazarus and the rich man) can be substituted for tax collector-sinner and Pharisee, respectively, and the story remains the same. Likewise the bi-polar reversal to be brought about by God remains the same. This parable serves as a warning: whatever brings self-exaltation—honor among others, possessions, or piety—puts one in opposition to God. One must choose the understanding characteristic of one who is helpless before God, in need of a Great Benefactor,[3] in order to experience God's exaltation.

It thus becomes clear that the theme of bi-polar reversal is directly related to the first-century cultural values of honor and shame. Although the terminology varies and the characters representing the two oppositions are seen in various circumstances, the underlying values of honor and shame are those ultimately reversed. The bi-polar reversal form is a message of hope to those without honor, and a message of warning

ing honor through generously disposing of what one has acquired among equals or *socially useful lower-class clients*' (italics added). The rich man's failure to act benevolently toward the beggar Lazarus accentuates the shameful condition of Lazarus—he was not even 'socially useful' to the rich man.

1. The Pharisee assumes his societal honor translates into honor before God and vice versa.

2. By labeling himself as a sinner, he understands his own position of dishonor/shame in society and before God.

3. Danker, *Luke*, 2nd edn, 20.

and exhortation to those in places of honor who are tempted to
rely on themselves instead of God. As the following examples of
implicit bi-polar reversal will show, the two sides characterized in these reversals are also sharply divided in their acceptance and rejection of Jesus. Most striking, however, will be
the pervasiveness of the theme in the ministry of Jesus, especially in the travel narrative where so much of the material
unique to Luke's account is found.

Simeon's Oracles (2.24)
The two oracles of Simeon are the final prophetic pronouncements made in the infancy narrative with regard to the
identity and destiny of the child Jesus. The scene of Jesus' presentation in the temple (2.25-38) appears to be modeled after
the presentation of Samuel (1 Sam. 1.24–2.11).[1] The parents
bring the infant to the temple where they perform the necessary sacrifices of purification and dedication. They are met by
two people, Simeon and Anna, both of whom are presented as
prophetic voices.[2] Both are old and expectantly awaiting
promised divine activity. Simeon is awaiting the 'consolation'
(παράκλησιν)[3] of Israel; Anna awaits the 'redemption'
(λύτρωσιν)[4] of Israel. The Holy Spirit has revealed to Simeon
that he would see the Lord's Christ before dying (v. 26). Thus,
when the Spirit directs Simeon to be in the Temple at the time

---

1. Cf. Brown, *Birth*, 451.
2. *Ibid*. Brown suggests the doubling of witnesses is attributable to
the author's ongoing interest in demonstrating the superiority of
Jesus to John. Only Anna is actually called a prophetess (v. 36); however, she has no direct speech in the account. Simeon's prophetic
authority is authenticated by the threefold reference to the Holy Spirit's
operation in his life prior to the first oracle (vv. 25-27). Brown also discusses at some length the portrayal of Anna and Simeon as examples
of *anawim* piety, which links them with the larger interest in the
anawim which Brown and others find particularly in the infancy narrative (see pp. 452-53). Cf. Drury, *Tradition*, 62.
3. Cf. 6.24, the only other use in the Gospel. Also see Isa. 40.1, the
probable background for the verse.
4. Cf. 1.68; also see 24.21, where the verb λυτρόομαι is used, again
with reference to the redemption of Israel. The only other use of
λύτρωσις in the New Testament is Heb. 9.12.

Jesus' parents are there with the child, Simeon testifies to the child's identity as the Lord's Christ (vv. 27ff.).

Simeon's first oracle is positive in tone, addressed to God and paraphrasing themes from Second Isaiah.[1] Simeon identifies himself as God's servant (δοῦλος),[2] asking God to grant his departure from this life in peace (v. 29).[3] The emphatic use of νῦν in v. 29 implies that the 'consolation' Simeon had awaited 'now' is fulfilled. Simeon has seen the promised salvation (v. 30);[4] 'the Lord's Christ' is the child held in Simeon's arms.[5] Verses 31-32 then introduce a programmatic element in Luke's understanding of this salvation which has come into the world. It is a salvation prepared 'in the presence of all the peoples' (πάντων τῶν λαῶν).[6] Rather than being only for the chosen people Israel, it is to be 'a light for revelation to the Gentiles' as well.[7] Here, for the first time in the Gospel, Gentiles are mentioned along with Israel as the recipients of God's salvation. It is not unimportant that in the parallelism of v. 32, the Gentiles are mentioned first.[8]

---

1. Brown (*Birth*, 458) lists the following passages to which Simeon's first oracle, the *Nunc Dimittis*, alludes: Isa. 40.5; 42.6; 46.13; 49.6; 52.9-10.

2. Cf. Mary's similar self-identity (δούλη) in 1.38, 48.

3. In contrast to Simeon calling himself a slave (δοῦλος), God is here called δέσποτα, an appropriate correlative to δοῦλος commonly found in classical and Hellenistic Greek literature and Josephus for the gods. Luke also uses the term in Acts 4.26. Cf. Fitzmyer, *Gospel*, 428. Tannehill suggests that Simeon's request to be dismissed 'in peace' probably indicates Simeon's place in the messianic peace celebrated in 1.79 and 2.14 (*Narrative Unity*, 39).

4. Cf. Isa. 40.5, quoted in Lk. 3.5. See the discussion of 'the salvation of God' in Tannehill, *Narrative Unity*, 40-41.

5. Creed, *Gospel*, 40. Cf. the use of νῦν in 6.20-26.

6. The singular λαός regularly refers to the Jews, as in v. 32 (cf. 1.10, 17, 21, 68, 77; 2.10 in the infancy narrative). This is the only use of the plural form in the Gospel and it is defined by the two groups mentioned in v. 32. Cf. Fitzmyer, *Gospel*, 428; Schweizer, *Good News*, 56.

7. It is noteworthy that the Gentiles are mentioned first in v. 32, and that the first mention of the salvation of Gentiles is placed in the setting of the Jewish temple (Isa. 2.1-3; Mic. 4.1). Cf. Brown, *Birth*, 453; Schweizer, *Good News*, 56. The repeated mention of Israel in vv. 25, 32, 34 recalls 1.54, 68.

8. Cf. Schweizer, *Good News*, 57. On the ambiguous syntax of this verse, see Tannehill, *Narrative Unity*, 42 n. 61.

The parents of the child are amazed (θαυμάζοντες) by the sayings of Simeon concerning the child (v. 33).[1] Simeon then addresses his second oracle to Mary,[2] and the tone dramatically shifts from glory and triumph (vv. 29-32) to prophetic warning:[3] 'this one is set (κεῖται)[4] for the falling (πτῶσιν)[5] and

---

1. Bultmann (*History*, 300) sees this verse as proof that 2.22-40 was originally an independent story since it suggests that Joseph and Mary had no prior knowledge of the child's destiny. Otherwise why would they be amazed? Schürmann, *Das Lukasevangelium*, 127, is correct in suggesting that the verse is a literary device used to draw attention to the inclusion of the Gentiles in God's salvation. Cf. Ellis, *Gospel*, 84.

2. The introductions to the two oracles are quite similar. In each case the phrase εὐλόγησεν... καὶ εἶπεν is used. The confident oracle of triumph begins with Simeon blessing God. The latter oracle begins with Simeon blessing 'them', i.e. both parents, but addressing the oracle specifically to Mary. Specifying Mary is in harmony with the rest of the infancy narrative which focuses throughout on the mother of Jesus.

3. Tiede (*Prophecy*, 26) writes: 'in phrases that ring with prophetic precedent (see esp. Isa. 8.14-15; 28) wherein God's plan of saving action also entails destruction for those who are found to oppose it, Simeon's word is strictly prophetic in this context. It is the first hint of future opposition.'

4. Marshall (*Commentary*, 122) remarks that κεῖται reflects the thought of Isa. 28.16 (Masoretic Text, not LXX). He thus agrees with a common conclusion drawn by scholars regarding the background of v. 34. Cf. Creed, *Gospel*, 42; Plummer, *Commentary*, 70; Schürmann, *Das Lukasevangelium*, 127; Grundmann, *Das Evangelium nach Lukas*, 91. The image is of the stone which is at the same time both a stumbling block and the head of the corner (cf. Rom. 9.33; 1 Pet. 2.6-8). Isa. 28.16 uses the foundation stone metaphor, and Isa. 8.14-15 uses the image of the stumbling stone. The problem with using these two texts as the background for 2.34 is that there is only partial reflection of the thought contained in the Old Testament passages. Marshall admits that the metaphor of the stone does not fit well with the 'rising' of v. 34. Furthermore, when Luke actually refers to the stone metaphor (Isa. 28.16) in 20.17-18, only judgment is emphasized (cf. Schweizer, *Good News*, 57, 304). Thus, while it is clear that the combination of the two Isaiah texts was current in the first century, saying as Drury does (*Tradition*, 62) that v. 34 is a 'free use' of Isa. 28.16 is an understatement. There is no certain link to either of the Isaiah texts in this verse. For further discussion, see Johnson, *Literary Function*, 90 n. 2; Drake, 'Reversal Theme', 136-37; Brown, *Birth*, 461; M.-J. Lagrange, *Evangile selon Saint Luc* (Paris: J. Gabalda, 1948), 88. If one is seeking 'allusions', is it possible the primary allusion is to the bi-polar reversal theme already introduced in the Magnificat?

rising (ἀνάστασιν)[1] of many in Israel, and for a sign (σημεῖον)
spoken against (ἀντιλεγόμενον)'. The terms πτῶσιν and
ἀνάστασιν imply the opposition high–low. 'Falling' suggests
going from high to low; 'rising' suggests going from a lower to
higher position. Thus, some sort of reversal is implied by the
terms, and Simeon states that the child is 'set', that is, in some
sense responsible for this action. The implied reversal involves
'many in Israel' and suggests what Jesus himself says later in
ch. 12: 'Do you think that I have come to give peace on earth?
No, I tell you, but rather division' (12.51).[2] The same child who
is identified earlier as the Lord's Christ and as God's salvation

5. πτῶσις is used only here in Luke; the other use in the New Testament is Mt. 7.27.
1. ἀνάστασις is normally used in the sense of resurrection (from the
dead) in Luke (cf. 14.14; 20.27, 33, 35, 36). Here the meaning 'rising' is
made clear by its juxtaposition with πτῶσις.
2. Cf. Brown (*Birth*, 460). Others who understand v. 34 as a reference
to two groups, one of which accepts Jesus and the other of which
rejects him, include: Johnson (*Literary Function*, 89-91), Tiede
(*Prophecy*, 30), Juel (*Luke–Acts*, 24), Creed (*Gospel*, 42) and Tannehill
(*Narrative Unity*, 43). Other scholars reject the idea of two groups,
believing that only one group is discussed, namely, those who accept
the Messiah. Caird, for example, says: 'The natural interpretation of
Simeon's words, and the one which is in better accord with the facts of
Luke's story, is that through the ministry of this one man Jesus the
many in Israel will fall before they can rise to the promised glory, will
pass through the valley of humiliation before they can ascend to the
hill of the Lord. For in the actual event it was not true that the coming
of Jesus meant the fall of some and the rising of others . . . We have
here the intimation of the great theme that will unfold throughout the
gospel and finally be expounded by the risen Jesus: that the Messiah,
because he comes to lead Israel to glory, must tread with her the path
of suffering' (*Saint Luke* [Philadelphia: Westminster, 1963], 64; see
also Marshall, *Commentary*, 122; Schweizer, *Good News*, 57). Caird's
position is not supported, however, by the Lukan presentation of bi-
polar reversal where there is clearly a division in Israel, where 'some
who are last will be first, and some who are first will be last'. Cf. the
conclusions of Johnson (*Literary Function*, 112): 'The shape of Luke's
narrative in chs. 9–19 continues the fulfillment of Simeon's prophecy
that many would rise and fall in Israel. Up to the Jerusalem ministry
we have seen that those who are falling, those who are being rejected
from the people, are the leaders of the people, in particular the Pharisees and lawyers.' Luke does in fact demonstrate the pattern of two
groups 'rising and falling' in response to Jesus.

(vv. 26, 29-30) is destined to be a sign 'spoken against'. As Tiede states, 'a conflict of wills with at least a part of Israel is anticipated and apparently no middle ground will remain between acceptance and rejection, obedience and disobedience, falling and rising'.[1] Following the parenthetic phrase directed to Mary,[2] the thought of upheaval among the Jews is continued in the phrase 'thus the thoughts (διαλογισμοί) of many hearts may be revealed' (cf. 12.1-2). The term διαλογισμός is repeatedly used in the Gospel in the context of the thoughts of those who either misunderstand Jesus or are opposed to him.[3] The emphasis on the opposition to Jesus in these verses suggests that, for the majority of Israel, the child is a sign of rejection, not acceptance. Coupled with the inclusion of the Gentiles in v. 32, Simeon's oracles provide a programmatic prophecy of the rest of Luke–Acts. As Johnson states:

> What makes the prophecy of Simeon so important as a key to the following narrative is that it directs us to see in the story of

---

1. *Prophecy*, 30. Tannehill translates the phrase σημεῖον ἀντιλεγόμενον 'destined to provoke contradiction' (*Narrative Unity*, 43). Cf. Acts 28.19, 22, where Paul and the Christian sect are also 'spoken against' by the Jews.

2. The meaning of the statement directed toward Mary, 'a sword will pierce through your own soul also', remains open to debate. For a discussion of the various theories that have been proposed, see Brown, *Birth*, 462-65. Brown's suggestion, also given by Fitzmyer (*Gospel*, 422), is most helpful, namely that even Mary will be included or excluded not on the basis of family but by passing the test of acceptance of Jesus as Messiah. The sword in this case represents 'a sword for discrimination and not merely for punishment' (Ezek. 5.1-2; 6.8-9; 12.14-16) (p. 464, with n. 58). Such a view fits well with the narrative that follows when Jesus is left behind in Jerusalem (2.41-51, esp. vv. 48-49), and with Luke's reference to Jesus being sought by his mother and siblings (8.19-21).

3. Cf. Tannehill, *Narrative Unity*, 43-44. In 5.21-22, Jesus recognizes the 'thoughts' (διαλογισμούς) of the Pharisees who oppose his healing the paralytic. In 6.8, it is the διαλογισμούς of the scribes and Pharisees which Jesus again recognizes when they oppose his healing the man with the withered arm. In 9.47-48 and 24.38, it is the disciples' thoughts which Jesus reveals and then seeks to change. The verb form, διαλογίζομαι, is used three times in Luke, referring to Pharisees in 5.21-22, the rich fool (12.17), and the wicked tenant farmers (20.14). Cf. Johnson, *Literary Function*, 91; G. Schrenk, 'διαλέγομαι', *TDNT*, II, 97-98.

Jesus a story as well of a people divided over the prophet, a division in which some are to rise and others are to fall.[1]

While the division of the people may be apparent, and the
conditions of 'falling and rising' actually stated, it is only by
implication in the context of other bi-polar reversal texts that
Simeon's oracle can be understood as an example of bi-polar
reversal. It is never certain in this context alone that a complete reversal of positions (high → low, low → high) is to take
place. Nor is the nature of the implied reversal apparent. Is it
to be a reversal of socio-economic, political, or spiritual—perhaps eschatological—positions? It is clear, however, that the
oracles together have several elements found in other reversal
texts, particularly word links and Old Testament allusions
that recall 1.46-55 and 3.4-6.[2] The 'now–not yet' eschatology
of the bi-polar reversal form is found in the 'now' of v. 32 and
the clearly futuristic nature of 'falling and rising'. Seen as a
variation of the larger repetitive form of bi-polar reversal,
Simeon's oracles provide new clues to the nature of God's salvation. Gentiles will be among those who receive the message
(cf. 13.26-30), and there will be a great division among those in
Israel. The characters involved in this rising and falling are
later made explicit in other bi-polar reversals.

The Mission of John the Baptist (3.4-6)
All four of the Gospels present the preaching of John the Bap-
tist as the fulfillment of Old Testament prophecy, specifically
Isa. 40.3.[3] Luke is the only writer to continue the quotation of
Isaiah 40 through v. 5 (Lk. 3.4-6).[4] The inclusion of the addi-
tional verses is often linked to Luke's interest in the salvation

1. *Literary Function*, 91.
2. See the chart of connecting themes in Tannehill, *Narrative Unity*,
42-43. Juel, *Luke–Acts*, 24, links the Magnificat and Simeon's second
oracle, remarking, 'The reversal God will bring about, heralded by
Mary, will occur with the people of God; the "enemies" from whom
God will deliver the people may well be enemies within the family'.
3. Cf. Mt. 3.1-6; Mk 2.2-6; Lk. 3.1-6; Jn 1.19-23.
4. The quotation is clearly from the LXX, with minor variations: in
Luke 3.4, αὐτοῦ is substituted for τοῦ θεοῦ ἡμῶν (LXX). In v. 5b, πάντα is
omitted (τὰ πάντα σκολιά, LXX); and ὁδοὺς λείας is found in place of LXX
πεδία (however, some MSS agree with the Lukan form). In v. 6 the first
half of Isa. 40.5 is omitted (καὶ ὀφθήσεται ἡ δόξα κυρίου).

of God being offered to 'all flesh' (Isa. 40.5), with v. 4 serving no
particular purpose.[1] Certainly the last verse of the quotation is
important and has ties to Luke's interest in God's salvation of
the Gentiles (cf. Lk. 2.30-31). However, if Isa. 40.4 serves no
purpose, it is odd that Luke chose to include it when clearly he
could have omitted the verse just as he did v. 5a (καὶ ὀφθήσεται
ἡ δόξα κυρίου). It is therefore probable that some metaphorical significance is intended, and the closest parallels to the
verse in Lukan thought are the bi-polar reversal texts.[2]

Verse 5 is composed of two couplets, the first of which contains antithetical parallelism, the second synonymous parallelism. In v. 5a (Isa. 40.4 LXX), 'Every valley will be filled up
(πληρωθήσεται)[3] and every mountain and hill will be made
low (ταπεινωθήσεται)',[4] the chiasm is similar to those seen in
the antithetic aphorisms.[5] The two verbs are theological
passives similar to those found in other bi-polar reversal texts.[6]
Furthermore the verb ταπεινόω links the verse with other bi-
polar reversals (1.52; 14.11; 18.14). The biggest problem with
calling the saying a bi-polar reversal is the fact that the verb
πληρόω is not a true opposite or even an obvious contrary to

---

1. Typical of this perspective is the treatment of Fitzmyer, *Gospel*,
450-61. He never mentions the content or purpose of v. 4, either in the
Comment or Notes. Ellis (*Gospel*, 89) states: 'The addition of Isaiah
40.4f. is important for Luke's theme. He wants to emphasize the salvation of God.' Ellis does not mention the content of v. 4. Similarly, see
Creed, *Gospel*, 50-51.

2. F.W. Danker (*Luke* [Atlanta: John Knox, 1982], 73) says that
Luke's addition of Isa. 40.4 is 'in harmony with his motif of the exalta-
tion of the lowly and humbling of the proud'. Cf. Tannehill, *Narrative
Unity*, 48; Marshall, *Commentary*, 137.

3. The Masoretic Text has the niphal imperfect form of *nasa* ('will be
lifted high'), which is a more obvious contrary to 'be made low'. On the
understanding of the Hebrew text of Isa. 40.4 as reversal, see J.P.
Fokkelman, 'Stylistic Analysis of Isaiah 40.1-11', *Oudtestamentische
Studiën* 21 (1981), 77.

4. Cf. the use of ταπεινόω, 1.52; 14.11; 18.14.

5.   A [low]   every valley (πᾶσα φάραγξ)
     B [high]   will be filled up (πληρωθήσεται)
     B′ [high]   every mountain and hill (πᾶν ὄρος καὶ βουνός)
     A′ [low]   will be made low (ταπεινωθήσεται)

6. Cf. 6.21; 14.11; 18.14.

ταπεινόω. On the surface the saying therefore appears to indicate a leveling of conditions rather than a reversal.[1]

The second couplet seems to support this conclusion. 'The crooked will be made straight (ἔσται τὰ σκολιὰ εἰς εὐθείαν) and the rough will be made smooth roads' (αἱ τραχεῖαι εἰς ὁδοὺς λείας). Both phrases suggest difficult travel conditions that will be eased by a smooth, straight path. Luke's later use of this imagery in Acts suggests that more than leveling is at stake, however. There it is used in the context of repentance and hardened opposition to the message of repentance (Acts 2.40; 8.21; 13.10).[2] Thus, as Tannehill says, 'This drastic transformation of a terrain that obstructs travel becomes a symbol of the repentance that the Lord's coming requires'.[3] It is precisely on this point that many of the bi-polar reversals turn. The unrepentant repeatedly are represented as the proud, self-exalted ones who will be brought down by God's divine reversal. The repentant ones, on the other hand, are the tax collectors and sinners, social outcasts, and needy—those who will be exalted in the Kingdom.[4]

Therefore, while the quotation of Isa. 40.4 is not an explicit example of bi-polar reversal, it is closely related to both the motifs and the form of bi-polar reversal found in the rest of the Gospel. It thus contributes to the continued rehearsal of the form in various guises and is another passage that shapes readers' expectations with regard to the form and its contents.

The Anointing of Jesus (7.36-50)
Narratives of the anointment of Jesus are found in all four Gospels,[5] but the Lukan account has peculiar characteristics

---

1. Cf. Schweizer, *Good News*, 70; Marshall, *Commentary*, 137.
2. In Acts 2.40, the term σκολιός is used: 'Save yourselves from this crooked (σκολιᾶς) generation'. In 8.21, Simon's heart is not 'right' (εὐθεῖα) with God. In 13.10, Paul denounces Elymas for trying to block Paul's efforts: 'You son of the devil, you enemy of all righteousness, full of all deceit and villainy, will you not stop making crooked (διαστρέφων) the straight (εὐθείας) paths of the Lord?'
3. *Narrative Unity*, 48.
4. See 5.20-27; 1.51-53; 10.26-30; 18.9-14.
5. Mt. 26.6-13; Mk 14.3-9; Lk. 7.36-50; Jn 12.1-8.

that distinguish it from the others.[1] Luke incorporates the story in a series of episodes that portray the reception given Jesus and his ministry by various persons or groups (7.1–8.3).[2] In the first episode Jesus heals the Gentile centurion's slave (7.1-10). The climax of the story comes in v. 9 when Jesus declares, 'Not even in Israel have I found such faith'. The faith of the Gentile, who continually understood himself as 'unworthy' to be in Jesus' presence (vv. 3, 6-7), is thus contrasted with the reception given Jesus by his own people.[3] In

---

1. In Matthew and Mark Jesus is anointed by an unnamed woman in the house of Simon the Leper, at Bethany, during the last week of Jesus' life. The woman uses an expensive ointment contained in an alabaster flask. The focus of the story is on the cost of the ointment; rather than being poured on Jesus' head, the disciples argue it should have been sold and the money given to the poor. In John, it is Mary, at the home of Mary, Martha, and Lazarus in Bethany, who anoints Jesus' feet and wipes them with her hair, early in the last week of Jesus' life. The focus again is on the expensive ointment which could have been sold, with the proceeds given to the poor. In Luke, an unnamed woman anoints the feet of Jesus with her tears and dries them with her hair, kisses his feet and anoints them with expensive ointment taken from an alabaster flask. This takes place in Galilee, at the home of Simon the Pharisee, early in Jesus' public ministry. The focus is not on the cost of the ointment, but the contrast in receptions of Jesus by the woman and Simon. Cf. R.F. O'Toole, *The Unity of Luke's Theology* (Wilmington, DE: Michael Glazier, 1984), 115; Talbert, *Reading Luke*, 84. For a discussion of the origins of the Lukan account and its relation to the accounts in the other Gospels, see Fitzmyer, *Gospel*, 684-86; R.E. Brown, *The Gospel according to John* (Garden City, NY: Doubleday, 1966), 449-52; Burton L. Mack and Vernon K. Robbins, *Patterns of Persuasion in the Gospels* (Sonoma, CA: Polebridge, 1989), 85-106. Especially note the rhetorical description of Lk. 7.36-50, pp. 100-104.

2. On the structure of ch. 7 and the close relationship it has to 4.16-30, and the use of Elijah/Elisha imagery in portraying Jesus as God's great Prophet, see Johnson, *Literary Function*, 96-99. Also see D.A.S. Ravens, 'The Setting of Luke's Account of the Anointing: Luke 7.2–8.3', *New Testament Studies* 34 (1988), 282-92.

3. Tannehill, *Narrative Unity*, 111, identifies this narrative as a quest story, a type of pronouncement story more common in Luke than in the other Gospels (7.36-50 is another quest story). He also notes the careful way in which the narrative assumes that a major social barrier exists between Jesus and the Gentile centurion, but the Gentile's humble attitude of faith and Jesus' commendation of his faith break down the barrier. 'When Jesus declares that the centurion is an

the second story of the series, Jesus raises from the dead the son of a widow (7.11-17). The narrative contains allusions to 1 Kgs 17.17-24, where Elijah also raises a widow's son.[1] The story concludes with the crowd's reaction to the miracle performed by Jesus. Glorifying God (v. 16), they declare, 'a great prophet has been raised in our midst' and 'God has visited his people'.[2]

The third section is a series of three smaller episodes involving Jesus and John the Baptist.[3] Verses 18-23 are reminiscent of 4.18 and the quotation of Isa. 61.1. In response to inquiries about Jesus' identity from John and his disciples, Jesus recounts the mighty works he is accomplishing: 'the blind receive their sight, the lame walk, lepers are cleansed, and the deaf hear, the dead are raised up, the poor have good news preached to them' (v. 22). Jesus confirms that he is more than a prophet like Elijah; he is the one who embodies the divine promises to be given to the unfortunate of society.[4] Verses 24-30 address the crowd's expectations of John as a prophet, with Luke (or his source) adding vv. 29-30 to the Q tradition. John and his message are presented as harmonious with Jesus, although inferior. While there is no one born of woman greater than John, the least in the Kingdom—which Jesus came to proclaim (4.43)—is greater. The people and the tax collectors justify God (ἐδικαίωσαν τὸν θεόν), having accepted

outstanding example of faith, it becomes difficult for any of his followers to deny this Gentile's share in the salvation which Jesus brings' (p. 115).

1. Note especially v. 15 (καὶ ἔδωκεν αὐτὸν τῇ μητρὶ αὐτοῦ) which is paralleled verbatim in 1 Kgs 17.23 (LXX). For a more complete treatment of the relationship between Lk. 7.11-17 and 1 Kgs 17, see T.L. Brodie, 'Towards Unraveling Luke's Use of the Old Testament: Luke 7.11-17 as an *Imitatio* of 1 Kings 17.17-24', *New Testament Studies* 32 (1986), 247-67. Cf. Schürmann, *Das Lukasevangelium*, 402; Creed, *Gospel*, 104; Grundmann, *Evangelium*, 159.

2. Fitzmyer, *Gospel*, 648, suggests this verse is the keynote of 7.1–8.3.

3. 7.18-23, 24-30, 31-35; cf. Mt. 11.2-19.

4. Fitzmyer, *Gospel*, 664, states that these verses depict Jesus rejecting the role of *Elias redivivus* and taking on the prophetic image of Isa. 61.1. However, the previous episode has just confirmed the link with Elijah (vv. 10-17). Johnson is correct is saying that Luke uses all the prophets, including Elijah/Elisha, as partial types of the prophet Jesus. See *Literary Function*, 97.

the preaching of John's baptism; the Pharisees and lawyers reject God's purpose (τὴν βουλὴν τοῦ θεοῦ ἠθέτησαν) by rejecting John's baptism.[1] The Pharisees/lawyers and the people/tax collectors are placed in opposition to each other by their rejection/acceptance of John and, implicitly, Jesus. The rejection of Jesus is more sharply stated in vv. 31-35, where the 'men of this generation' (v. 31) are accused of rejecting John the Baptist and Jesus alike. The proverb of v. 32 and the descriptions that follow in v. 33 appear to address directly the Pharisees and lawyers, those who reject John as an eccentric, and Jesus as a friend of tax collectors and sinners.[2] Verse 35 again uses the verb δικαιόω linking the verse with v. 29 (ἐδικαίωσαν [v. 29]—ἐδικαιώθη [v. 35]). Both verses refer to those who acknowledge God's authority in John and in Jesus, i.e. the people and tax collectors (v. 29), tax collectors and sinners (v. 35).[3]

The narrative of the anointment of Jesus illustrates a number of issues raised in the preceding episodes.[4] Tannehill identifies the form as a quest pronouncement story that incorporates a parable in vv. 41-43.[5] The episode begins with Jesus

1. On the concept of 'justifying' God, see Talbert, *Reading Luke*, 84-85.
2. The accusation against the Son of man in v. 34 recalls 5.27ff., where Jesus dines with Levi the tax collector and a collection of others. There the Pharisees complain to Jesus' disciples, saying, 'Why do you eat and drink with tax collectors and sinners?' (v. 30).
3. Talbert, *Reading Luke*, 85. Talbert also suggests that 'Wisdom' (v. 35) 'is a periphrasis for God or for the "purpose of God"' (v. 29) (p. 84).
4. The Pharisee of the story partakes of the character of the Pharisees of v. 29; the woman is a sinner (ἁμαρτωλός), recalling v. 34 (also 5.8, 30, 32); Simon's question concerning Jesus' prophetic character recalls the statement of the crowd in v. 16; and the social position of the woman as an 'outsider', and her faith (v. 50) are placed opposite the 'insider' position of the host Pharisee, with his lack of faith. This recalls the outsider Gentile (v. 9) whose faith was greater than any found in Israel.
5. *Narrative Unity*, 111, 116-18. 'In the synoptic quest story someone approaches Jesus in quest of something very important to human well-being. This quest is a dominant concern of the story; its importance is shown by the fact that the episode does not end until we are told whether the quest is successful or not' (p. 111). See further, Tannehill, 'Synoptic Pronouncement Stories: Form and Function', *Society*

being invited to dine at the home of an as yet unnamed Pharisee.[1] Upon entering the Pharisee's house and reclining at table
with him,[2] the scene immediately shifts from the host to 'a
woman who was in the city a sinner' (γυνὴ ἥτις ἦν ἐν τῇ πόλει
ἁμαρτωλός, v. 37).[3] The woman learns that Jesus is dining
with the Pharisee and she enters,[4] bringing with her an

of *Biblical Literature 1980 Seminar Papers*, ed. P. Achtemeier (Chico,
CA: Scholars Press, 1980), 51-57. Here, Tannehill notes that quest sto-
ries 'function to change attitudes on the part of hearers and readers.
The stories end in a way that challenges common social values' (p. 54).
Also see 'Introduction: The Pronouncement Story and Its Types',
Semeia 20 (1981), 1-13; and 'Varieties of Synoptic Pronouncement Sto-
ries', *Semeia* 20 (1981), 101-19.
    1. On the compositional influence of the symposium for the Lukan
redaction of this story and the other accounts of Jesus dining with
Pharisees, see Delobel, 'L'Onction par la pécheresse', 415-75; Steele,
'Jesus' Table-Fellowship', 59-68. This is the first of three such occasions found only in Luke where Jesus dines with a Pharisee (cf. 11.37-
52; 14.1-24). In all three instances Jesus ends up at odds with the host.
In each case the authority and identity—therefore also the honor—of
Jesus is put to the test. In ch. 7, it is clear that the Pharisee of v. 36 is to
be identified with the Pharisees of 7.29-30 who rejected the purpose of
God. Beginning in 5.17, the Pharisees are presented in Luke as
opposed to Jesus and his message. They complain when he and his
disciples eat with tax collectors and sinners (5.30; cf. 7.34); they look for
a means to accuse him when he heals on the Sabbath (6.2, 7).
    2. Jeremias (*Parables*, 126) argues that the term κατεκλίθη suggests
a banquet setting rather than a simple meal where people would otherwise sit erect. The banquet and implied home ownership suggest some
degree of wealth for the Pharisee.
    3. The most likely meaning of the phrase is that the woman was a
known prostitute in the community. Cf. Fitzmyer, *Gospel*, 688;
Jeremias, *Parables*, 126; J.D.M. Derrett, *Law in the New Testament*
(London: Darton, Longman & Todd, 1970), 267-68. The term ἁμαρτωλός
is first used of Peter (5.8) and becomes in Luke a technical term for the
religious outcasts whom Jesus repeatedly befriends, since he understands his mission to include calling sinners to repentance (5.32; cf.
5.30; 7.34; 15.1-2, 7, 10; 18.13; 19.7). By identifying the woman as a
'sinner' Luke makes clear her shameless status in the presence of
Pharisees and Jesus.
    4. For a discussion of the open dining room setting which allowed
outsiders entrance to banquet settings, see Bailey, *Poet and Peasant*, 4-
5; Talbert, *Reading Luke*, 86. The narrative only implies the woman's
entrance, using the aorist participles κομίσασα and στᾶσα to place her
in the room with Jesus. This heightens the 'insider-outsider' opposition of the woman and the Pharisee. Luke has already made it plain

alabaster flask of ointment.[1] Standing behind Jesus at his feet—an understandable position since Jesus was reclining—she weeps (κλαίουσα, cf. 6.21), wetting Jesus' feet and drying them with her hair. Then she kisses his feet and anoints them with the ointment (v. 38).

The scene then shifts back to the Pharisee who invited Jesus and has just witnessed the woman's actions. His response is to doubt the prophetic character of Jesus, concluding that a true prophet would recognize the woman for what she was, a sinner![2] He assumes that a prophet is clairvoyant.[3] Since Jesus allowed this woman's actions he must not realize what kind of woman she is. More importantly, Simon's question threatens Jesus' authority and honor. By accepting the actions of a shameless person, Jesus was bringing shame to himself.[4] He therefore could not possibly be God's prophet. However, the story makes clear that Jesus can read thoughts by recounting Jesus' answer (ἀποκριθείς, v. 40) to Simon's thoughts.[5] Moreover, rather than losing his own honor, Jesus restores the honor of the woman.

that a Pharisee would never have any dealings with a 'sinner', much less invite one to a banquet or purposely allow one to enter into his home as Jesus does (εἰσελθὼν εἰς τὸν οἶκον, v. 36).

1. Derrett (*Law*, 268) suggests the ointment would have been a tool of her trade, probably purchased by her from her earnings.

2. The Pharisee thus is placed in opposition to the people's response to Jesus in v. 16: 'A great prophet has arisen among us'. The term ἅπτω ('touch', v. 39) can have a secondary reference to sexual touching or intercourse (cf. 1 Cor. 7.1; see BAGD, 102). Bailey (*Poet and Peasant*, 11) suggests sexual overtones are a part of the Pharisee's usage.

3. Cf. G. Friedrich, 'προφήτης', *TDNT*, VI, 844 n. 400.

4. 'The shameless person is one with a dishonorable reputation beyond all social doubt, one outside the boundaries of acceptable moral life, hence one who must be denied the normal social courtesies. To show courtesy to a shameless person makes one a fool, since it is foolish to show respect for boundaries when a person acknowledges no boundaries, just as it would be foolish to continue to speak English to a person who does not know the language at all' (Malina, *New Testament World*, 44-45).

5. The Pharisee speaks to himself (εἶπεν ἐν ἑαυτῷ, v. 39); Jesus answers, thus demonstrating his prophetic powers. The Pharisee is finally named in v. 40. The delay in naming him may be due to the narrator's desire to focus on the opposition of Pharisee/sinner, rather than a particular individual.

Jesus first tells the parable of the two debtors (vv. 41-42). The implication is that the woman, a sinner, loves more because she was forgiven more.[1] When Simon admits that one forgiven more loves more (v. 43), Jesus makes the contrast between Simon and the woman concrete, juxtaposing Simon's failures as a host and the woman's hospitable actions.[2] Simon gave no water for footwashing; the woman washed his feet with her tears. Simon did not greet Jesus with a kiss; the woman has not ceased kissing his feet. Simon did not anoint Jesus' head with oil; she anointed his feet with ointment.[3] The one who had sought to be a host of Jesus is thus shown to be less hospitable than the sinful woman of the city: she is the truly hospitable one in the story.[4] Therefore, her sins are forgiven, seeing that she loved much (v. 47).[5] He who is forgiven little,

---

1. Fitzmyer (*Gospel*, 687) says, 'The parable of the two debtors... not only carries its own message about the relation between forgiveness and love (that the sinner turns out to be the one who manifests to God greater gratitude than the upright, critical Pharisee), but also allegorizes the narrative. Repentance for the sins of the woman's life has made her more open to God's mercy than the stingy willingness of the host who wanted to honor Jesus with a dinner.'

2. Tannehill (*Narrative Unity*, 116-17), notes the careful way in which the contrast is set up by plotting in the narrative: 'The narrator has withheld relevant information about the Pharisee's attitude toward Jesus until it can be used to contrast the woman and the Pharisee. Only in vv. 44-46 do we learn that the host did not supply water for washing of feet, nor a kiss, nor oil for anointing when Jesus arrived at dinner.' Thus, the new honorable position of the woman is contrasted to the shamed position of the Pharisee.

3. The contrast is not only in the anointing but in the substance used as well—comparatively inexpensive olive oil and expensive ointment. Cf. Marshall, *Commentary*, 312.

4. There is disagreement among scholars regarding the failures of Simon being typical requirements of a host. For the view that Simon intentionally insults Jesus by his failures as a host, see Bailey, *Poet and Peasant*, 8. At the opposite end of the spectrum, see Derrett, *Law*, 268, for the view that Simon's behavior was simply conventional for the time. For a more balanced approach, cf. Marshall, *Commentary*, 312; Fitzmyer, *Gospel*, 685-86; Talbert, *Reading Luke*, 87.

5. The wording of v. 47a is ambiguous and has been understood in two different ways: 1. Because the woman loves much, she is forgiven. Forgiveness is therefore conditioned upon the woman's loving actions. The problem is that this interpretation is opposite to what is stated in the parable (vv. 41-42). 2. The woman's love is proof of her forgiveness.

however, loves little. The contrast is now complete. The woman obviously loves much; the Pharisee has loved little. Her demonstration of faith brings about honor; his failure leaves him shamed before his guests.

Jesus' announcement in v. 48, 'Your sins are forgiven' (cf. 5.20), removes all doubt about the woman's state of forgiveness, and suggests a certain interplay between love and forgiveness. Love may be the result of forgiveness (v. 42), but it may also bring about forgiveness.[1] The primary use of the saying, however, appears to be as a lead-in to the reaction of the other guests in v. 49 as they ponder the identity of one who even forgives sins (cf. 5.21). Jesus then tells the woman to go in peace; her faith has saved her.[2] The woman's faith recalls the faith of the Gentile centurion in 7.9 and proclaims her acceptance of Jesus as the one with authority to forgive sins. Her acts of love toward Jesus are seen to be a result of faith that saves. Simon, on the other hand, doubts Jesus is a true prophet, loves little, and is forgiven little; and in the end Simon appears as one who rejects the purpose of God (7.30) by failing to accept the true identity of Jesus.

The story presents a reversal of the roles initially presented in the narrative. In the beginning the Pharisee is the host, the woman is a sinner. He is inside; she is outside. He has honor; she is shameless. As the story develops, she acts hospitably; he fails to show any special kindness towards Jesus. She understands him to be a prophet; he rejects Jesus' prophetic character. She is forgiven much and loves much; he is forgiven little and loves little. Her faith saves; by implication, Simon's lack of faith means the rejection of salvation. She now has honor;

This interpretation is in harmony with the parable, it is a possible reading linguistically, and is the one most often chosen by modern commentators. Cf. Tannehill, *Narrative Unity*, 117; Fitzmyer, *Gospel*, 686-87; Marshall, *Commentary*, 306-307; Talbert, *Reading Luke*, 87; Bailey, *Poet and Peasant*, 18. The greatest difficulty with this view is that it requires a prior meeting of Jesus and the woman, or at least some prior understanding on her part that she had received forgiveness from the one sent to earth to forgive sins.

1. On this reciprocal relationship, see Tannehill, *Narrative Unity*, 117.

2. The phrase ἡ πίστις σου σέσωκέν σε is otherwise used in healing narratives in Luke. Cf. 8.48; 17.19; 18.42.

Simon is shamed. The outsider has become an insider; Simon, the supposed insider, has become an outsider.

This variation in the reversal form focuses not on eschatological reversal but on response to Jesus in the present.[1] The character opposition is Pharisee/sinner, found in a number of other Lukan texts.[2] Rejection of Jesus means that the religious insider becomes an outsider, and suffers shame before his guests.[3] Acceptance of Jesus means forgiveness for the sinful woman, salvation through her faith in him, and restoration of honor through Jesus' acceptance of her actions.

The Good Samaritan (10.25-37)

The parable of the Good Samaritan (10.25-37) is the first of six Lukan parables that Crossan defines as parables of reversal.[4] Crossan's list of reversal parables corresponds closely to Bultmann's category of exemplary stories.[5] However, Crossan

---

1. Tannehill (*Narrative Unity*, 117) states, 'Jesus, the person of authority in Luke's Gospel and the dominant speaker in this scene, puts the Pharisee in a negative light and the woman in a positive light, reversing the situation which existed before Jesus intervened. Apart from Jesus the Pharisee was the person of status in the community and was presumably in control of events in his own home. The woman was a despised sinner in the town who had made herself especially vulnerable by her presence and behavior in the Pharisee's house. Jesus' commendation of the woman's strange behavior turns the initial situation upside down'.

2. Cf. 5.30ff.; 15.1ff.; 18.9-13.

3. In his discourse analysis of 7.36-50, J. Louw speaks of the intentional level of interpretation and writes: 'It seems that Luke uses the events to convey a message of utter irony. Jesus and his preaching is not for people (like the Pharisee) who regard themselves as righteous. Jesus came to minister to the underdogs, the outcasts, the sinners. His message is understood by these very people, while the respected of society, the privileged, the powerful, stand aloof. Those who can be expected to appraise the preaching of Jesus do not understand his message at all, while the despised and rejected really comprehend the essence of the message' ('A Semiotic Approach to Discourse Analysis with Reference to Translation Theory', *The Bible Translator* 36 [1985], 106).

4. *In Parables*, 57.

5. Bultmann lists the following Lukan parables as exemplary stories: The Good Samaritan (10.30-37); The Rich Fool (12.16-21); The Rich Man and Lazarus (16.19-31); Pharisee and Publican (18.10-14); The Wedding Guest (14.7-11); The Proper Guests (14.12-14); see *History*, 178-79.

seeks to demonstrate the reversal character found in the reconstructed parables of the historical Jesus.[1] In the case of the parable of the Good Samaritan, Crossan limits his discussion, therefore, to vv. 30-36.[2] The reversal about which he speaks is a reversal of hearers' expectations.[3] The Lukan narrative, however, creates a different set of expectations than those posited by Crossan, and the audience clearly is different from Crossan's 'historical' audience of the authentic parable. Rather than attempting to identify the Lukan audience, or create a new category of 'hearer expectations reversal', the task at this point is to identify features in the parable and its

Crossan's parables of reversal include all of the above plus the parable of the Prodigal Son (15.11-32). See *In Parables*, 55-78.

1. *Ibid.*, p. 56.

2. However, Crossan believes that the surrounding context, vv. 25-29, 37, reflects a pre-Lukan tradition rather than Lukan redaction, concluding that this material was already in one context in Q. See *In Parables*, 59-60. There is great diversity of opinion on the origins of the parable and its placement in the context of the lawyer's question. For example, J. Drury (*The Parables in the Gospels* [New York: Crossroad, 1985]) believes that Luke adapted Matthew and Mark himself (p. 133). Drury further implies that the parable may be a creation of Luke based on 2 Chron. 28.14f. (pp. 134-35). Fitzmyer (*Gospel*, 877, 883) suggests that vv. 25-28 and 30-37 are from Luke's L source, with Luke redactionally adding v. 29 to link them together. Funk (*Language*, 218) believes that the authenticity of the Lukan context is not decisive for the meaning of the parable, i.e. the meaning of the parable is clear apart from the context. However, the context does support the proper understanding of the parable. J. Lambrecht (*Once More Astonished* [New York: Crossroad, 1981], 75-77) and E. Linnemann (*Parables of Jesus* [London: SPCK, 1966], 51-58), both argue that the meaning of the parable is changed considerably in the edited version now found in Luke. On the other hand, Manson (*Sayings*, 259-60) and Marshall (*Commentary*, 440-41) affirm the basic unity and authenticity of the entire unit (vv. 25-37).

3. See his more detailed analysis, 'The Good Samaritan: Towards a Generic Definition of Parable', *Semeia* 2 (1975), 93-96. Cf. Drake, 'Reversal Theme', 245-51, who follows Crossan in categorizing the reversal in the parable as a reversal of hearers' expectations. Also see Funk, *Language*, 212ff., for a discussion of the importance of hearer expectations; and Sandra Wackman Perpich, *A Hermeneutic Critique of Structuralist Exegesis, with Specific Reference to Lk 10.29-37* (Lanham, MD: University Press of America, 1984), 200-206.

context that implicitly demonstrate features of bi-polar reversal we have seen in other Lukan narratives.

The larger context for the parable must begin with the
inception of the travel narrative (9.51) and the first mention of
Samaritans in the Gospel. 'Having set his face toward
Jerusalem', Jesus attempts to enter into a village of Samaritans (9.52).[1] The Samaritans refuse to receive Jesus because
'his face was proceeding to Jerusalem' (v. 53).[2] However,
when James and John are indignant and seek permission to
call fire down from heaven to consume the village (cf. 2 Kgs
1.10-12), Jesus rebukes them, not the Samaritans (vv. 54-55).
The scene demonstrates the hostility between Samaritans and
Jews but creates ambiguity regarding the Samaritans and
Jesus. The Samaritans encounter only Jesus' disciples, and
they refuse to receive him because of his destination rather
than on account of his personal identity or message.[3] Jesus'
rebuke of James and John suggests that animosity towards
the Samaritans is in some sense wrong. The scene appears to
serve, therefore, as an introduction to a character group—
Samaritans—who later will reappear with greater clarity and
precision in the narrative.[4]

The immediate context of the parable of the Good Samaritan
is a dialogue between Jesus and a lawyer.[5] The lawyer asks
Jesus a question, testing him: 'Teacher, what shall I do to
inherit eternal life?' (διδάσκαλε, τί ποιήσας ζωὴν αἰώνιον

1. This is the first of three references to Samaritans in Luke; the
others are 10.33 and 17.16. In Acts, the Samaritans are viewed positively, and serve as a bridge between the mission to the Jews and the
mission to the Gentiles (cf. 1.8; 8.4-25). See the discussion of this point
in Lambrecht, *Astonished*, 77-78.
2. On the possible link to 2 Sam. 17.11 LXX, see Marshall, *Commentary*, 406.
3. Cf. Fitzmyer, *Gospel*, 830.
4. In Acts, Luke often does this, e.g. with Barnabas (Acts 4.36),
Stephen (6.5), Saul (8.1), and John Mark (12.12).
5. Luke uses the term νομικός 7 times (cf. Matthew once, Mark none).
In the other six references, lawyers are grouped with the Pharisees
and are clearly hostile to Jesus and his message (cf. 7.30; 11.45, 46, 52,
53; 14.3). True to that antithetical character the lawyer in this case
stands to put Jesus to the test (ἐκπειράζων; cf. 4.2; 11.16, 29).

κληρονομήσω, v. 25).[1] Unlike a similar situation in Mark and
Matthew,[2] Jesus does not recite the two great commandments
himself but asks the lawyer to answer from his own understanding of the law. The lawyer responds by quoting Deut. 6.5
and Lev. 19.18. Jesus tells him, 'You have answered correctly;
do this and you will live' (ὀρθῶς[3] ἀπεκρίθης· τοῦτο ποίει καὶ
ζήσῃ). The present imperative ποίει answers the lawyer's
original question of v. 25, τί ποιήσας, with a call to continuous
action rather than a specific requirement which the aorist
tense (ποιήσας) suggests.[4]

The lawyer wishes to justify (δικαιῶσαι)[5] himself, and asks
Jesus, 'Who is my neighbor?' (τίς ἐστίν μου πλησίον).[6] Since he
is to love his neighbor as himself in order to have life, the
lawyer seeks greater specificity regarding the identity of those

1. Jeremias (*Parables*, 202) notes the unusual situation created by a
lawyer—a professional—addressing a layman as 'teacher' and asking
a question about the Law. The wording of the question is identical to
the question asked by the rich ruler in 18.18.
2. Cf. Mt. 22.35-40; Mk 12.28-31. There are a number of differences in
the accounts. In Mark, a scribe asks the question, 'Which commandment is first of all?' Jesus responds by quoting Deut. 6.4-5—the latter
verse is actually identical in wording to Josh. 22.5 LXX—and Lev. 19.18.
The scribe replies, telling Jesus he has answered well, and then he
paraphrases the commandments himself. Jesus then tells him that he
is not far from the kingdom of God. In Matthew, a lawyer who is one of
the Pharisees asks a question to test (πειράζων) Jesus: 'Teacher, which
is the great commandment in the Law?' Jesus responds, quoting Deut.
6.5 (Josh. 22.5) and Lev. 19.18, and then summarizes by saying, 'On
these two commandments depend all the law and the prophets'. In
Matthew the lawyer makes no further comment. Luke's account thus
has certain features in common with each account and distinctive differences from each. There is no longer a scholarly consensus on the
relationship of the three texts. Cf. the discussions of Fitzmyer, *Gospel*,
877-78; Manson, *Sayings*, 259-61; Bultmann, *History*, 22-23; Crossan,
In Parables, 58-59.
3. Cf. Lk. 7.43. Jesus tells Simon, ὀρθῶς ἔκρινας. ὀρθῶς is found only
four times in the New Testament, three of which are in Luke (the other
reference is 20.21), one in Mark (7.35).
4. K. Bailey, *Through Peasant Eyes* (Grand Rapids: Eerdmans, 1980),
38.
5. Cf. 7.29-30, 16.15, 18.9, all of which demonstrate a similar self-
interest on the part of lawyers and/or Pharisees.
6. πλησίον is used only three times in Luke, all of which are in this
context (vv. 27, 29, 36).

whom he is called to love. Jesus answers by telling the story of a man traveling from Jerusalem to Jericho who is attacked by robbers, and left stripped, beaten, and half dead (v. 30). Three different individuals are then presented in succession who come upon the man and make a choice either to help him or ignore him. The first two are religious leaders of the Jews, a priest and a Levite.[1] For reasons not given,[2] each chooses to pass by the injured man without giving aid. The third man is a Samaritan who, upon seeing the injured man, has compassion (ἐσπλαγχνίσθη) and administers aid. He binds and treats the man's wounds, carries him to an inn and takes care of him (v. 34). The next day he makes provision with the innkeeper to continue caring for the man until he is well and pledges to pay whatever additional expenses the innkeeper may sustain (v. 35).[3]

Jesus then asks the lawyer to identify which one of the three acted as neighbor (γεγονέναι πλησίον)[4] to the man who was

---

1. ἱερεύς is used four other times in Luke, all in contexts which speak of their cultic responsibilites rather than particular attitudes toward God or Jesus (1.5; 5.14; 6.4; 17.14). The term Λευίτης is found two other times in the New Testament, once in John (1.19) and once in Acts (4.36). Fitzmyer says that Levites of the first century enjoyed a privileged status along with the priests, and were entitled to tithes for priestly service (*Gospel*, 883, 887). Some prior understanding of their function as religious leaders along with the priests seems necessary to fully understand the story.

2. A common assumption made by scholars is that the priest and Levite chose not to attend to the battered man either out of fear or obedience to ritual purification laws. See Bailey, *Through Peasant Eyes*, 44-47; Derrett, *Law*, 211-17; Jeremias, *Parables*, 203-204; Fitzmyer, *Gospel*, 887.

3. The Samaritan's hospitality towards a foreigner is perhaps greater than often assumed. Douglas E. Oatman argues that 'Two denarii, in summary, represent around three weeks' worth of food for one person or about 1% of an ancient Palestinian's annual budget' ('The Buying Power of Two Denarii: A Commentary on Luke 10.35', *Forum* 3/4 [1987], 37).

4. The difference in the lawyer's question (v. 29) and Jesus' question in v. 36 is often noted. The 'neighbor' in the lawyer's question is the object of action. In Jesus' final question the neighbor is the subject who acts. The change in usage has been treated in a variety of ways. For example, Ellis (*Gospel*, 160) and Creed (*Gospel*, 151) argue that the parable implies an answer to the lawyer's question, viz. aiding anyone

robbed and beaten. The lawyer has little choice but to confirm that it was 'the one having done mercy with him' (ὁ ποιήσας τὸ ἔλεος μετ' αὐτοῦ).[1] Jesus then commands him to 'Go and do likewise' (πορεύου καὶ σὺ ποίει ὁμοίως). The use of ποιέω in vv. 36 and 37 links the concluding command to the lawyer's initial question and Jesus' answer in v. 28. Loving one's neighbor becomes synonymous with showing mercy to a half-dead stranger. More important in the Lukan context, however, is the implication that acting as the Samaritan did means inheriting eternal life. The repeated use of ποιέω in vv. 25, 28, 36, and 37 links the initial question to the actions of the Samaritan. The call to 'Do this and you will live' (v. 28) is given specification by the Samaritan's actions, and it is repeated in the final command to 'Go and do likewise'.[2]

It is with regard to the issue of inheriting eternal life that the implicit bi-polar reversal takes place in this narrative. The lawyer, a religious leader himself, poses the question, 'What shall I do to inherit eternal life?' The lawyer answers from the

---

in need is the proper object of neighborly love. Jülicher (*Gleichnis-reden*, 596) used the discrepancy as a basis for separating the parable from the Lukan context, as did Bultmann (*History*, 178). Lambrecht (*Astonished*, 79) claims that the discrepancy came about as an unintentional oversight in Luke's editing. Marshall (*Commentary*, 450), on the other hand, believes the change is historical and intentional, to avoid further argument with the lawyer. Funk (*Language*, 210) believes that to infer an answer to the lawyer's question, as Ellis, Creed and others do, produces an answer out of harmony with the main thrust of the parable. He concludes that without somehow reworking the question or the parable there must be discontinuity between the two questions (vv. 29, 36). When the context is viewed as a whole, however, 'doing' that which will bring eternal life is of central importance. Since that is the major focus of the narrative, the lawyer's question is seen as a subdivision of his first question. Jesus' question in v. 36 changes the lawyer's secondary question in order to force the lawyer to answer his own primary question regarding what he must 'do'—he must act as the outsider Samaritan acted.

1. Funk (*Language*, 212) notes the great incongruity faced by the lawyer in response to Jesus' parable. Over against the priest and Levite, who normally would be his associates, he must identify with the despised Samaritan. In response to Jesus' question the lawyer cannot bring himself to utter the name Samaritan. He can only refer to 'the one' who acted mercifully.

2. Cf. Crespy, 'Parables', 37-38; Lambrecht, *Astonished*, 76.

Law, saying that he should love God and love his neighbor;
Jesus confirms his answer and tells him to do this and live.
When the lawyer tries to vindicate himself, Jesus tells a parable which, as Luke uses the story, contrasts the actions of two
esteemed and honorable Jews with the act of a shameful foreigner. The story suggests that an outsider, the Samaritan, is
capable of inheriting eternal life, but religious leaders, like the
priest and Levite, are incapable. The religious insiders may
indeed be following certain demands of the Law, but they fail
in the weightier matters (cf. 11.42). By their exclusivist
actions, they are excluding themselves from the Kingdom.
The outsider, by his act of mercy, does that which is necessary
to inherit eternal life.[1] The shameful Samaritan is shown to be
honorable by his actions; the honored Jews are shameful
because of their inaction.

In a similar way to the anointing story in ch. 7 and the
parable of the Pharisee and the Publican in ch. 18, this story
suggests that religious outcasts have a better understanding of
God than the religious insiders. In the overall context of Luke,
therefore, the 'surprise reversal of hearer expectations' often
mentioned in relation to this parable is not so surprising. The
group of Jewish religious leaders who fail to 'do' that which
will bring life is expanded by the use of a priest and a Levite as
examples, but their failure to act as neighbor fits well with
Luke's presentation of Pharisees and lawyers who 'reject the
purposes of God' (7.30), fail to show hospitality to Jesus (7.44-
46), and who later are described as justifying themselves
before men (16.15) and trusting in themselves that they are
righteous (18.9).

The parable itself has only a temporal dimension, but the
Lukan context creates eschatological overtones. Present
action or inaction leads to future inclusion or exclusion from
'life'. Inheriting eternal life becomes the goal of the narrative

---

1. In ch. 17, where the third and last mention of Samaritans occurs
in the Gospel, only the Samaritan leper—called a 'foreigner'
(ἀλλογενής, v. 18)—responds with gratitude to Jesus' healing. The nine
Jewish lepers do not 'return and give praise to God' (v. 18). Thus,
while the first encounter with the Samaritans in the text is ambiguous, the next two clearly view the 'foreigner' in a more positive light
than the Jewish counterparts.

and 'doing mercy' as the Samaritan did becomes the way to achieve life. The lawyer, who begins by testing Jesus and seeking to justify himself, is forced to identify with the outcast Samaritan and admit that showing compassion to a half-dead stranger is what leads to life. Acting as neighbor now takes on eschatological meaning. This is quite characteristic of the reversal texts in Luke which continually integrate 'now' and 'not yet'. The narrative implies that the outcast Samaritan, by acting as neighbor, has life; the religious insiders, with whom the lawyer would otherwise identify himself, fail to act neighborly and thus to inherit eternal life.

Table-Fellowship Instructions (14.17-24)
Luke 14 includes the last of three incidents in Luke that portray Jesus dining with the Pharisees (vv. 1-24).[1] There are four units of material woven together around the setting of Jesus going to eat bread (φαγεῖν ἄρτον) at the home of 'one of the rulers of the Pharisees on the Sabbath' (τινος τῶν ἀρχόντων τῶν Φαρισαίων σαββάτῳ).[2] Funk notes that the four units are linked by the catchword 'invite' (καλέω),[3] as well as the phrases 'to eat bread' (14.1, 15), and 'a great banquet' (14.16

1. See the earlier discussion of the symposium and its relation to the Lukan narratives of Jesus dining with Pharisees in the study of 14.11 in Chapter 2. Also see Josef Ernst, 'Gastmahlgespräche: Lk 14.1-24', in *Die Kirche des Anfangs* (ed. R. Schnackenburg, J. Ernst, and J. Wanke; Freiburg: Herder, 1978), 57-78, esp. 57-63. On the rhetorical importance of the repetition in the three narratives (7.36-50; 11.37-54; 14.1-24), see T.M. Noel, 'Parables in Context: Developing a Narrative-Critical Approach to Parables in Luke' (Ph.D. dissertation, The Southern Baptist Seminary, 1986), 159-60. Also see Tannehill's discussion of these three texts as an example of type-scenes in Luke. Tannehill defines a type-scene as 'a basic situation which recurs several times within a narrative. Each occurrence has a recognizably similar set of characteristics, sometimes highlighted by the repetition of key phrases, but this similarity permits—even requires, if boredom is to be avoided—new variations in the development of the scene' (*Narrative Unity*, 170-71).
2. The four units are are: Jesus healing the man with dropsy on the Sabbath (vv. 1-6); proper behavior of guests at banquets (vv. 7-11); behavior of hosts (vv. 12-14); the Great Supper (vv. 15-24).
3. Forms of the verb καλέω are found in vv. 7, 8 (twice), 12, 13, 16, 17, 24.

reflects both 14.12 and the wedding feast in 14.8).[1] The four
stories each present a different teaching and successively
depict Jesus addressing Pharisees and lawyers (14.3) who
were dining with him (14.1), those invited with him to dine
(14.7), the host (14.12), and one of the guests at table with him
(14.15).[2] The characters are typical of those found in the symposium genre: the master of the house, the guest of honor and
main speaker, the invited guests, and the uninvited.[3] The
details of v. 1 apply to all four stories: the time is the Sabbath;
Jesus is dining at the home of a ruler of the Pharisees;[4] they
are 'watching him' (παρατηρούμενοι αὐτόν).[5]

The first unit (vv. 1-6) sets the stage for the following verses
and recalls two previous accounts in which Jesus healed
someone on the Sabbath (6.6-11; 13.10-17).[6] In the first inci-

1. Funk, *Language*, 172.
2. *Ibid*. Crossan (*In Parables*, 70) argues that the unity of vv. 1-24 is
artificial and he seeks to place each of the last three stories in isolated,
historical contexts. De Meeus ('Composition') has shown that these
verses are indeed a highly structured literary unity composed with
clear reference to the symposium genre (see esp. 852, 855-59). For the
Lukan audience this unity therefore is not to be ignored but understood
in the context of the symposium. This has implications for how one
understands the characters of the text—primarily the Pharisees—and
the reversals that are presented. Cf. Smith, 'Table-Fellowship', 622
n. 28. Also see Noel, 'Parables in Context', 150, for the validity of reading the parables of vv. 7-24 in context.
3. De Meeus, 'Composition', 852, 855-56; Smith, 'Table-Fellowship',
621.
4. The fact that the Pharisee was a 'ruler' (τινος τῶν ἀρχόντων)
denotes both honor and wealth for the host of the banquet. Tannehill
notes that 'the scribes and Pharisees whom Jesus meets at dinner par-
ties are understood to be persons of wealth who need instruction in
their social responsibility to the poor' (*Narrative Unity*, 183).
5. Cf. 11.53-54.
6. This three-fold repetition of healings on the Sabbath also is a type-
scene in Luke. Cf. Tannehill, *Narrative Unity*, 171. There are a number of parallels between both of these accounts and 14.1-6. In 6.7,
scribes and Pharisees were 'watching' (παρετηροῦντο) Jesus (cf. 14.1);
in 6.9 Jesus asked them if it was lawful to do good on the Sabbath (cf.
14.3); in both stories the diseased person was healed. In 13.14, a ruler
of the synagogue voices opposition to Jesus' actions (in 14.1 it is a ruler
of the Pharisees who hosts Jesus); in 13.15 Jesus argues, 'Does not
each of you on the sabbath untie his ox (βοῦν) or his ass from the
manger, and lead it away to water it?' In 14.5 Jesus says, 'Which of

dent, Pharisees and scribes were outraged by Jesus' action and discussed what they might do to Jesus (6.11). In the second account a ruler of the synagogue (ἀρχισυνάγωγος) was indignant because of Jesus' actions; however, Jesus put to shame all his adversaries (κατῃσχύνοντο πάντες οἱ ἀντικείμενοι αὐτῷ, 13.17). In this third instance, Jesus leaves his critical audience of Pharisees and lawyers silent as he heals a man with dropsy.[1] The story presents the different attitudes taken by Jesus and the Pharisees toward social outcasts: Jesus wishes to heal the man; the Pharisees are more interested in the failure of Jesus to properly observe the Sabbath.[2]

Verse 7 serves as a transition from the first unit to the second and also functions as a counterpoint to v. 1. Whereas the Pharisees were 'watching' Jesus in the opening scene, Jesus also had been watching the way in which the other guests chose the places of honor (πρωτοκλισίας).[3] He tells them that choosing the route of self-honor at a marriage feast is danger-

you, having a son or an ox (βοῦς; the only other use of βοῦς in Luke is 14.19; the term is not found in Matthew or Mark) that has fallen into a well, will not immediately pull him out on a sabbath day?'

1. The scene depicts Jesus, the supposedly honored guest, with his honor and authority on trial before the watchful Pharisees and lawyers. The man whom he heals has a disease which was dishonorable and one which would have prevented Pharisees from contact with such a person. Cf. Strack–Billerbeck, II, 203-204; Steele, 'Jesus' Table-Fellowship', 70. Jesus heals the man, thus restoring his honor, and demonstrates his authority and honor before the silent critics.

2. Talbert, *Reading Luke*, 196, finds the following chiastic pattern in vv. 1-24:

A   Unconcern about others (human) while having the appearance of being religious (vv. 1-6)
B   Self-seeking as a guest (vv. 7-11)
B′   Self-seeking as a host (vv. 12-14)
A′   Unconcern about others (God) while having the appearance of being religious (vv. 15-24)

3. Cf. 11.43; 20.46. The Pharisees' love for the 'first couches' also recalls 13.30, where 'some who are last will be first (πρῶτοι), some who are first will be last'. The question of seating at places of honor is common within the symposium genre. Cf. Plutarch, *Table Talk*, 1.2, 1.3. See the discussion of Smith, 'Table-Fellowship', 618-20, who notes that in Plutarch the issue is settled by the philosophical principles of friendship and order; in Luke the answer is the Biblical virtue of humility.

ous, since a more eminent one (ἐντιμότερος) may arrive. The host would then say, 'Give your place to this one' (δὸς τούτῳ τόπον). Rather than receiving honor in the first seat, one would be shamed (αἰσχύνης, v. 9), ending up in the last place (ἔσχατον τόπον).[1] Jesus suggests instead that one should sit in the last seat so that when the host comes and says, 'Friend, go up higher', the guest will be honored by all.

The story implies that a reversal of one's actions will bring about the status originally desired but lost through improper self-evaluation. The common scene of the banquet and the values of honor and shame would have been well known to the Lukan audience. In the setting of the symposium of ch. 14, they are used to teach the Biblical virtue of humility. The implicit bi-polar reversal of vv. 9-10 is made explicit in the aphorism of vv. 11 where the self-exalted will be humbled and the humbled exalted.[2] The wisdom saying also adds a theological dimension to the double reversal, implying that the double reversal is ultimately a divine principle.[3]

The aphorism also influences the meaning of Jesus' instructions to the host (vv. 11-14). Again the values of honor and shame are important,[4] as Jesus advises against the normal

1. Cf. 13.28-30. The person who lost the honor challenge at this table resembles those who are destined to lose out at the eschatological banquet in 13.28ff. In *Table-Talk* 1.2, Plutarch relates that at a banquet held by his brother Timon, the decision was made to allow guests to recline wherever they wished. However, when an especially honored guest arrived late, he was insulted that no place worthy of his honor was left and therefore departed angrily.

2. There is no suggestion in the narrative that those choosing the places of honor at the meal attended by Jesus actually experienced such a reversal. The 'parable' serves as a warning that such self-seeking could result in loss of honor and position, thus bringing about a reversal of one's social standing at a banquet. By choosing the lowest seat first, however, one might insure the opposite reversal which would in turn bring about the desired honor in the presence of the other guests.

3. Cf. the use of the aphorism in 18.14. On the use of the theological passive, 'will be humbled', 'will be exalted', see above, Chapter 2.

4. Malina (*New Testament World*, 55) argues that, in the first century, one's personhood was not determined individually but in relationship to others; he terms this dyadism. 'A dyadic personality is simply one who needs another continually in order to know who he or she is ... Such a person internalizes and makes his own what others

procedure of reciprocity and advocates hosting those unable to repay. The host is instructed not to invite those individuals through whom his personhood is affirmed, those to whom he normally gives honor who in return show him honor. These include his friends, brothers, kinsmen, and rich (πλουσίους) neighbors—those who naturally would reciprocate. Honor is thus maintained and enhanced among one's equals and superiors. Rather, he is to invite those who cannot repay—the poor, the maimed, the lame, the blind (v. 13).[1] The latter group cannot reciprocate nor do they appear to be socially advantageous in a patron-client relationship. They are the dishonored of society. Such a guest list would mean that the host not only was inviting those who could not repay, but also he would be associating with the dishonored ones of society, thereby bringing shame to himself.

In return for inviting such guests, the host would be blessed (v. 13) and be repaid at the resurrection of the just (v. 14).[2]

---

say, do, and think about him because he believes it is necessary, for being human, to live out the expectations of others. That person would conceive of himself as always interrelated to other persons while occupying a distinct social position both horizontally (with others sharing the same status, moving from center to periphery) and vertically (with others above and below in social rank). Such persons need to test this interrelatedness, with the focus of attention away from ego, on the demands and expectations of others who can grant or withhold reputation. Pivotal values for such persons would be honor and shame, not guilt.' Cf. G. Bornkamm, *Jesus of Nazareth* (trans. I. and F. McLuskey with J.M. Robinson; New York: Harper and Row, 1960), 80.

1. J.A. Sanders has shown the relationship this list has to the lists of people with whom one is forbidden to associate according to Lev. 21.17-23; 1QS^a 2.5-22; 1 QM 7.4-6. All three lists include the blind, lame and physically injured. Sanders notes that the Qumran lists could not include the πτωχοί since that was a self-designation of their piety. Sanders also notes that the seating arrangement at a banquet (vv. 7-11) is inverted in comparison to Qumran. See 'Luke's Great Banquet Parable', in *Essays in Old Testament Ethics*, Festschrift for J. Philip Hyatt (ed. J.L. Crenshaw and J.T. Willis; New York: Ktav, 1974), 261-65.

2. The reward for the host's decision to humble himself by inviting those beneath his own social status, therefore, is not temporal but eschatological. This suggests that v. 11 should also not be taken solely as a statement of reversals to present conditions but as a bi-polar reversal with eschatological overtones. Cf. Tannehill, *Narrative Unity*, 184;

Both of these divine responses indicate that proper human
interaction brings about spiritual rewards. For the host to
include such guests suggests the host must step outside the
honor/shame conventions, humbling himself in order to
receive his reward at the resurrection of the just. By choosing
to humble himself the host is promised divine exaltation (cf.
v. 11). Significant links between vv. 7-11 and vv. 12-14 suggest
that more than the aphorism applies to both teachings. The
parallels between the two sets of instructions are striking:

14.8-10	14.12-14
When you are invited by any-one to a marriage feast	When you give a dinner or a banquet
Do not sit down in a place of honor	Do not invite your friends or your brothers
Lest a more eminent man than you be invited by him	Lest they also invite you in return
And then you will begin with shame to take the lowest place	And you be repaid
But when you are invited Sit in the lowest place	But when you give a feast Invite the poor, the maimed, the lame, the blind
You will be honored in the presence of all	You will be blessed because they cannot repay you

Jeremias, *Parables*, 193. The eschatological content of the sayings is
reinforced by vv. 15ff., where Jesus tells the parable of the great banquet in response to the statement of one at table with him, 'blessed is
he who shall eat bread in the kingdom of God' (cf. 13.28-29). However,
Fitzmyer (*Gospel*, 1044-45) correctly warns against abandoning too
quickly the practical advice of vv. 7-14 for the present in the lives of
Christian disciples. There is, to be sure, an important link between
present attitudes and actions and the future reversal expressed by the
aphorism. But Fitzmyer himself notes the use of the 'theological passive' in v. 11, which 'expresses God's judgment as the source of the
honor' (p. 1045).

Everyone who exalts himself
will be humbled; everyone
who humbles himself will be
exalted.[1]

You will be repaid at
the resurrection of the just.

In the comparison, seeking self-honor as a guest is like seeking the honor one receives from inviting friends, kinsmen and rich neighbors. Similarly, choosing the last place at a banquet is like inviting the poor, lame, maimed and blind to one's feast. The person who seeks honor in either case is admonished to humble himself, either by choosing the last seat or by inviting the social outcast. Both teachings are thus illustrative of the aphorism in 14.11.

What apparently is a set of instructions about table manners in vv. 7-13 takes on spiritual and eschatological dimensions in v. 14. The reward for proper behavior is to be given at the resurrection of the just. The aphorism, which parallels this verse, also becomes more than temporal wisdom.[2] The instructions to guests and the host are calls to reflect in human behavior what will ultimately be the eschatological act of God. In the case of the behavior of the host, the actions of God achieve greater clarity through the telling of the final parable in the literary unit, the parable of the great banquet (vv. 16-24).[3]

The final parable is given as a response to a statement by one of the guests, 'Blessed is he who shall eat bread (ὅστις φάγεται

---

1. This parallel structure is given by Noel, 'Parables in Context', 152, who credits Alan Culpepper, *Pentecost 2* (Philadelphia: Fortress, 1986), 38, with a similar analysis. Tannehill (*Narrative Unity*, 183), notes that vv. 12-14 are formally parallel to vv. 8-10, but he gives no details.

2. Cf. Jeremias, *Parables*, 192-93; Tannehill, *Narrative Unity*, 184; Noel, 'Parables in Context', 152; Creed, *Gospel*, 189-90. Against finding eschatological overtones in vv. 8-11 is Fitzmyer, *Gospel*, 1044. When the verses are read in isolation from vv. 12-14, Fitzmyer is correct. However, the literary context which links these texts together suggests that the practical advice on table manners has taken on a larger religious meaning.

3. The repetition of the list of social misfits to be invited in the parable (cf. vv. 13 and 21) demonstrates the close relationship intended between vv. 12-14 and vv. 16-24. Cf. O. Glombitza, 'Das grosse Abendmahl Luk. xiv 12-24', *Novum Testamentum* 5 (1962), 10-16; Ernst, 'Gastmahlgespräche', 69-75; Jeremias, *Parables*, 44-45.

ἄρτον; cf. 14.1) in the kingdom of God' (v. 15).[1] The guest's statement makes the eschatological element of the banquet scene explicit. Within this context, the parable of the Great Banquet takes on specific meaning in relation to the previous units and in relation to the immediate audience of Pharisees and lawyers.[2] With Jesus already having given instructions to fellow guests and the host which had eschatological implications, the guest's statement turns the discussion to the King-

---

1. Verse 15 links the parable to the previous setting of Jesus dining with the Pharisee, and also recalls the words of 13.26-30, in which people will come from all directions to sit at table in the Kingdom of God while those who thought they were 'in' will be thrust out. While Bultmann, *History*, 335, may be correct that the saying of v. 15b is a traditional statement editorially placed on the lips of a guest, the statement still has a particular function for the Lukan audience within the literary unity of vv. 1-24.

2. The parable is also found in Matthew (22.1-14) and the *Gospel of Thomas* (§64) with significant variations in each. In Matthew, the audience is also the Pharisees—along with the chief priests (21.45ff.)— but the parable itself is more allegorical. An eschatological banquet scene is described in which two separate invitations are refused by those invited. In the second rejection, the invited ones 'paid no attention' (ἀμελήσαντες), one going away to his farm, another to his business; the host's servants are treated shamefully and killed by the rest of the invited guests (v. 6). In anger the king sends troops and destroys those who refused the invitation (v. 7). The servants are then sent (only one time) to the highways to invite 'as many as you find'. Both 'bad and good' are gathered and brought to the feast and the wedding hall is filled (v. 10). Matthew's version then has the parable of the wedding garments appended (vv. 11-14), giving the parable of the Great Banquet a distinctive conclusion. In the Gospel of Thomas, the setting is more urban than in Luke. A man already had received visitors and prepared a dinner for them. However, when the servant was sent to invite the guests to dine, each in turn asked to be excused. The first had business dealings with merchants to which he must attend; the second had just bought a house and had no spare time; the third had a friend about to be married and he was to prepare the banquet. Upon learning of his guests' refusal, the master said to his servant, 'Go outside to the streets and bring back those whom you happen to meet so that they may dine. Businessmen and merchants will not enter the Places of My Father' (trans. in Funk, *Gospel Parallels*, II, 153). In the latter account the triad of excuses is similar in form to Luke, but the excuses themselves are different. The version in Thomas, like Matthew's account, has only one invitation to the uninvited, whereas Luke has two.

dom banquet. Jesus' final parable demonstrates the relationship between human behavior and entrance into the Kingdom.

Jesus tells the story of a man who prepared a feast (δεῖπνον)[1]
and invited (ἐκάλεσεν) guests. When the time came for the
banquet, he sent his servant (δοῦλον)[2] to those invited
(κεκλημένοις),[3] saying, 'Come, for all is now ready' (v. 17). All
of those invited began to make excuses (ἤρξαντο ἀπὸ μιᾶς
πάντες παραιτεῖσθαι): the first had bought a field that he 'must'
(ἀνάγκην) go to inspect;[4] he therefore asked to be excused. The
second had purchased five yoke of oxen which he needed to
examine;[5] he likewise asked to be excused. A third simply said,
'I have married a wife and cannot come'.[6] The three excuses

1. Although Luke often makes reference to eating situations in the
Gospel and Acts, δεῖπνον is used only in ch. 14 (vv. 12, 16, 17, 24) and
20.46.
2. Cf. the plural δούλους in Mt. 22.3, 4; singular in the *Gospel of
Thomas*.
3. Bailey suggests that the second invitation was a common courtesy
in the oriental culture and therefore a natural part of the process of
having guests for a banquet. See *Through Peasant Eyes*, 93-94;
Jeremias, *Parables*, 176. The double invitation also removes doubt as to
the awareness of the impending banquet by those invited—there was
no surprise involved which prevented their acceptance.
4. The use of ἀνάγκην suggests that the man had little choice in the
matter (Marshall, *Commentary*, 589). However, the double invitation
suggests that, with prior knowledge of the impending feast, the man's
interest in possessing the field was greater than his interest in the
banquet. Buying a field suggests a rural setting—as opposed to the
urban setting reflected in the *Gospel of Thomas*—and a person of some
means financially.
5. Jeremias (*Parables*, 177), notes that the typical farmer had enough
land to support the use of 1–2 yoke of oxen. A person who could pur-
chase 5 yoke had considerable wealth and landholdings.
6. Linneman (*Parables*, 89, 164), argues that the third excuse is secondary, since there is no parallel to it in the other versions. She further suggests that the emphasis is not on failure to attend at all but
being excused for being late. The problem, aside from no textual evidence for omitting the third excuse and the fact that such triads are
common in Luke, is that such an emphasis does not explain the reaction of the host. Such a view also seems doubtful when the use of
παραιτέομαι is considered. Cf. BAGD, 616; G. Stahlin, 'παραιτέομαι',
TDNT, I, 195. Literary links between the three excuses and the following discourse on discipleship (vv. 25-33) should also be noted. Whereas

are often compared to the causes for exemption from Holy
War listed in Deut. 20.5-8.[1] Whether or not the Holy War
exemption list provides the background, the characteristic of
each individual is his involvement in the cares and concerns of
life. Each is too preoccupied with a recent acquisition
(possessions, wife) to hear the call to dine.[2]

In response to the guests' refusal, the host is understandably
angry;[3] his honor would be severely damaged by such a mass
refusal.[4] He therefore sends his servant out to the streets of the
city to invite the societal outcasts—the poor and maimed and
lame and blind (cf. v. 13)[5]—into his feast. When the banquet

in the parable the invited guests were too concerned with possessions
and family relations to accept the invitation, Jesus calls those who
would be his disciples to hate (μισεῖ) all of those close to them, including τὴν γυναῖκα (v. 25). In v. 33 Jesus summarizes by saying that whoever does not renounce all of his possessions (πᾶσιν τοῖς ἑαυτοῦ ὑπάρχ-
ουσιν) cannot be his disciple.

1. Cf. Derrett, *Law*, 136-37; J.A. Sanders, 'Ethic of Election', 256-57;
P.H. Ballard, 'Reasons for Refusing the Great Supper', *Journal of
Theological Studies* n.s. 23 (1972), 345-50. However, Fitzmyer (*Gospel*,
1056) argues that such an interpretation is eisegetical. He claims that
to scrutinize the excuses in such a manner misses the story-telling
technique: three persons, three sendings of the invitation, three
excuses.

2. Johnson, *Literary Function*, 147.

3. Bailey (*Through Peasant Eyes*, 100) attempts to argue that the
host's response is one of grace, since he turns to the socially outcast
and invites them to the feast. However, it is difficult to ignore the wording: 'in anger' he told his servant to bring in the poor and maimed and
lame and blind.

4. Jeremias (*Parables*, 178-79) argues that Jesus was making use of a
well-known story of a rich tax collector and a poor scholar. The rich
tax collector died and was given a splendid funeral; the poor scholar
died and no one took notice. The reason for such care and concern for
the tax collector stemmed from his one good deed. Once he had
arranged a banquet for the city leaders but they had not come. So he
invited the poor to come and eat lest the food be wasted. Therefore the
town showed honor and respect at his funeral. The major difference in
this story and the parable in Luke has to do with the host's honor. The
tax collector would have had no honor in the first place and thus was
rejected, receiving honor only after death. In the Lukan story, the
honor of the host is not questioned until the refusal of the guests to
attend.

5. While the lists of outcasts to be invited are the same, the circumstances of the latter invitation clearly are different from that suggested

hall still is not filled the host sends his servant out a second time,[1] 'to the highways and hedges', to compel (ἀνάγκασον)[2] people to enter, in order that his house might be filled. The two groups invited are often linked to Luke's interest in the twofold spread of the gospel—to the Jews who could 'hear' first, then to those outside the city, the Gentiles.[3] While Luke and his audience may or may not have made such a distinction, the message to the immediate audience—the Pharisees and lawyers—is made clear in the final verse: 'For I tell you, none of those who were invited shall taste my banquet'.

The use of the plural 'you' (ὑμῖν) in the final sentence, for the Lukan audience at least,[4] confirms Jesus as host of the eschatological banquet. The message for the Pharisees is unmistakable: they are in danger of losing their invitation (cf. 13.26-30). The Pharisees and lawyers were the people of wealth and honor who expected to be invited to a great banquet. However, their failure to have concern for the outcast (14.1-6), complaints about Jesus eating and drinking with tax collectors and sinners (5.30; 7.34; 15.1-2), their pursuit of honor (14.7), and love of money (16.14), all were combining to separate them

in v. 12. In the parable the larger vision of the messianic banquet and the negative message being sent to those refusing—in context, the Pharisees—distinguishes the parable from the previous instructions.

1. The second invitation is generally considered a secondary addition to the parable, added either by Luke or his source. See Jeremias, *Parables*, 64; Bultmann, *History*, 175. Marshall (*Commentary*, 590) concedes this is the general consensus, but seeks to make the verse's authenticity at least plausible. Aside from Marshall's attempt to place the words on Jesus' lips, however, it should be noted that the two invitations are balanced, literarily, by the two invitations originally sent (vv. 16-17).

2. Cf. ἀνάγκην, v. 18. The imperative ἀνάγκασον indicates only that these people should be urged to come in. Understandably the uninvited outcasts would at first be hesitant to receive such an unexpected invitation. Cf. Grundmann, *Evangelium*, 300; Fitzmyer, *Gospel*, 1057.

3. See Drake, 'Reversal Theme', 206; Jeremias, *Parables*, 64; Creed, *Gospel*, 192; F.H. Borsch, *Many Things in Parables* (Philadelphia: Fortress, 1988), 50.

4. Fitzmyer (*Gospel*, 1057) suggests that in the original parable, if this phrase was included at all—an assumption doubted by many—it would have been simply a generic parable conclusion. However, in later stages of transmission, certainly in the form found in Luke, the entire verse took on eschatological meaning.

from their place in the Kingdom. In the context of vv. 1-24 human action is challenged to imitate divine action; proper behavior as guest and host is to imitate the actions of God at the Great Banquet.[1] Failure to do so is symptomatic of those who will refuse their invitation and thus lose it altogether.

The final verse also implies the completion of a double reversal presented throughout the parable. The originally invited guests now will be excluded. The originally uninvited—the outcasts—have been included in place of those invited. God's banquet hall is filled, but not with those who expected to be there. Those concerned with their own possessions and honor are outside; those without possessions and honor are inside. In the setting of a banquet, the two oppositions repeatedly seen in the bi-polar reversal are used to demonstrate proper ethical behavior in the present and attitudes that will likewise lead to eschatological inclusion or exclusion. The self-seeking, self-interested pursuit of honor and possessions, as exemplified by the Pharisees,[2] is contrasted with the decision to act in humility, sacrificing honor in the present for future honor. By associating with the poor and maimed and lame and blind—the people in society without honor—one may be included in the eschatological banquet. For the Lukan audience, the aphorisms of 13.30 and 14.11 would be heard throughout the scene

---

1. Robert L. Brawley (*Luke–Acts and the Jews: Conflict, Apology, and Conciliation* [Atlanta: Scholars Press, 1987], 103) says, 'From the perspective of Luke's readers, Jesus' announcement of this reversal of values takes on the character of proclamation, exhortation, and an appeal to adopt God's values'. Cf. H.J. Cadbury, *The Making of Luke-Acts* (New York: Macmillan), 262-63.

2. Steele argues that in Luke the presentation of Jesus' relationship to the Pharisees, outside of the three occasions in which he dines with them, is so antithetic that he doubts such an occasion could ever arise. Steele claims that the three scenes are Lukan redactions—neither he nor his audience knew or cared much about the historical Pharisees. See 'Jesus' Table-Fellowship', 130-32. Similarly, Smith, 'Table-Fellowship', 622 n. 28, writes: 'The critique of the Pharisees and its relation to the table fellowship theme reaches beyond these texts alone, however, as will be seen throughout this study. In the majority of these cases, as here, the Pharisees seem to function primarily as a literary stereotype or as a foil for Jesus' proclamation of his message. Thus, the relation of Luke's portrayal of the Pharisees to the actual historical sect seems much less clear than is often suggested.'

of the symposium: some are last who will be first; some are first who will be last. He who exalts himself will be humbled; he who humbles himself will be exalted.

Although such a reversal might have been unexpected by Jesus' immediate audience[1], the Lukan audience would hardly have been surprised. The word links with previous bi-polar reversals and repeated character traits so often seen in opposition place the entire literary unit within the bi-polar reversal form. The humiliation/exaltation reversal is seen as more than a question of temporal honor and shame but as an eschatological question of being inside or outside the Kingdom. The choices made with regard to honor and shame in the present become determinative for the question of honor and shame at the Messianic Banquet.

The Father's Two Sons (15.11-32)
Luke 15 forms another literary unit within the central section of Luke's Gospel. Following Jesus' discourse on discipleship addressed to the crowds (14.25-35), the audience for the three parables in ch. 15 shifts back to the Pharisees (cf. 14.1; 15.1-2). The grumbling (διεγόγγυζον)[2] of the Pharisees and scribes regarding Jesus' association with tax collectors and sinners restates the controversy first mentioned in 5.30-32 and

---

1. J. Resseguie concludes his discussion of vv. 1-24 by remarking, 'Besides divisions among the characters, an abrupt and unexpected reversal of positions comes to expression with the parables. Those who are humiliation-oriented displace quite unexpectedly those who are exaltation-oriented, and those who are later invited to the great banquet displace those who are initially invited. The dramatic reversal of positions illustrates well the narrative's belief that only one point of view is acceptable' ('Point of View in the Central Section of Luke', *Journal of the Evangelical Theological Society* 25 [1982], 46). It is true that two perspectives are being opposed to each other throughout the Gospel, and that only one is acceptable. However, the repeated presentation of those perspectives in the bi-polar reversal form makes these instances almost expected rather than surprising.
2. Cf. 19.7, the only other use of διαγογγύζω in the New Testament; and 5.30 (γογγύζω). C.H. Giblin, 'Structural and Theological Considerations on Luke 15', *Catholic Biblical Quarterly* 24 (1962), 16, notes the thematic links between ch. 15 and the story of Jesus and Zacchaeus, particularly v. 10: 'For the son of Man came to seek and save the lost' (τὸ ἀπολωλός; cf. 15.4, 6, 8, 9, 24, 32).

repeated in 7.29-30.[1] By associating with the dishonorable
people of society Jesus' own honor and authority were called
into question. The three parables grouped together in the
chapter are a response to the Pharisees' critical attitudes
towards the tax collectors/sinners and Jesus himself.[2]
  The three parables are linked together with the catchwords
'lose' (ἀπόλλυμι) and 'find' (εὑρίσκω).[3] The first two parables

1. See also 7.34. Cf. Dupont, *Les Béatitudes*, II, 234 n. 2; Johnson, *Literary Function*, 109.
2. The setting provided in vv. 1-2 is almost universally considered to
be redactional. So, e.g., J. Jeremias, 'Tradition und Redaktion in
Lukas 15', *Zeitschrift für die neutestamentliche Wissenschaft* 62
(1971), 185-89; I. Broer, 'Das Gleichnis vom verlorenen Sohn und die
Theologie des Lukas', *New Testament Studies* 20 (1973/74), 455; Bultmann, *History*, 334-35; Dupont, *Les Béatitudes*, II, 233-37; Marshall,
Commentary, 599. The first parable (The Lost Sheep, vv. 4-7) is probably from Q (cf. Mt. 18.12-14). The second parable (vv. 7-10) is usually
thought to have been part of Luke's special source, although Conzelmann (*Theology*, 103) and Drury (*Tradition*, 155ff.) attribute the verses
to Lukan composition. Bultmann (*History*, 171) suggests the verses
were a secondary addition to the parable of the Lost Sheep already
found in the tradition used by Luke. The debate over the final parable
concerns the authenticity of the last half of the parable (vv. 25-32). J.T.
Sanders is the most recent to doubt the authenticity of the verses—a
question first raised by Wellhausen. Sanders rejects the category of
zweigipfelig parables and argues on linguistic grounds that the latter
half of the parable is a Lukan addition. See 'Tradition and Redaction in
Luke xv. 11-32', *New Testament Studies* 15 (1968/69), 433-38. However,
the works of Jeremias ('Tradition', 172-81) and J.J. O'Rourke ('Some
Notes on Luke xv. 11-32', *New Testament Studies* 18 [1971/72], 431-33)
refute Sanders's linguistic argument. Schottroff claims that vv. 11-32
are a unit created by Luke himself. See L. Schottroff, 'Das Gleichnis
vom verlorenen Sohn', *Zeitschrift für Theologie und Kirche* 68 (1971),
27-52; also Drury, *Tradition*, 156. Against this view, see Marshall's
discussion of Schottroff's position in *Commentary*, 605-606, and C.E.
Carlston, 'Reminiscence and Redaction in Luke 15.11-32', *Journal of
Biblical Literature* 94 (1975), 368-90. Carlston's conclusion (p. 390), represents the current consensus: the parable should be viewed as a unit,
with minor redactional changes by Luke, which was part of Luke's
source material and probably part of the earliest tradition, perhaps
from Jesus himself. Cf. Jeremias, *Parables*, 128-32; Fitzmyer, *Gospel*,
1085; Bultmann, *History*, 196; M.A. Tolbert, *Perspectives on the Parables: An Approach to Multiple Interpretations* (Philadelphia: Fortress,
1979), 98-101.
3. Forms of these verbs are used eight times each in the chapter:
ἀπόλλυμι (vv. 4 [twice], 6, 8, 9, 17, 24, 32); εὑρίσκω (vv. 4, 5, 6, 8, 9 [twice],

are often called 'twin similitudes' since their structures are
almost identical.[1] The first concerns a male figure; the second
a female. The first setting is rural—a field; the second is
domestic—a house.[2] In both the pattern of losing, searching,

24, 32). The use of these terms in vv. 24, 32, leads Fitzmyer (*Gospel*
1090) to suspect the verses are redactional, intended to create the links
with the previous two parables. Cf. E. Klostermann, *Das Lukasevangelium* (Tübingen: Mohr, 1929), 160.

1 Lambrecht, *Astonished*, 26-27, shows the parallels between the
parables, dividing each into three sections:

(1) *Search*

What man of you, having	Or what woman, having
a hundred sheep,	ten silver coins,
if he has lost one of them,	if she loses one of them,
does not leave the ninety-nine	does not light a lamp
in the wilderness and go after	and sweep the house and seek
the one which is lost,	diligently
until he finds it?	until she finds it?

(2) *Actions after the finding*

And when he has found it	And when she has found it
he lays it on his shoulders,	
rejoicing.	
And when he comes home,	
he calls together his friends	she calls together her
and his neighbors,	friends and neighbors, saying,
saying to them,	'Rejoice with me,
'Rejoice with me,	for I have found the coin
for I have found my sheep	which I had lost'.
which was lost'.	

(3) *Application*

Just so, I tell you	Just so, I tell you,
there will be more joy	there is joy
in heaven	before the angels of God
over one sinner who repents	over one sinner who repents.
than over ninety-nine	
righteous persons who need	
no repentance.	

2. Jeremias (*Parables*, 133) argues that the 10 drachmas were part of
the woman's dowry, her headdress; therefore the great concern. However, Klostermann (*Evangelium*, 157) and others since have pointed
out that there is no textual evidence at all for such an identification.
The woman's concern over the loss of one drachma, the equivalent of a
denarius, does not necessarily indicate the woman was miserly, as
Fitzmyer (*Gospel*, 1080) suggests. The tendency to regard a drachma
as a trivial amount is a modern assumption about the worth of 'a day's
wages'. Cf. the worth of two denarii in Oakman, 'Buying Power', 37.

148   *The Last Shall Be First*

finding, rejoicing, is followed by a comparison to God's love for a sinner (ἁμαρτωλός) who repents (μετάνοια, v. 7, μετανοέω, v. 10).[1] Both parables present one-sided reversals—the lost is found (vv. 6, 9). In the context of 15.1-2, each parable serves as justification for Jesus receiving sinners and tax collectors.

The third parable in the literary unit expands on the theme of joy over finding that which was lost, no longer dealing with possessions lost and found, but persons. In v. 11 the subject of the parable is introduced with the stock beginning for the narrative parables in Luke, 'A certain man (ἄνθρωπός τις)[2] had two sons'. Although the father is the subject,[3] the rest of the parable focuses on the attitudes and actions of the two sons.[4] The younger son (νεώτερος) is discussed first.[5] He asks his

1. Cf. the use of ἁμαρτωλός in 15.1, and Jesus' statement in 5.32: 'I have not come to call the righteous (δικαίους, cf. 15.7) but sinners (ἁμαρτωλούς) to repentance (μετάνοιαν)'.

2. Cf. 10.30; 12.16; 14.16; 16.1, 19.

3. Jeremias was perhaps the first to call attention to this, changing the title of the parable from the more traditional 'prodigal son' to the 'parable of the Father's love' (*Parables*, 128). Bernard B. Scott's interpretation focuses particularly on this fact; it is the father's relationship as father to two sons which is central to the entire parable. See *Jesus, Symbol-Maker for the Kingdom* (Philadelphia: Fortress, 1981), 47-58.

4. Tolbert provides a structural outline of the parable, determined by the manner of discourse (narrated discourse is ND; direct discourse is DD), which demonstrates the unity of the parable:

I.   ND: Introduction, v. 11
II.   DD: Younger son's request that divides the family, v. 12a
III. ND: Younger son's journey away, vv. 12b-16
      DD: Younger son's decision to return, vv. 17-19
      ND: Father's reception of younger son, v. 20
      DD: Younger son's confession and father's response, vv. 21-24a
      ND: Elder son's return home, vv. 24b-26
      DD: Servant's explanation, v. 27
      ND: Father's reception of elder son, v. 28
      DD: Elder son's accusation and father's response, vv. 29-32

Tolbert further develops the parallels in part three of the outline, showing the verbal links between the descriptions of the two sons. See *Perspectives*, 98-100.

5. A number of commentators have pointed out the preponderance of stories in the Old Testament in which the younger brother is given preference over the older, e.g. Cain and Abel, Ishmael and Isaac, Esau and Jacob, Joseph and his brothers, David and Solomon—both

father for his share of the inheritance, which according to
Deut. 21.15-17 would have been one-third of the estate.[1] Such
a division of the estate was legal and perhaps practiced with
some regularity in Palestine,[2] although the son's decision
would have meant a certain loss of honor. He was breaking up
the family estate and the family.[3]

The father granted the son's request and the son soon left to
seek his fortune (vv. 12b-13), thus breaking family ties completely. Rather than prospering, however, he squandered
(διεσκόρπισεν)[4] his goods living a profligate life (ζῶν ἀσώτως).[5]
To compound matters, when he had spent everything
(δαπανήσαντος), a famine came over the land and he 'began to
be in want' (ὑστερεῖσθαι). His first attempt to solve his problem
was to attach (ἐκολλήθη) himself to one of the citizens of the
country. This landowner assigned him the task of feeding the
pigs (v. 15). In becoming a swineherd, the son severed whatever ties remained with his Jewish heritage since such ani-
mals were unclean.[6] Even then, he longed to be filled (ἐπεθύμει
χορτασθῆναι)[7] from the pigs' food since no one offered him
anything. In that desperate situation, he 'came to himself' (εἰς
ἐαυτὸν ἐλθών),[8] realizing that even his father's hired servants

were younger brothers who were chosen king. It is suggested that
such a preference is also being shown in this parable. Whether or not
the Lukan audience would have made the connections with the Jewish
stories is open to question. It is more probable that Jesus' audience
would have. See the discussions on this point in Scott, *Jesus, Symbol-
Maker* 49-50; Drury, *Tradition*, 75-76; P. Perkins, *Hearing the Parables
of Jesus* (Ramsay, NY: Paulist, 1981), 153-54.

1. On the legal aspects of the son's request and the amount and kind
of inheritance settlement given by the father, see Derrett, *Law*, 104-11.
2. See D. Daube, 'Inheritance in Two Lukan Pericopes', *Zeitschrift
der Savigny-Stiftung für Rechtsgeschichte* 72 (1955), 334.
3. See Malina, *New Testament World*, 78, 102.
4. Cf. 16.1; also see 1.51, the only other use in Luke and part of the bi-
polar reversal.
5. ἀσώτως is found only here in the New Testament.
6. Cf. Lev. 11.7; Deut. 14.8.
7. Cf. 16.21—the poor beggar Lazarus 'longed to be filled' (ἐπιθυμῶν
χορτασθῆναι) from the scraps of the rich man's table. Also see 6.21.
8. Jeremias (*Parables*, 130) states this phrase in Aramaic is an
expression of repentance. Cf. Strack–Billerbeck, II, 214-15; Scott,
Jesus, Symbol-Maker, 51; Drake, 'Reversal Theme', 219.

(μίσθιοι)[1] were better off than him. They had food to spare, but he was perishing (ἀπόλλυμαι) with hunger. He therefore decided to return to his father's house, confess his sin, and ask for reinstatement into the household not as a son but as a servant (vv. 18-19).

While he was still on the road towards home, his father recognized him, had compassion (ἐσπλαγχνίσθη),[2] and ran to meet him, embraced him and kissed him. The father's actions signified his forgiveness and acceptance of the son before the son could even make his proposal.[3] The son then followed through with the proposal he had come to make: 'Father, I have sinned against heaven and before you; I am no longer worthy (ἄξιος) to be called your son' (v. 21; cf. v. 19).[4] As though not hearing the son's confession, the father disregarded the son's efforts to return as anything less than a son, instead calling for the best robe, a ring, and shoes—symbols of the father's generosity and the son's status as son, not slave.[5] In celebration, the fatted calf was killed,[6] and the party was prepared ('let us eat and make merry' [εὐφρανθῶμεν]).[7] The father then expressed the reversal that had taken place: 'this

1. The term is use only here and in v. 19 in the New Testament.
2. Cf. 10.33; 7.13. All three uses of σπλαγχνίζομαι are unique to Luke's account; Luke omits the word when it is used in shared material in Matthew and Mark.
3. Cf. Jeremias, *Parables*, 130.
4. The son's expression of unworthiness (dishonor) is characteristic of someone seeking the benefaction of a superior. Cf. Malina, *New Testament World*, 78.
5. Jeremias (*Parables*, 130) says that the shoes were a sign of freedom, signifying the opposite answers to the son's requested status of servant. K.H. Rengstorf (*Die Re-Investiture des verlorenen Sohnes in der Gleichniserzählung Jesu Luk. 15.11-32* [Köln: Westdeutscher Verlag, 1967]) argues that the son was legally cut off from his family by his squandering the inheritance and by his subsequent shameful acts. The robe, ring, and shoes were the signs of his formal reinstatement into the family as a son again.
6. Scott (*Jesus, Symbol-Maker*, 52) notes that red meat would have been eaten only on rare occasions.
7. Cf. 12.19; 16.19. In both of these cases, εὐφραίνω is used in a negative context of merriment made at the expense of others. The term is used four times in the present context (vv. 23, 24, 29, 32), all in the positive context of a party-like atmosphere celebrating the younger son's return.

my son was dead (νεκρός) and is alive again (ἀνέζησεν);[1] he was lost (ἀπολωλώς), and is found' (εὑρέθη). With relationship restored, the party could begin (v. 24b).

With the conclusion to the younger son's story, the scene shifts to the elder brother, whose existence has been implied from the opening sentence of the parable, but who is not actually mentioned until v. 25.[2] When the younger son returned and the party began, the older son was in the field; as he returned he heard the sounds of the celebration (συμφωνίας καὶ χορῶν), and inquired from a servant (ἕνα τῶν παίδων) what it was about.[3] Rather than entering the house to participate in his brother's return, the elder son was angry and refused to enter (v. 28a). When his father left the party to come outside and entreat him (παρεκάλει αὐτόν) to enter, he responded not in tones of sonship but servanthood: 'These many years I have served (δουλεύω) you and I never disobeyed your command' (ἐντολήν σου παρῆλθον).[4] Faithfully performing his duties had never led the father to kill a goat[5] so that he might enjoy merry-making (εὐφρανθῶ) with his friends. Yet when his 'father's son' (ὁ υἱός σου)[6] had returned from consuming the family inheritance with harlots,[7] the father had killed the fatted calf.

1. Any doubts about the serious nature of the younger son's departure from the family are put to rest with the comparison to death. The son's relationship had been severed completely, but now was restored.
2. Scott, *Jesus, Symbol-Maker*, 53.
3. *Ibid.* Scott points out the importance of the elder son discovering the news through a servant rather than looking in the house himself. Within the story, he must remain on the outside. The servant therefore is the means of communicating the younger son's return without the elder brother entering to see for himself.
4. By speaking only of the legal requirements by which he 'served', the elder son demonstrates his own estrangement from the father-son relationship.
5. A male goat (ἔριφον) clearly was inferior to the fatted calf given the younger brother. Cf. Fitzmyer, *Gospel*, 1091.
6. Again the elder son demonstrates his outsider status in the family, rejecting the younger son as his brother.
7. The elder son's specification of the younger brother as ζῶν ἀσώτως indicates the elder son's contempt for the shameless acts of his brother.

Having listened to his older son demonstrate his own estrangement from the family, the father said to him, 'Son (τέκνον),[1] all that is mine is yours' (v. 31).[2] The father thus reinforced the inheritance rights of the elder brother and emphasized his desire for the elder brother's inclusion in the family. The rest of the father's response is not just a restatement of v. 24, but a final challenge to the elder brother to enter into the celebration.[3] 'It was necessary' (ἔδει) to make merry and rejoice because 'this your brother (ὁ ἀδελφός σου οὗτος) was dead (νεκρός) and is alive (ἔζησεν); he was lost (ἀπολωλώς) and is found (εὑρέθη)'. The parable ends with the focus on the younger son's return and father's joyous acceptance. But there is also a question left unsolved. The elder brother still stands outside the feast, and must decide whether to be included in the family or excluded.

In the first part of the parable the younger son experiences a series of reversals common to the plots of ancient comedy—his situation goes from good to bad, back to good again.[4] The son

1. Jeremias (*Parables*, 131) points out the affectionate address of the father in calling the elder brother τέκνον, 'my dear child'. While it is true that the term indicates the father's effort to emphasize the familial relationship, it is noteworthy that the same term (τέκνον) is the form of address used by Abraham when he speaks to the rich man from across the great gulf separating them (16.25). The only other instance of the vocative use of τέκνον in Luke also precedes a rebuke (2.48).

2. Scott (*Jesus, Symbol-Maker*, 54) correctly sees that the surprise experienced by the audience in this story is not over the reversal of fortunes experienced by the younger son. Rather it comes as a surprise when the father seeks to block the estrangement of the elder brother. Scott maintains that the audience perceives the elder brother as the real scoundrel of the story and they expect him to end up on the outside while the rogue-like younger brother enjoys restoration into the family. While the father's effort to block the elder brother's exclusion is important for understanding the nature of the father, it is necessary to remember that the parable ends with the elder brother's decision in doubt.

3. Although the father makes clear his desire to have a relationship with both of his sons, the elder son's refusal to enter the house and his reference to 'this son of yours' indicate his decision to refuse relationships with both brother and father.

4. Cf. Dan O. Via, *The Parables: Their Literary and Existential Dimension* (Philadelphia: Fortress, 1967).

that chose to leave family behind, and thus became lost, is found and welcomed again into the family. The reversal fits well with the previous parables of the lost sheep and lost coin, apart from the owner's search—in the last parable 'finding' depends on the son 'coming to himself'. The other half of the bi-polar reversal—the 'found' becoming lost, i.e. the older brother being excluded from the family—is never stated. However, the parable ends with his status in doubt, not because of the lack of response by the father but because of attitudes and decisions made by the older son. Two clues in the narrative point to the elder son's exclusion. first, when the younger brother decided to return, he wished only to be granted the status of one of the hired servants (μίσθιος). Instead he was accepted as a υἱός. However, when the elder brother arrived on the scene, he spoke of his own relationship in terms of servanthood, not sonship. He had served (δουλεύω) dutifully, fulfilling all the legal demands of his service. The estranged son who wished to be a servant became a son. The son who had always been there saw himself not as a son but as a servant. The second indication of the elder brother's exclusion is his refusal—to the end of the parable—to enter into the house. The banquet (cf. 14.16-24) was held in celebration of the younger son's return, but the elder brother refused the invitation and entreaty of his father and was left standing outside.

Within the context, the Lukan audience surely associated the younger brother with the sinners and tax collectors. The father's loving response to the profligate son was justification for Jesus' own loving actions toward the outcasts of his day. Likewise, the elder brother represented the Pharisees[1] who stood in danger of being excluded from the feast because of their own exclusionary practices toward outcasts. Just as

---

1. Schottroff ('Das Gleichnis', 35, 39, 52) argues against any reference to Pharisaism in the parable. This is understandable in view of her belief that Luke wrote the entire parable for his Christian audience. As Carlston points out, however, it is Luke's own context that creates the anti-Pharisaic association. See 'Reminiscence and Redaction', 387. It may be true that for Luke and his audience the Pharisees serve as foils throughout the Gospel. In any case it is the 'Pharisaic character' that is presented in ch. 15 as analogous to the elder brother.

Luke's Gospel never closes the door on the Pharisees,[1] so that fate of the elder brother is never completely disclosed. The implication, however is not positive. The son who lost his status and returned was granted sonship again; the son who remained but viewed his sonship as slavery and refused to accept his 'father's son' as brother is left to decide whether to join the celebration or remain outside.[2] The emphasis in both halves of the parable is on the human attitudes and actions of the two brothers with regard to their relationship to the father. In the end, the brother who recognized his unworthiness to be called a son had a relationship. One is left to wonder, however, about the brother who met the legal demands of sonship but ended up outside, unwilling to enter his father's house.

The Rich Ruler (18.18-30)
The aphorism that concluded the parable of the Pharisee and the publican (18.14) continues to shape the understanding of the two episodes that follow in ch. 18.[3] Although the material in vv. 15-17 and 18-30 resumes Luke's use of Mark as a source,[4] the call to humility in v. 14 gives the material a particular Lukan flavor. In vv. 15-17, the call to humility is stated as a call for adults to become like children. Children should be allowed to come to Jesus because 'to such belongs the Kingdom' (v. 16). Thus, anyone wishing to enter the Kingdom must receive it 'like a child' (ὡς παιδίον).

Likewise, the aphorism of v. 14 is echoed in the story of the rich ruler and the ensuing discussion about wealth (vv. 18-30).

---

1. It is important to remember that in Acts, the Pharisees are often viewed positively, e.g. Gamaliel (5.34ff.) and especially Paul (23.6; 26.5).
2. The question of eschatology in this implicit example of bi-polar reversal is answered on the basis of how much allegorization one chooses to impose upon the parable. When the father of the story becomes God (e.g. Jeremias, *Parables*, 131), it is easy to equate the return home and ensuing celebration with scenes of eschatological banqueting. But in this context, it is Jesus' reception of sinners and tax collectors in the present that is being defended, and thus should be seen as the primary focus of the parable.
3. Cf. the way in which the same aphorism shapes one's understanding in the two episodes which follow in ch. 14 (vv. 12-14, 15-24).
4. Cf. Mk 10.13-16, 17-31 (par. Mt. 19.13-15, 16-30).

3. *Implicit Bi-Polar Reversal in Luke*

The narrative in Luke is very similar to that in Mark, but the changes made by Luke, though few in number, demonstrate Luke's own interests. By not removing the rich man from the scene (v. 23; cf. Mk 10.22; Mt. 19.22), Luke creates a single unified scene in which the failure of the rich man is sharply contrasted with the success of the disciples.[1]

As in Mark and Matthew, Luke's placement of the account of the rich man after v. 17 creates a contrast with ὡς παιδίον.[2] Luke heightens the tension by identifying the person coming to Jesus as an ἄρχων.[3] The mention of his position is no accident,[4] for it enhances the man's social and economic status.[5] He is a man of recognized honor and authority in his community. He comes to Jesus, whom he recognizes as a person of religious authority,[6] and asks, 'Good Teacher, what shall I do to inherit eternal life?'[7] Jesus first responds to the fact that the ἄρχων addresses him as διδάσκαλε ἀγαθέ. 'Good' (ἀγαθός) ultimately must be viewed from the perspective of God, the prime example of the good. Even Jesus therefore renounces such praise for himself.[8] Having reminded the ἄρχων of that fact, Jesus then responds to his question by rehearsing the commandments of the Law (Deut. 5.16-20).[9]

1. Cf. Tannehill, *Narrative Unity*, 120. By eliminating the aphorism found at the conclusion of Mark's account (10.31, par. Mt. 19.30), the scene begins with a question about inheriting eternal life and ends with Jesus' promise regarding eternal life.

2. Johnson, *Literary Function*, 144.

3. Cf. 8.41; 14.1; 23.13, 35; 24.20. All of these uses refer to Jewish leaders in contexts which portray the ἄρχων negatively, in some sense opposed to Jesus. Cf. Tannehill, *Narrative Unity*, 187.

4. Cf. Dupont, *Les Béatitudes*, III, 155; Johnson, *Literary Function*, 145.

5. Pilgrim, *Good News*, 120.

6. This recognition is seen in his addressing Jesus as διδάσκαλε ἀγαθέ.

7. Cf. 10.25. The discussion between Jesus and the lawyer (10.25-29) parallels closely 18.18-21, except that in ch. 10 the lawyer quotes from the Law; in ch. 18, Jesus quotes the Law.

8. Danker, *Jesus and the New Age*, 2nd edn, 299.

9. Both Matthew and Luke omit the fifth commandment in Mark's list, 'You shall not defraud'. Fitzmyer attributes this to independent editing by Matthew and Luke (*Gospel*, 1199).

The ἄρχων responds by saying, 'All these I have kept from my youth' (v. 21). In his fidelity to the Law, the ἄρχων demonstrates that his piety is just cause for honor along with his social standing. He no doubt expects praise for his diligence from the honorable teacher.[1] Instead of receiving praise and honor, however, he is faced with a terrible dilemma. Jesus tells him that one thing still remains: He must sell all that he has (πάντα ὅσα ἔχεις πώλησον),[2] distribute (διάδος)[3] it among the poor (πτωχοῖς)—noting that he would instead have treasure in heaven—and come follow Jesus. At that news, the man is dejected (περίλυπος[4] ἐγενήθη) because he is exceedingly rich (πλούσιος σφόδρα).[5]

Jesus' announcement that the ἄρχων must sell all his possessions would not just mean the loss of wealth, but the loss of honor and importance as well. More than possessions are at stake—he must sacrifice his status as well. In distributing his wealth among the πτωχοί he must associate himself with the social outcasts—the beggars like Lazarus (16.19) who cannot reciprocate and are of no social value (14.13). Perhaps worse, he must follow after a man who consistently spends his time with such people.[6] It is little wonder that Jesus looks at him[7]

1. Danker says that, in the Graeco-Roman world, 'Men and women of exceptional merit and distinction would on occasion be praised for manifestation of virtue "from their youth". This official desires to improve his reputation for extraordinary merit, and Jesus is an authority on what constitutes merit' (*Jesus and the New Age*, 2nd edn, 300).

2. The demand to sell 'all' (πάντα) is found only in the Lukan version; cf. Mk 10-21; Mt. 19.21.

3. διαδίδωμι is used only four times in the New Testament, three of which are in Luke–Acts (11.22; 18.22; Acts 4.35). Cf. the reference to the church's use of proceeds from such sales of possessions in Acts 4.34-35. Also see the similar statements of Jesus in 12.33-34; 14.33.

4. This term is used only here by Luke. Cf. Mark's statement by Jesus (περίλυπός ἐστιν ἡ ψυχή μου ἕως θανάτου, 14.34, par. Mt. 26.38).

5. It is not unimportant that, in telling the story, the man's wealth is disclosed only at the end of the narrative. Up to that point, the focus is on his honorable position of status and his piety. When the third aspect of his character is added, he becomes a composite of the characters repeatedly doomed to downfall in previous reversals. The ἄρχων is described as πλούσιος only by Luke; Mark and Matthew both say he had 'many possessions' (κτήματα πολλά).

6. Danker, *Luke*, 2nd edn, 118.

and says, 'How hard it is for those who have riches (οἱ τὰ χρήματα ἔχοντες)[1] to enter (εἰσπορεύονται)[2] the kingdom of God! For it is easier for a camel to go through the eye of a needle than for a rich man to enter the kingdom of God.'[3]

The hyperbole creates tension for the rest of Jesus' audience whose surprise is evidenced by their response: 'Then who can be saved?'[4] Jesus reminds them that with God all things are possible (v. 27). By leaving the rich man on the scene, Luke keeps him within hearing distance of Jesus' remarks and reminds his audience that hope does exist for all—including the πλούσιοι—because God does the impossible (cf. 1.37). That it is indeed possible to leave one's possessions behind is seen in the verses that follow. Whereas the ἄρχων was apparently unwilling to humble himself, Peter says, 'Lo, we have left τὰ ἴδια and followed you' (v. 28). The disciples have done what the rich ἄρχων could not do (cf. 5.11, 28). Jesus responds favorably

---

7. Jesus speaks to the disciples in Mark and Matthew, after the rich man has walked away.

1. Luke uses χρῆμα only here in the Gospel—this statement, along with the following hyperbolic comment, is quoted almost verbatim from Mark, 10.23—but the term is found four times in Acts (where πλούσιος is never used). See Acts 4.37; 8.18, 20; 24.26.

2. Luke replaces the future tense εἰσελεύσονται of Mark (10.23) with the present tense (cf. 6.20), again placing entrance into the Kingdom in the context of 'now' rather than only the future. Combined with v. 30, this passage preserves the 'now–not yet' tension seen in other bi-polar reversal texts.

3. Cf. 6.24. Jesus' comments thus equate in some sense the desire of the ἄρχων for eternal life and entrance into the Kingdom of God. Pilgrim observes that the point of the hyperbole of the camel going through the eye of a needle demonstrates the basic incompatibility between the abundance of wealth and faithful discipleship (*Good News*, 120); cf. Otto Michel, 'κάμηλος', *TDNT*, III, 593.

4. Paul Minear suggests this is a question not of poor followers of Jesus but wealthy Christians. He therefore sees it as a secondary addition ('The Needle's Eye: A Study in Form Criticism', *Journal of Biblical Literature* 61 [1942], 166). Pilgrim suggests, on the other hand, that the question reflects the great surprise of Jesus' hearers who probably believe that wealth is a sign of God's blessing instead of a handicap (*Good News*, 121). For the Lukan audience the 'surprise' in Jesus' statement likely comes from the severity of the comparison. The preceding accounts of the difficulties of the πλούσιοι in entering the Kingdom presuppose the fate of the rich man in this story.

to Peter, saying, 'There is no one who has left house or wife or brothers or parents or children,[1] for the sake of the Kingdom, who will not receive manifold more in this time,[2] and in the age to come eternal life'. Those who have humbled themselves for the sake of the Kingdom will be exalted.

The aphorism that explicitly defined the reversal experience of the Pharisee and the publican fits well the experiences of the rich ἄρχων and the disciples.[3] The ἄρχων comes to Jesus as a man of great wealth and honor seeking eternal life. When told he must abandon his wealth—which ultimately means loss of honor—he is unable to respond. The disciples, on the other hand, with less honor to lose and a belief that through Jesus honor will be gained, have left τὰ ἴδια to follow Jesus. It is to them that the promise of eternal life is given.

That the rich ἄρχων's plight is more a problem of honor than wealth is demonstrated by the story of Zacchaeus (19.1-10). Zacchaeus also is described as πλούσιος (v. 2). Rather than being an honored ἄρχων, however, he is a shameless 'chief tax-collector'.[4] The shameless status of Zacchaeus in the community is further emphasized by his inability to get through the crowds to see Jesus. He is short of stature (ἡλικίᾳ μικρὸς ἦν) and must climb a tree and wait for Jesus to walk by in order to get a glimpse of him.[5] To his surprise, and the

1. See the similar list in 14.26, and the parallels in Mk 10.29, Mt. 19.29. Only Luke includes a wife (γυναῖκα) in the list.

2. Cf. Mk 10.30; Mt. 19.29. Pilgrim (*Good News*, 123) correctly notes that 'manifold more in this time' is not a reference to the tradition of Job, but 'a new community where the needs of one person are met by the gifts of another, where there is a common sharing of possessions according to need, where a supportive community suffers and rejoices with one another, and where one can trust God without fear or anxiety over earthly needs'. This is Luke's description of the church in Acts 4.32-37.

3. Schottroff and Stegemann, *Jesus von Nazareth*, 100-101, make a similar comparison when they link 18.18-30 to the beatitudes and woes, 6.20-26. Also see W.P. Loewe, 'Towards an Interpretation of Lk. 19.10', *Catholic Biblical Quarterly* 36 (1974), 327, who compares the reversal of Zacchaeus's situation to 1.52-53.

4. See Malina's discussion of tax collecting as a shameless (*sic*) profession, *New Testament World*, 83.

5. Having to climb a tree indicates not only Zacchaeus' size, but his separation from the rest of the crowd. Tannehill, *Narrative Unity*, 123,

crowd's, Jesus stops, addresses him by name, and invites himself to Zacchaeus' house (σήμερον γὰρ ἐν τῷ οἴκῳ σου δεῖ με
μεῖναι).[1] The crowd's reaction is reminiscent of previous reac-
tions to Jesus' association with tax collectors and sinners. They
grumble (διεγόγγυζον) because Jesus is the guest of a
ἁμαρτωλός.[2]

Zacchaeus demonstrates his repentance[3] by telling Jesus
(τὸν κύριον) that he will give half of his goods (ὑπαρχόντων) to
the poor (πτωχοῖς) and restore fourfold whatever he has
defrauded (v. 8).[4] For Zacchaeus, giving up his wealth indeed
signifies repentance. But it is a reflection of honor restored
rather than honor lost. Jesus confirms this by telling him,
'Today (σήμερον),[5] salvation has come to this house, since he

suggests that the crowd's hostility toward Zacchaeus in v. 7 is also
implicit in v. 3: 'that is, Zacchaeus was unable to see Jesus because
people were not willing to make room for him at the front, as they
would for honored members of the community'.

1. On the use of the divine δεῖ with reference to Jesus going to Zaccha-
eus' house, see J. O'Hanlon, 'The Story of Zacchaeus and the Lukan
Ethic', *Journal for the Study of the New Testament* 12 (1981), 15; C.H.
Cosgrove, 'The Divine ΔΕΙ in Luke–Acts: Investigations into the
Lukan Understanding of God's Providence', *Novum Testamentum* 26
(1984), 175.

2. Cf. 15.1-2; 5.30-32. For Luke's audience the reaction of the crowds
thus serves as a preview of Zacchaeus' salvation.

3. Zacchaeus' statements of repentance follow Jesus' acceptance of
him just as the profligate son's confession follows the father's acceptance of him (15.20-21).

4. On the Old Testament demands of restitution, see Lev. 6.1ff., Exod.
21.37. Cf. Grundmann, *Evangelium,* 360; Marshall, *Commentary,* 698.
For similar Roman laws, see Derrett, *Law,* 284; Schottroff and Stegemann, *Jesus von Nazareth,* 138. Pilgrim, *Good News,* 132-33, distinguishes between Jesus' admonitions elsewhere in Luke to renounce
all possessions (14.33; 12.33-34; 18.22) and the lesser—though beyond
the demands of law—amount given by Zacchaeus. Tannehill (*Narrative Unity,* 124) argues that in fact Zacchaeus does renounce all when
the total is added up. Both of these arguments fail to address the underlying value of honor. For the rich ruler, wealth is directly related to
honor; he therefore is unwilling to give it up. Wealth has nothing to do
with honor for Zacchaeus and is more easily given up.

5. The placement of σήμερον in emphatic position again demonstrates the present time quality of σωτηρία, i.e. access to the Kingdom.

also is a son of Abraham'.[1] He was a shameless outcast, no longer worthy of his Jewish heritage; now honor and heritage are restored. Jesus' final comment sums up not just the story of Zacchaeus but his earthly ministry: 'For the son of man came to seek and save the lost'.[2]

The message of bi-polar reversal is seen in the combination of the narratives in 18.18-30 and 19.1-10. The story of Zacchaeus provides a second opposition to the rich ἄρχων. The ἄρχων seeks eternal life but is unable to gain it because he is unwilling to part with his wealth. Jesus implies, on the other hand, that the disciples who have left τὰ ἴδια will have eternal life. Zacchaeus is then presented as a person of wealth who also receives salvation. The question of honor is a controlling factor in the different scenarios of the different individuals. The one without honor (Zacchaeus) and those who give up honor (the disciples) have access to eternal life. On the other hand, the one unable to humble himself (and those grumbling because Jesus associates with sinners?) implicitly are excluded from the Kingdom.

Conclusion

In material either unique to Luke's account or adapted to the Lukan context by editing, the theme of bi-polar reversal moves from repetitive form to conventional form. The reader is conditioned to expect that certain, defined character types will experience a positive divine reversal. Other individuals, also with well-defined characterizations, will experience a negative reversal. Both groups are defined by their position of honor or shame in society. Those with prestige, power, wealth, piety, or combinations thereof reject Jesus; those who are without honor, status, wealth, or religious appearance in the present readily respond to Jesus and his message. The principles explicitly set forth through wisdom sayings are expanded

---

1. The reference to Abraham is not so much an indicator of Zacchaeus' Jewishness as it is a sign of his worthiness. Cf. Marshall, *Commentary*, 698; O'Hanlon, 'Story of Zacchaeus', 25 n. 62.

2. Cf. 4.21; 5.32. See Tannehill, *Narrative Unity* 132; Pilgrim, *Good News*, 130. Also compare the uses of ζητέω, σώζω, and ἀπόλλυμι in 19.10 with 9.24 and 17.33.

and given concrete expression through these implicit examples. The different texts function inductively, broadening the reader's understanding of both the form and the theme it articulates. At the same time the close relationship to more explicit examples causes the reader to bring closure to the reversal form, thereby further developing the form and confirming the reader's understanding of the theme.

Beginning with Simeon's song Luke informs the reader not only that God's salvation includes 'a light for revelation to the Gentiles', but also that a bi-polar reversal is going to overturn the fortunes of many in Israel. John the Baptist's quotation of Isa. 40.4 metaphorically reflects the humbling and exalting found in the Magnificat, and echoes Simeon's inclusion of the Gentiles ('all flesh will see the salvation of God'). The story of Jesus' anointing at the house of a Pharisee verifies what already was suspected in 5.30-32, viz. Jesus restores honor to shame the self-serving Pharisees. In ch. 10, the piety of Jewish leaders is contrasted with the compassion of a Jewish outcast. It is the outcast who demonstrates the qualities necessary for the reception of eternal life.

In ch. 14, seeking honor and maintaining it through hosting others are both repudiated by Jesus as he teaches that self-humbling is the way to achieve honor. It is not through human exaltation but God's exaltation. This is made explicit in the great banquet where, once again, the shameless people are inside, those interested in themselves are outside. In ch. 15, the lost son who brought shame to himself and his family is restored as a son; the elder brother, who despises 'that son of yours', stands outside the house, in danger of being estranged himself. In ch. 18, the pious and rich are seen together as the same type of character. Reliance upon their own accomplishments and possessions as sources of honor and righteousness leaves both the Pharisee and the ἄρχων separated from the Kingdom. On the other hand, the tax collector-sinner and those who have left their own things to follow Jesus find acceptance from God.

As the narrative progresses, the element of surprise is not so much in the reversal of fortunes as it is in variations of the form. For example, the father's continued efforts to include the elder brother goes against the expectation created by the form that the elder brother is lost. Similarly, it is a surprise that a rich man can indeed enter the Kingdom, if we base ourselves on the narratives preceding the account of Zacchaeus. What becomes clear in the former example is that the father's willingness to accept the elder brother is not the issue. Rather, the question left unanswered is the elder brother's willingness to remain a son and accept the 'lost' brother that was found. Human action is called upon to imitate the divine action of God. In their respective contexts, the aphorisms call forth the same kind of mirroring. In the case of Zacchaeus, the salvation of a wealthy person is possible because there is no honor attached to the wealth. He is a shameless person whose honor is restored by Jesus. Giving up possessions is therefore a simple matter for Zacchaeus. This is in contrast to the ἄρχων, for whom giving up his wealth also meant losing his honor; it was a price too high to pay.

Honor and shame, pivotal values in the culture, are seen to be embedded in the bi-polar reversal theme. Throughout these narratives, already existing conditions of honor or shame are central to attitudes taken toward Jesus. In his coming and presence, Jesus overturns the means by which honor is to be achieved and maintained. In the Kingdom those without honor according to the culture's standards are the honored ones. Jesus came 'to seek and save the lost; in order to achieve that salvation one must therefore 'lose his life', 'humble himself', become 'last'.

Finally, with regard to eschatology, these stories demonstrate present conditions that are reversed, but the reversal is linked to acceptance or rejection of Jesus as the bearer of the Kingdom in the present. Present reversals are portents of things to come. The Pharisee and the publican experience a reversal of their present spiritual circumstances before God, but the present is immediately tied to the eschatological future by the aphorism (18.14). The parable of the good Samaritan and the narrative of Jesus' encounter with the ἄρχων center on the question of eternal life. The narrative in ch. 18 ends with the familiar 'now–not yet' promise (v. 39).

For the Lukan audience the theme of bi-polar reversal constantly reminds them that human action is to mirror the value system of God. God reverses the human understanding of the values of honor and shame. The proper human response is therefore to reverse those values in one's self-understanding and in the treatment of others. Those who do so 'will receive manifold more in this time, and in the age to come eternal life'.

Chapter 4

BI-POLAR REVERSAL AND AUDIENCE EXPECTATIONS:
THE FORM CONTEXTUALIZED
IN THE MEDITERRANEAN WORLD

The Composition of Luke's Audience
In Chapter 1, the question of audience expectations surfaced
often in connection with previous studies on reversal in Luke.
However, there was seldom clarification about the audience
being considered—modern, Lukan, or auditors of the historical Jesus. Throughout this study the focus has been on the presentation of bi-polar reversal within the Lukan narrative.
Audience expectations must therefore be defined in terms of
the auditors or readers of that narrative.[1] The consensus of
scholarship has been that Luke–Acts was written for a Christian audience composed predominantly of Gentile converts[2]

1. It is understood that in a late first-century setting most of those
having contact with Luke–Acts would hear it rather than actually
having a copy to read. Yet because it is a written text, for convenience
and consistency the term reader(s) will be used in reference to Luke's
audience.
2. See the lengthy discussion of the Lukan community and its identity
in Esler, *Community and Gospel*, 24-33. An exception is Drury (*Tradition*) who argues for a Jewish audience. J. Jervell (*Luke and the People of God* [Minneapolis: Augsburg, 1972]) did much to rehabilitate the
Lukan interest in the Jews and Israel in Luke–Acts, but admitted the
audience of the Gospel was primarily Gentile Christian (see pp. 68,
146-47, 174-75). Esler argues on the basis of the descriptions of Gentile
conversions in Acts and the preponderance of OT references and allusions in the Gospel that the majority of the Gentiles in Luke's community already were attached to the synagogue and had some background
in the LXX. See *Community and Gospel*, pp. 36-45; cf. Fitzmyer, *Gospel*,
57-59. Danker, *Luke*, 2nd edn, 47-48, and *Jesus and the New Age*, 2nd
edn, 2-3, wishes to leave the question of Luke's audience more open-
ended. He suggests that the Hellenistic literary techniques would have

sometime in the last forty years of the first century.[1] Studies of the rich–poor motif have suggested that Luke's Gospel was intended for poor Christians in need of comfort and consolation. Some scholars have suggested the opposite—that the community was composed of wealthy Christians in need of warning and exhortation regarding their use of possessions.[2] That both Jewish and Gentile Christians and both socio-economic circumstances could be found in Luke's audience seems most likely.[3] The question that remains is how this audience 'heard' or understood the bi-polar reversal texts. The concept of intertextuality in text-linguistics is important for ascertaining the answer. This has to do with the texts or background understandings of reversal which the author and audience have in common.[4] The way in which the audience

been well understood by a non-Jewish audience just as the OT references would have been best understood by Jewish Christians. He therefore opts for a mixture of Jewish and Gentile Christians.

1. Although the lack of reference to Paul's death has influenced some scholars to assign an early date to Acts (and therefore Luke), a post-70 date seems most likely, on the basis of Lk. 21.20-24. See Danker, *Jesus and the New Age*, 2nd edn, 17-18; Esler, *Community and Gospel*, 27-30; Fitzmyer, *Gospel*, 53-57.

2. For the former position, see Degenhardt, *Lukas*. For the latter, see Karris, 'Rich and Poor'; Schottroff and Stegemann, *Jesus von Nazareth*. Cf. Talbert, *Reading Luke*, 112-25; Esler, *Community and Gospel*, 165-200.

3. Cf. Danker, *Jesus and the New Age*, 2nd edn, 2-3, who refers to the author of Luke as a 'Cultural Bridgebuilder'. Also see the conclusions of Esler, *Community and Gospel*, 183-87. However, as the above analysis of texts suggests, wealth and poverty are representative of two more important values in the culture, namely honor and shame. The rich-poor motif serves to highlight the theme of bi-polar reversal by juxtaposing the honorable rich with the shameless poor. From the Lukan perspective, wealth is 'honorable' only when used in beneficent settings, to aid the shameless of society, thereby laying up treasure in heaven (12.33-34; 16.10-13).

4. For a discussion of intertextuality as one of seven standards of textuality, see R. de Beaugrande and W.U. Dressler, *Introduction to Text Linguistics* (New York: Longman, 1981), 11-12, 182-206. De Beaugrande and Dressler state that intertextuality 'concerns the factors which make the utilization of one text dependent upon knowledge of one or more previously encountered texts' (p. 11). With regard to bi-polar reversal this has importance in two ways: the relationship of the bi-polar reversals in Luke to prior or contemporary texts which

and the author understand bi-polar reversal will be shaped by previous experiences or readings of the form. By the same token, the understanding of different texts within the Gospel narrative that reflect varying degrees of the bi-polar reversal form will also be affected in terms of each other. Initial encounters of the form will shape the reader's understanding of later accounts in the narrative. The complete form will also become the background for understanding partial or incomplete aspects of the form.

In terms of audience expectations, the repetition of bi-polar reversal, explicitly and implicitly, creates a conventional form within the Gospel. What was perhaps at first a surprise or 'reversal of expectations' in the Magnificat loses its value as a surprise when the form is many times repeated. It is true that the variations in the form continue to broaden the characterizations and each additional nuance may be informative and perhaps even surprising. It is also true that what no longer is a surprise within the narrative may still involve a 'reversal of world' for the Lukan audience.[1] But as these reversals are heard in relationship to each other, audience expectations within the narrative shift. Informativity declines as familiarity with the form and expectations regarding the appearance of the form increase.

Variations of the Form in Luke–Acts
The bi-polar reversal form, once established in the mind of the reader, becomes the vehicle that shapes the reader's expectations in successive episodes, so that the reversal of fortunes for the rich man and Lazarus, for example, is no surprise at all. It is expected, confirming Jesus' statements in the beatitudes and woes. What is informative about the story comes not from the double reversal but from the extended details and circumstances that continue to broaden the scope of the two oppositions. It also seems unlikely that the reversals presented in the aphorism of self-exaltation versus self-humiliation function to

demonstrate similar form; and the repeated occurrence of the form in the Gospel itself.
	1. The need for such repetition and the variations in characterization of the two contrasting sides make it apparent that the divine principles indeed involved a reversal of the societal standards.

surprise the reader/hearer with a shocking reversal. In both contexts (chs. 14 and 18) the character oppositions and the reversals already are implied in the larger narrative and in the specific examples and stories to which the aphorism is attached.[1]

By the time the reader has finished chs. 14 through 16, the oppositions of rich/poor and Pharisee/sinner-tax collector have been brought together and represent the same polarities. It is no surprise therefore that in ch. 18 the judgment implied against the Pharisee and the rich ruler is the same, or that the justification of the publican is similar to Jesus' commendation of the disciples who have left all. Thus, each successive example of the form is shaped for the reader by the prior experiences of the form. Likewise later variations of the form are 'read back' into previous examples so that each example is intensified and enlightened by the others in Luke's Gospel.

As was seen in the case of the parables of the rich fool, the lost sheep, the lost coin, and the story of Zacchaeus, the theme of bi-polar reversal establishes a framework for other narratives and sayings in Luke that reflect only one half of the bipolar form. Particularly with regard to overturning the cultural values of honor and shame, many of the healings performed by Jesus reflect not just Jesus the miracle worker and Great Benefactor[2] but also Jesus the agent of God who reverses the plight of the shameless by making them whole participants in society again. In this regard, the quotation of Isa. 61.1-2 in the programmatic sermon at Nazareth[3] is seen

1. The same lack of surprise seems true of the other aphorisms as well, since each serves to confirm a reversal already suggested in the narrative. While such 'surprises' may occur in the narrative, the recurring pattern must inevitably change the reversals into confirmations of the form rather than individual surprise reversals in the narrative.

2. See Danker's discussion of the healing episodes as a function of Jesus the Beneficent Savior in *Luke*, 2nd edn, 30-37.

3. The importance of this passage is universally acknowledged. See J. Kodell, 'Luke's Gospel in a Nutshell (Lk 4.16-30)', *Biblical Theology Bulletin* 13 (1983), 16-18; Johnson, *Literary Function*, 91 n. 3; Tiede, *Prophecy*, 19.

as a statement of reversals to be brought about by Jesus.[1] The captives (αἰχμαλώτοις) and the oppressed (τεθραυσμένους) are promised release (ἄφεσις) from their misery.[2] The societal ostracism caused by being blind (τυφλός) is removed; Jesus proclaims recovery of sight (ἀνάβλεψις).[3] Along with the πτωχοί who have good news preached to them, these groups represent the miserable of society who are to have their fortunes reversed. The repetition of a similar list in 7.22[4] confirms the authenticity of Jesus as the beneficent healer who reverses the physical maladies and misfortunes that ostracize and leave one without honor.

The three sabbath day healings (6.6-11; 13.10-17; 14.1-6) demonstrate not only Jesus as Lord of the sabbath, but also Jesus as benefactor of the shameless diseased. Each of the persons healed is socially unacceptable before Jesus' actions. Yet the response of the Jewish leaders is not new acceptance of these individuals but animosity towards Jesus for his violation of the Sabbath. In ch. 7, the widow left without kin by the death of her son has her honor restored when Jesus raises the son from the dead (7.11-17). The unworthiness of the Gentile centurion is reversed to worthiness when Jesus heals the man's servant (7.1-10).[5]

In ch. 8, the Lukan account of two healing narratives includes details that are specifically reversed by Jesus' actions. The Gerasene demoniac (8.26-39) is described as a man from

1. Cf. L. Keck, 'Jesus' Entrance upon his Mission', *Review and Expositor* 64 (1967), 478. He says, 'Here the theme of eschatological reversal appears... Fulfillment is good news to these folk because it brings rectification to their situation. The dawn of God's Day does not confirm and consummate the present but overturns it.'
2. Luke uses the term ἄφεσις three other times in the Gospel (1.77; 3.3; 24.27) and five times in Acts (2.38; 5.31; 10.43; 13.38; 28.18), all in relation to the forgiveness (release) of ἁμαρτίαι, sins'.
3. Cf. 7.22; 14.13, 21; 18.41ff; and cf. Johnson, *Literary Function*, 133.
4. The list of wonders performed by Jesus includes healing the deaf, lepers being cleansed, and the dead being raised.
5. Only in Luke does the centurion send Jewish messengers ahead to proclaim his worthiness (ἄξιος, v. 4), while he remains at home and does not want Jesus to come to his house because of his own 'unworthiness' (οὐ ἱκανός εἰμι, v. 6). The centurion's son is healed following Jesus' proclamation to the crowd, 'Not even in Israel have I found such faith' (v. 9).

the city (ἐκ τῆς πόλεως) who wore no clothes (οὐκ ἐνεδύσατο ἱμάτιον) and lived 'not in a house but among the tombs' (v. 27). Having often been driven into the desert by demon possession (v. 29), he was 'saved' (ἐσώθη, v. 36) and 'clothed (ἱματισμένον) and in his right mind', able to return to his home in the city and 'declare what God had done' (v. 39).[1] The story of Jesus' healing the woman with a flow of blood—embedded in the story of Jesus' raising Jairus' daughter in all three synoptic accounts—is recast in Luke to emphasize the reversal of the woman's conditions.[2] The account of Jesus' raising the daughter of Jairus is the second time in two chapters that Jesus brings a dead child back to life (one male, one female).

When Jesus heals the ten lepers (17.11-19) the reader is not only witness to the reversal of the outcast condition of the lepers but also reminded of the anomaly that 'foreigners' (ἀλλογενής) are more responsive to the beneficence of God in Jesus than the sons of Israel (cf. 10.29-37).[3] The blind beggar in ch. 18 epitomizes the proper response of the disabled person whose physical malady is healed and his honor restored. When Jesus says, 'receive your sight (ἀνάβλεψον),[4] your faith has saved you' (ἡ πίστις σου σέσωκέν σε),[5] the man immedi-

---

1. Only Luke includes the details specifically reversed in the story: a man of the city who wore no clothes lived outside the city among the tombs, and was often 'driven' by the demon into the desert; when healed, he was clothed, in his right mind, and he returned to the city.

2. Only Luke records that the woman had 'a flow of blood' (οὖσα ἐν ῥύσει αἵματος) which 'could not be healed' (οὐκ ἴσχυσεν ἀπ' οὐδενὸς θεραπευθῆναι). Upon touching Jesus' garment, 'immediately the flow of blood ceased' (παραχρῆμα ἔστη ἡ ῥύσις τοῦ αἵματος αὐτῆς); later the woman declares how she had 'immediately been healed' (ὡς ἰάθη παραχρῆμα 8. 47). See the discussion of this point in V.K. Robbins, 'The Woman who Touched Jesus' Garment: Socio-Rhetorical Analysis of the Synoptic Accounts', *New Testament Studies* 33 (1987), 511.

3. Cf. H.D. Betz, 'The Cleansing of the Ten Lepers (Luke 17.11-19)', *Journal of Biblical Literature* 90 (1971), 319.

4. Cf. 4.18 (ἀνάβλεψις); 7.22.

5. Cf. 8.36, 48, 50; 18.42; in each case the verb σώζω is used in a context of healing. Also see 7.50. Fitzmyer defines salvation as 'the deliverance of human beings from evil, physical, moral, political, or cataclysmic. It connotes a victory, a rescue of them from a state of negation and restoration to wholeness or integrity' (*Gospel*, 222). The last sentence of the definition fits well the aspect of shame reversed in the narratives of healing.

ately 'received his sight and followed him, glorifying God'.[1]
Being healed by Jesus brought about a restoration not only of
physical well-being but honor as well and called forth thanksgiving and discipleship. The healing episodes reflect the reversal of present conditions brought about by Jesus as the instrument of God's beneficence as Jesus ushers in the New Age. The
use of salvific terms in conjunction with some of these narratives suggests that the reversal of present physical conditions
also involves a greater spiritual salvation in the future.[2]

Beyond the healing narratives there are other texts in
which aspects of bi-polar reversal can be heard. On two occasions the disciples of Jesus argued over which of them was the
greatest (μείζων; see 9.46-48; 22.22-27). In the first instance,
near the close of the Galilean section of the Gospel, Jesus compares greatness in the Kingdom to a little child and says,
'Whoever receives this child in my name receives me, and
whoever receives me receives him who sent me; for he who is
least (ὁ γὰρ μικρότερος)[3] among you all is the one who is great
(οὗτός ἐστιν μέγας)'.[4] In this instance a reversal of standards
about greatness is implied through the comparison to a little
child[5] and the comparison of μικρότερος/μέγας. The saying
serves as a warning to the disciples who had recently received
δύναμις καὶ ἐξουσία (9.1). In ch. 22, the scene of the disciples'
argument follows the last supper. This time Jesus compares

1. See Danker's discussion of Jesus as instrument of God the
Supreme Benefactor. The normal response to such beneficence would
be the praise and thanksgiving regularly mentioned following a healing account (*Luke*, 2nd edn, 36-37).

2. On the relationship of healings to reversal, see Drake's discussion
of the variety of terms used to denote healing in Luke and the way in
which the terms reflect reversals of specific conditions ('Reversal
Theme', 256-57).

3. On the use of the comparative form as a superlative, see M. Zerwick, *Biblical Greek* (Rome: Biblical Institute, 1963), §146.

4. Compare Mk 9.33-37; Mt. 18.1-5. The Lukan version of this saying
is modified considerably. In Mark the comparison with the child follows the aphorism, 'If any one would be first, he must be last of all and
servant of all' (εἴ τις θέλει πρῶτος εἶναι, ἔσται πάντων ἔσχατος καὶ πάντων
διάκονος, v. 35b). The oppositions in Mark (πρῶτος/ἔσχατος) are more
sharply defined than in Luke. See Crossan's discussion of this aphorism in its variety of uses in the Gospels in *In Fragments*, 287-90.

5. Cf. 17.2, where Jesus refers to a small child as μικρός; 18.15-17.

greatness in the Kingdom with greatness in a society ruled by Gentiles.[1] The βασιλεῖς of the Gentiles exercise lordship (κυριεύουσιν) and the ones in authority (οἱ ἐξουσιάζοντες) are known as benefactors (εὐεργέται).[2] However, the disciples are to adopt a different mode of leadership. The greatest (μείζων) is to become as the youngest (νεώτερος);[3] the one who leads (ὁ ἡγούμενος) as one who serves (ὁ διακονῶν).[4] Jesus emphasizes the radical nature of this new style by comparing the one who sits at table with the one who serves; it is obvious to all that the one who sits at table is greater (μείζων) than the one who serves (ὁ διακονῶν). Yet he (Jesus) is among them as one who serves. The disciples are thus called to imitate the one whose leadership style reversed the ways of worldly rulers in accordance with God's divine principle—the humble servant will be exalted (1.47-55).[5]

The most important reversal portrayed in the Gospel is that which takes place in the life of Jesus. He is the son conceived by the Holy Spirit, empowered by the Spirit to reverse the plight of all those without honor, the one transfigured in the presence

---

1. Cf. Mk 10.41-45; Mt. 20.24-28. In contrast to Luke placing this episode at the close of the last supper, Mark and Matthew both include this dispute in Jesus' ministry, when Jesus responds to a request of James and John—their mother Mary makes the request in Matthew—that they be seated in the seats of honor beside Jesus.

2. The reference to εὐεργέτης demonstrates Luke's familiarity with the benefaction system and supports Danker's claim that Luke is portraying Jesus as the Great Benefactor (cf. Acts 10.38). Danker argues that Jesus is satirizing the Gentile attitude. By understanding καλοῦνται as the middle voice, the emphasis falls on the self-interest of the Gentile authorities. See *Luke*, 2nd edn, 31-32.

3. As in 9.48, Luke's terminology reflects a comparison between adult and child. Cf. Acts 5.6, where the young men (νεώτεροι) have the menial task of carrying out the dead. A similar kind of comparison is made in Lk. 10.21, where Jesus says, 'I thank you, Father, Lord of heaven and earth, that you have hidden these things from the wise and understanding (σοφῶν καὶ συνετῶν) and revealed them to babes (νηπίοις)'.

4. The synonymous parallelism intensifies the one-sided reversal of leadership styles which the disciples are to emulate:

μείζων	νεώτερος
ὁ ἡγούμενος	ὁ διακονῶν

5. Cf. Talbert, *Reading Luke*, 210; E. LaVerdiere, *Luke* (Wilmington, DE: Michael Glazier, 1980), 260-61.

of disciples, the one who proclaims the good news of the Kingdom. Yet he is destined (δεῖ) to suffer a shameful death on the
cross.[1] By humbling himself, however, he prepares for God's
great exaltation—the resurrection and his ascension into
heaven.[2] Jesus thus becomes the model to be followed (9.22ff.;
14.26ff.; 17.25ff.) for those wishing to experience the exaltation
side of God's bi-polar reversal.

In Acts, bi-polar reversal as a theme gives way to a community in which the divine principles have been enacted. It is
therefore the positive side of the two poles that is idealized.
There are no longer πλούσιοι and πτωχοί in the community,
for now all share equally and everyone's needs are met
(2.43ff.; 4.32). Likewise, tax collectors (τελῶναι) and sinners
(ἁμαρτωλοί) disappear and the Pharisees are seen in an
entirely different light. They are those who come to the
defense of the Apostles on trial—first Gamaliel speaks in
behalf of Peter, John and the others (5.34ff.); later Paul uses
his own heritage as Pharisee in his defense speeches.[3] The one
bi-polar opposition that develops in Acts is that of the Jews and
Gentiles within Paul's missionary preaching. In confirmation
of Luke 13.26-30, when the Jews who received the message
first fail to accept the good news, Paul and company turn to
the Gentiles—the last ones to hear.[4]

Only when someone fails to live by the principles of losing or
humbling themselves do they experience a negative reversal.
Thus, Barnabas receives commendation when he sells his
property; Ananias and Sapphira are sentenced to death when
they 'lie to the Holy Spirit' (4.36–5.11). Simon tries to buy the
Holy Spirit and is rebuked by Peter for seeking such self-exaltation (8.18ff.). The only other instance in which both halves of

1. Cf. 9.22; 17.25; 18.32.
2. Juel observes that a 'most stunning reversal occurs when God
raises Jesus from the dead, making of the rejected stone the "head of
the corner"' (*Luke–Acts*, 50). Cf. 20.17; Acts 4.11.
3. Cf. 23.6-9; 26.5. The only other mention of Pharisees is 15.5 where
disciples who once belonged to the party of the Pharisees are arguing
that Gentile believers should be circumcised. While their perspective is
rejected, it is still important to note that these are Pharisaic disciples,
believers rather than rejecters of Jesus.
4. Acts 13.44-47; 18.6; 28.25-28. Cf. J.T. Sanders, *The Jews in Luke–
Acts* (Philadelphia: Fortress, 1987), 134-35.

bi-polar reversal are placed together is in ch. 12. Peter's miraculous escape from prison through the guidance of an angel is contrasted with Herod's being struck by an angel for his failure to give glory to God (vv. 6-11, 20-23). As Adams demonstrates, the 'turning of the tables' in Acts most often reflects the triumph of the faithful in the face of their suffering and impending humiliation.[1] God's promised reversal for those who 'lose themselves for my sake' is seen in Stephen's vision of heaven as he is about to be stoned (7.56ff.), and in the repeated miraculous escapes of Peter and the apostles—then Paul and his companions—as the Kingdom spreads throughout the Empire.

To paraphrase Danker, there is almost no end to reversal in Luke–Acts![2] The bi-polar form establishes a new value system that is not only maintained through repetition of the entire form but also seen in partial expression throughout the Gospel. In Acts the triumph of the value system means that the positive side—God's exaltation—is normally seen. Within the narrative of Luke–Acts, the theme of bi-polar reversal in its specific repetitions thus has great impact on the rest of the narrative.

Graeco-Roman Perceptions of the Form in the First Century
The question that remains unanswered is the background understanding of bi-polar reversal shared by author and audience prior to writing/reading the narrative. Jewish Christians or Gentiles who were former God-fearers well versed in the Septuagint would be drawn to the many parallels between bi-polar reversal in Luke and God's acts of reversal in the Old Testament.[3] Such people also might be acquainted with the

---

1. *The Sufferings of Paul*, 22-27, 293.
2. The brief discussion above is not intended to be inclusive of 'all' reversals in Luke–Acts. A comparison with Danker's list (*Luke*, 2nd edn, 37-47) and Drake ('Reversal Theme') demonstrates the different reversals others would add to the list. If one is not careful, however, reversal becomes so diffuse there is no longer any relationship to the theme of bi-polar reversal.
3. See Drake's chapter on reversal in the Old Testament, 'Reversal Theme', 75-117; also the references to similar OT texts in the analyses in Chapters 2 and 3 above. For such people Dahl's comment would

apocalyptic reversals of *1 Enoch* 92–105.[1] Those without such knowledge, living in a Hellenistic environment apart from prior contact with the Jewish synagogue, would draw on a variety of backgrounds in formulating their understanding. The reversal of values related to honor and shame would no doubt have come as a surprise. The repetition would therefore have been necessary to reinforce the new value system.[2]

With regard to the reversal form itself, the discussion of Graeco-Roman parallels has too quickly stopped with Greek tragedy and comedy, and the plot device of περιπέτεια.[3] Both tragedy and comedy have, as a part of the plot, a single-sided reversal—either from good to bad or bad to good.[4] The reversal in tragedy, as described by Aristotle, was that of a person of high renown—but neither virtuous nor inherently evil—whose misfortune was brought about by some great error or frailty.[5] Such a characterization may have some application in the reversals in Luke, but it does not illuminate the bi-polar form. Danker recognized the need to look elsewhere for help in understanding the Lukan reversals in a Hellenistic environment when he suggested the literary device of 'now–then'[6] and the common human progression of *koros–hybris–atē* (satiety–insolence–retribution).[7] The latter is relevant only to

seem appropriate: reversal 'represents God's normal way of dealing with his people' ('Purpose of Luke–Acts', 91).

1. Cf. Nickelsburg, 'Riches', 338-44; Esler, *Community and Gospel*, 189-91.

2. On the value of repetition in establishing and maintaining expected behavior, see the discussion of Leo Perdue and John Gammie in 'Paraenesis: Act and Form', *Semeia* 50 (1990).

3. Cf. Drake, 'Reversal Theme', 44-74; Crossan, *In Parables*, 55; Via, *Kerygma and Comedy*, 44-49, 94-103.

4. As Drake points out, comedy reflects more of a U-shaped movement (good–bad–good). That does not change the fact that only one half of bi-polar reversal is ever involved in the comedic reversal of fortunes. See 'Reversal Theme', 69.

5. Cf. *Poetics*, 13.2-4.

6. Cf. *Luke*, 2nd edn, 53-55.

7. *Ibid.*, 55. This progression is hinted at but not stated in Aristotle's view of the value of wealth (πλοῦτος) in *The Art of Rhetoric*, 2.16. 'The characters which accompany wealth are plain for all to see. The wealthy are insolent (ὑβρισταί) and arrogant (ὑπερήφανοι), being mentally affected by the acquisition of wealth, for they seem to think that

the negative pole of reversal, however, and the 'now–then' motif must be turned in a number of directions to encompass the aspects of past–present–future found in bi-polar reversal.

When one turns to more specific textual parallels of the bi-polar form in Graeco-Roman literature—some of which were cited in the previous chapters—reversals are found that are strikingly similar to the bi-polar forms expressed as chiastic aphorisms. In the earlier Greek literature the reversals are attributed to the gods. For example, Danker quotes the 7th-century BC poet Archilochos:

> The deities are ever just. Full oft they raise those who lie prostrate on the darkened earth. Full oft the prosperous are tripped, their bellies to the sky; and miseries untold attend them. Mindless, in aimless poverty they wander.[1]

A similar reversal is described by Hesiod (7th century BC) at the beginning of *Works and Days*, in which he attributes the reversal to Zeus:

> Muses of Pieria who give glory through song, come hither, tell of Zeus your father and chant his praise. Through him mortal men are famed or unfamed, sung or unsung alike, as great Zeus wills. For easily he makes strong, and easily he brings the strong man low; easily he humbles the proud and raises the obscure, and easily he straightens the crooked and blasts the

they possess all good things; for wealth is a kind of standard of value of everything else, so that everything seems purchasable by it. They are luxurious and swaggerers, luxurious because of their luxury and the display of their prosperity, swaggerers and ill-mannered because all men are accustomed to devote their attention to what they like and admire, and the rich suppose that what they themselves are emulous of is the object of all other men's emulation... In a word, the character of the rich man is that of a fool favoured by fortune' (trans. J.H. Freese; Loeb Classical Library; Cambridge, MA: Harvard University Press, 1926), 259.

1. Cited in *Luke*, 2nd edn, 48-49. Danker's source is E. Diehl, *Anthologia Lyrica Graeca* (Teubner, 1925). Danker dismisses the parallel because 'the destinies of the mighty and lowly are not defined from a moral perspective, nor are they conceptualized in terms of an adversarial relationship' (p. 49). However, the similarities should not be dismissed too quickly because of the differences. The concern here is to identify those elements which would have contributed to the conceptual framework of bi-polar reversal.

proud,—Zeus who thunders aloft and has his dwelling most high.[1]

Xenophon (4th century BC), in *Anabasis* 3.2.10, refers to his hopes for deliverance from the enemy by saying:

> it is fair to assume that the gods are their foes and our allies— and the gods are able speedily to make the strong weak and, when they so will, easily to deliver the weak, even though they be in dire perils.[2]

In Euripides' *Trojan Women* (5th century BC), Hecuba says at one point, 'I see the work of the gods who pile tower-high the pride of those who were nothing, and dash present grandeur down'.[3] Hecuba's statement implies an attitude of envy by the gods that is often cited as the reason for such reversals.[4] Thus Herodotus (5th century BC) describes the efforts of Polycrates to appease the gods following his good fortune by throwing into the sea his most prized possession, a signet ring. When by chance the ring comes back to him, his friend who advised him to appease the gods ends the friendship, lest he be found mourning Polycrates' inevitable demise.[5]

With the decline of traditional Greek religion in the fifth and fourth centuries BC, the role of the gods in the fortunes of life receded and was slowly replaced by the the capriciousness of

1. Trans. H.G. Evelyn-White in *Hesiod: The Homeric Hymns and Homerica* (Loeb Classical Library; Cambridge, MA: Harvard University Press, 1943), 3. Also see the statement cited in Diogenes Laertius, *Lives* 1.69: 'When Chilon the Lacedaemonian asked Aesop what Zeus was doing, he got the answer, "He is humbling the proud and exalting the humble"' (trans. by R.D. Hicks; Loeb Classical Library; New York: G.P. Putnam, 1925), 70-71.

2. Xenophon, *Hellenica, Books VI & VII*; *Anabasis, Books I-III* (trans. C.L. Brownson; Loeb Classical Library; New York: G.P. Putnam, 1932), 441.

3. *Euripides III: Four Tragedies* (trans. Richmond Lattimore; Chicago: University of Chicago Press, 1958), 149.

4. Cf. G.J.D. Aalders, 'The Hellenistic Concept of the Enviousness of Fate', *Études préliminaires aux religions orientales dans l'empire romain* (ed. M.J. Vermaseren; Leiden: Brill, 1974), 1-2.

5. Cf. Herodotus, *The History*, 3.40-43 (trans. David Grene; Chicago: University of Chicago Press, 1987), 229-30.

chance (Τύχη).[1] Herodotus gives evidence of this shift in his description of a true rich man (πλούσιος):

> For he that is greatly rich is not more blessed than he that has enough for the day unless fortune (τύχη) so attend him that he ends his life well, having all those fine things still with him. Moreover, many very rich men are unblessed and many who have a moderate competence are fortunate. Now he that is greatly rich but is unblessed has an advantage over the lucky man in two respects only; but the latter has an advantage over the rich and unblessed in many. The rich and unblessed man is better able to accomplish his every desire and to support such great visitation of evil as shall befall him. But the moderately rich and lucky man wins over the other in these ways. True, he is not equally able to support both the visitation of evil and his own desire, but his good fortune (εὐτυχίη) turns these aside from him; he is uncrippled and healthy, without evils to afflict him, and with good children and good looks. If, in addition to all this, he shall end his life well, he is the man you seek, the one who is worthy to be called blessed; but wait till he is dead to call him so, and till then call him not blessed but lucky (εὐτυχής).[2]

1. Cf. Aalders, 'Hellenistic Concept', 4; Iiro Kijanto, 'Fortuna', *Aufstieg und Niedergang der römischen Welt*, 17.1 (ed. Wolfgang Haase; New York: Walter de Gruyter, 1981), 527, says, '*Tyche* was a dominant figure in the literature of the hellenistic period. Two factors contributed to her popularity. The Olympic gods were rapidly losing ground. This created a religious vacuum, which was in part filled by *Tyche*. Again, the time of Alexander the Great and of the Epigoni was a period of great upheavals. Many great states, e.g., the Persian Empire, fell to pieces, and new ones were founded instead. The success of an individual seemed often to depend more upon chance than upon his own efforts. This may explain why Fickle *Tyche*, the personification of blind chance, gained so important a position in men's minds.'

2. *The History* 1.32 (trans. Grene, 47). Grene comments in the introduction, 'On the whole, I think that Herodotus believes that the Divine is altogether jealous and prone to trouble us because it controls a world in terms that we cannot understand and that distort the outcome we would want; but it is not necessary that we believe that the Gods have personal vindictiveness against those who are destroyed. What is decisive is the impersonal hinge of fate. Particular Gods may at times be represented as the unwilling asssistants as the hinge of fate turns. But fate in its compulsive patterns depends on the potency of single events or blocks of events' (pp. 26-27).

By the third and second centuries, *Tyche* was personified as a powerful goddess who controlled human destinies.[1] The power of *Tyche* is noted by Polybius (second century BC) at the close of his *Histories*. Having returned to Greece, he asks all the gods to let his present circumstances continue for the rest of his life, noting 'that fate (τύχη) is powerful in conceiving envy against men and displays its power especially in those spheres in which man thinks that he is most successful and prosperous in his life'.[2] In the Roman world, Greek Τύχη overlaid the Latin *Fortuna*, thus broadening and continuing the rule of the capricious goddess.[3] Belief in the power of *Tyche* is strongly stated by Pliny the Elder in the first century AD:

> Everywhere in the whole world at every hour by all men's voices Fortune alone is invoked and named, and we are so much at the mercy of chance that Chance herself, by whom God is proved uncertain, takes the place of God. [Fortune is] alone accused, alone impeached, alone pondered, alone applauded, alone rebuked and visited with reproaches; deemed volatile and indeed by most men blind as well, wayward, inconstant, uncertain, fickle in her favors and favoring the unworthy. To her is debited all that is spent and credited all that is received, she alone fills both pages in the whole of mortals' account.[4]

1. Luther Martin, *Hellenistic Religions: An Introduction* (New York: Oxford University Press, 1987), 22. Cf. Gilbert Murray, *Five Stages of Religion* (New York: Columbia University Press, 1925), 164ff.; M.P. Nilsson, *Geschichte der Griechischen Religion*, II (Munich: C.H. Beck, 1961), 201-203.

2. *Histories*, 39.8.2 (trans. W.R. Paton; Loeb Classical Library; Cambridge: Harvard University Press, 1921), 453. Aalders ('Hellenistic Concept', 1) writes, 'It is clear from this that Polybius was convinced that fate, Τύχη, was capricious and incalculable and that he was apprehensive that the situation might change, as it so often did after success and good luck'.

3. Kijanto, 'Fortuna', 521, 525-32.

4. *Natural History*, 2.5.22 (trans. H. Rackham; Loeb Classical Library; Cambridge: Harvard University Press, 1938), 183-85. Commenting on Pliny's remarks, Martin (*Hellenistic Religions*, 22) says, 'The universal recognition of Fortune's effects is often viewed as the final stage in the secularization of Hellenistic religion, in which, as Pliny notes, the personification of the unpredictable and the unexplained 'takes the place of God'. But she has also been described as the most important deity of the Hellenistic era because of her universal sovereignty over mortals and immortals alike.' Cf. Nilsson,

The power of reversal attributed to *Tyche* is seen in the Orphic hymn addressed 'To *Tyche*': 'In you lies the great variety of men's livelihood. To some you grant a wealth of blessings and possessions, while to others against whom you harbor anger, you give evil poverty.'[1] The role of *Tyche* is seen most clearly in Apuleius' *Golden Ass* (2nd century AD), where *Fortuna* is a *Leitmotif*.[2] The opening story is suggestive of the role that Fortune plays in the events of Lucius' life, as seen in Martin's synopsis:

> In this tale Aristomenes, a chance companion of Lucius, tells him of his own chance meeting with a long-lost friend, Socrates, who had come into some bad luck and had become a beggar. Attacked by bandits while on a business trip to Macedonia, Socrates finally escapes to an inn, only to fall under the power of the wicked sorceress, Meroe. Ultimately, however, Socrates does not blame Meroe for his present condition; rather he blames Fortune and Aristomenes. 'O my friend..., now perceive I well that you are ignorant of the whirling changes, the unstable forces and slippery inconstancy of fortune' (*Met.* 1.6).[3]

As Lucius' own story unfolds, he too falls prey to the capricious actions of Fortune, being buffeted by Fortune until finally saved by the savior goddess of Good Fortune ('Αγαθὴ Τύχη), Isis.[4] Like other goddesses that emerged from regional locales

---

Geschichte, 202; Everett Ferguson, *Backgrounds of Early Christianity* (Grand Rapids: Eerdmans, 1987), 190.

1. Cited in Martin, *Hellenistic Religions*, 101.
2. Kijanto, 'Fortuna', 542.
3. Martin, *Hellenistic Religions*, 21. See Apuleius, *The Golden Ass: Being the Metamorphoses of Lucius* (trans. W. Adlington, rev. S. Gaselee; Loeb Classical Library; Cambridge: Harvard University Press, 1947), 11.
4. Martin, *Hellenistic Religions*, 23. See *The Golden Ass* 11.15, which contains the following summary by the priest of Isis: 'O my friend Lucius, after the endurance of so many labours and the escape of so many tempests of fortune, thou art now at length come to the port and haven of rest and mercy. Neither did thy noble lineage, thy dignity, neither thy excellent doctrine anything avail thee; but because thou didst turn to servile pleasures, by a little folly of thy youthfulness, thou hast had a sinister reward of thy unprosperous curiosity. But howsoever the blindness of fortune tormented thee in divers dangers, so it is that now by her unthoughtful malice thou art come to this present felicity of religion. Let fortune go and fume with fury in another place;

in this period, the great claim of Isis was her superiority over capricious *Tyche*. By embodying 'Good Fortune' she offered salvation to Lucius and those like him.[1]

The universal rule of *Tyche* was approached in different ways by the philosophers. Stoic philosophy, especially, sought to disarm *Tyche* by asserting the superiority of the human spirit over *Tyche*.[2] The Epicureans sought to experience pleasure as a means of offsetting the ambiguities of Fortune.[3] Perhaps most interesting are the statements found in Plutarch's *Moralia* (1st century AD) in his 'Letter to Apollonius'. Plutarch first speaks of the different circumstances in life that can bring about a reversal of fortunes:

> For as there are in plants at one time seasons of fruitage and at another time seasons of unfruitfulness, and in animals at one time fecundity and at another time barrenness, and on the sea both fair weather and storm, so also in life many diverse circumstances occur which bring about a reversal of fortunes.[4]

Plutarch then quotes Menander, as saying, 'To sum up all I say, you are a man, than which no thing that lives can swifter be exalted high and straight brought low'.[5] The quotation seems to suggest that such reversals are simply a rule of life. Plutarch then comments:

> But, in spite of this condition of affairs, some persons, through their foolishness, are so silly and conceited, that when only a little exalted, either because of abundance of money, or importance of office, or petty political preferments, or because of position and repute, they threaten and insult those in lower station, not bearing in mind the uncertainty and inconstancy of fortune, nor yet the fact that the lofty is easily brought low and the humble in

---

let her find some other matter to execute her cruelty; for fortune hath no puissance against them which have devoted their lives to serve and honour the majesty of our goddess... Know thou that thou art safe, and under the protection of that fortune that is not blind but can see' (*Golden Ass*, 563).

1. Cf. Martin, *Hellenistic Religions*, 84.
2. Kijanto, 'Fortuna', 534.
3. Martin, *Hellenistic Religions*, 38.
4. *Moralia*, vol. II (trans. F.C. Babbitt; Loeb Classical Library; New York: G.P. Putnam, 1928), 114-15.
5. *Ibid.*

turn is exalted, transposed by the swift-moving changes of fortune.[1]

The importance of this text for the discussion of bi-polar reversal in Luke is not only the similarity in the wording of two-sided reversals, but also the suggested relationship between reversal and moral values. It is thought foolish, when only slightly exalted, to take pride in one's station and look upon those of lower station with condescension and insults. For Plutarch Fortune (τύχη) is not envious or malicious, but inconstant, uncertain. Yet one who would despise others after minimal exaltation begs to be brought low.

The point of this lengthy description of *Tyche* is not to suggest a direct link between the reversals attributed to the gods or to *Tyche* and bi-polar reversal in Luke, although as a participant in the culture Luke probably was aware of such beliefs. Rather it is to suggest that the attribution of human reversals of fortune to the gods would have been common in literature of the first century. More importantly, such an understanding of *Tyche* would have been part of the Gentile world in the first century.[2] The reversals brought about by *Tyche* were understood to be temporal, and in Plutarch there are even links to moral behavior. It was at a time when and in a world where *Tyche* controlled human fortunes that Luke's Gospel was written. The form of bi-polar reversal found in Luke would have been immediately recognized. The distinc-

---

1. *Ibid.*, 116-17.
2. Knowledge of similar beliefs among the Jews of the late first century is seen in Josephus' distinctions among the various Jewish sects. He describes each in relationship to their views of εἱμαρμένη ('Fate'), a belief in the deterministic actions of cosmological forces in human affairs. See Martin's discussion, *Hellenistic Religions*, 106-107. Josephus remarks, 'as for the Pharisees, they say that certain events are the work of Fate (εἱμαρμένη), but not all; as to other events it depends upon ourselves whether they shall take place or not. The sect of Essenes, however, declares that Fate is mistress of all things, and that nothing befalls men unless it be in accordance with her decree. But the Sadducees do away with Fate, holding that there is no such thing and that human actions are not achieved in accordance with her decree, but that all things lie within our own power, so that we ourselves are responsible for our well-being, while we suffer misfortune through our own thoughtlessness' (*Antiquities* 13.172-73).

tive Lukan claim was that God is the power behind the reversal, not blind chance. God's divine reversals are not capricious but ordered, brought about at the advent of the New Age through the appearance of his son Jesus. Rather than being left to chance, one's future could be determined by acceptance or rejection of the value system advocated by Jesus. The proud, self-righteous and wealthy who relied on themselves and despised others would be brought down—in this time and in the age to come. Those choosing to lose themselves for his sake, or those already without honor, received honor in the present and in the age to come, eternal life. Luke's 'now–not yet' eschatology thus would have served as a middle ground between the apocalyptic claims of reversal in the New World and the temporal reversals commonly attributed to *Tyche* in the first century.

Conclusion

In the introductory chapter three areas surfaced with regard to the study of reversal in Luke that needed further exploration: (1) the need to demonstrate the pattern or form of double or bi-polar reversal and to analyze the texts that explicitly or implicitly represent the form; (2) the need to clarify the eschatological content of those reversals; (3) the need to clarify what is meant by audience expectations in relation to reversal. Chapters 2 and 3 demonstrated, through the use of a rhetorical definition of form, that bi-polar reversal explicitly and implicitly set forth divine principles which express a theme in Luke. This theme was related more to the values of honor and shame than to particular physical conditions often characterized by the two opposing positions seen in the reversal texts. This does not detract from either the physical or spiritual circumstances of the characters involved but rather indicates the sphere in which these circumstances were deemed important in the first-century world. Luke presents Jesus as the inaugurator of the Kingdom, in whose presence the future breaks into the present. The reversal texts thus display the now–not yet eschatology found in the rest of the Gospel. The focus shifts in the various texts between present reversals of one's situation and future reversals. The healing

stories, especially, reflect the restoration of honor brought to
the dishonored and shameless by Jesus in the present time. On
the other hand, the promise of future exaltation in the 'age to
come' is never far removed from view.

In this chapter, the repetitive force of bi-polar reversal was
examined with regard to audience expectations. It was argued
that such repetition would naturally have lessened the
'surprise' or shock typically attributed to the bi-polar texts.
However, the repetitive pattern also would have served to
solidify the value system inherent in the divine principle. Also
in this chapter, an attempt was made to highlight the impact
of bi-polar reversal on the rest of the Gospel narrative and
Acts, and to suggest alternative understandings of reversal for
an audience perhaps not aware of the Septuagint and other
Jewish literature reflecting reversal as God's normal mode of
action. In the first century the concept of bi-polar reversal
would have been a popular belief most often attributed to
Tyche/Fortuna in the Graeco-Roman world. Luke used the
form to communicate a radical shift in the means by which
one either attained or maintained honor and shame. He also
demonstrated that *Tyche/Fortuna* was not the source behind
the reversal of fortunes in people's lives. The God who sent his
son into the world to inaugurate the New Age was the ultimate cause. Furthermore, these reversals were not temporal
only but had eternal consequences.

For the person with a Jewish background, especially one
who viewed the coming of the Son of man apocalyptically,
Luke's use of bi-polar reversal signaled the arrival of the
Kingdom in the present. One need not wait for the destruction
of this world and the creation of the new world. The Kingdom
was already here. Reversals already had taken place through
God's anointed one, Jesus. The dead were raised, the socially
outcast and physically disabled had their health and honor
restored.

Participation in the Kingdom was therefore dependent on
acceptance of Jesus as God's anointed. Acceptance meant a
radical shift of values in imitation of the divine principle of
reversal for those already enjoying honor and position in this
life. Greatness now meant servanthood, self-humiliation,
association with the outcasts of society. Failure to reverse

those values in imitation and acceptance of Jesus meant God's divine reversal would bring it about later with eternal conse-quences. On the other hand, for those who left all to follow Jesus or had no honor in the first place, acceptance of Jesus meant the arrival of the Kingdom now. Bi-polar reversal would have communicated well to Jew and Gentile alike and must be seen as an important theme in Luke's portrayal of the gospel of exaltation. The Lord of glory was first God's anointed one who humbled himself and endured the shame of the cross.[1] For the person in Luke's audience still living under the value system of the world, enjoying honor and prestige and despising the outcast, Luke's message was one of harsh warning. For the societal misfits and poor who had believed in the Christ, Luke's Gospel offered a message of confirming hope. The theology of glory so often attributed to Luke first required a reversal of the values of honor and shame in order for one to participate in the final exaltation.

1. Cf. the remarks by Marshall, *Luke: Historian and Theologian*, 209-11, in response to the assertion of Käsemann that Luke's *theologia glo-riae* necessitates Luke–Acts being characterized as 'early catholic'. See E. Käsemann, 'New Testament Questions of Today', in *New Tes-tament Questions of Today* (trans. W.J. Montague; Philadelphia: Fortress, 1969), 22.

BIBLIOGRAPHY

Aalders, G.J.D. 'The Hellenistic Concept of the Enviousness of Fate'. *Études préliminaires aux religions orientales dans l'Empire Romain*. Ed. M.J. Vermaseren. Leiden: Brill, 1974, 1-8.

Aalen, S. 'St. Luke's Gospel and the Last Chapters of I Enoch'. *New Testament Studies* 13 (1966), 1-13.

Adams, David. 'The Sufferings of Paul and the Dynamics of Luke–Acts'. Ph.D. dissertation, Yale University, 1979.

Albertz, R. 'Die »Antrittspredigt« Jesu im Lukasevangelium auf ihrem alttestamentlichen Hintergrund'. *Zeitschrift für die neutestamentliche Wissenschaft* 74 (1983), 182-206.

Alter, Robert. *The Art of Biblical Narrative*. New York: Basic Books, 1981.

Apuleius. *The Golden Ass: Being the Metamorphoses of Lucius*. Loeb Classical Library. Cambridge, MA: Harvard University Press, 1947.

Aristotle. *Poetics*. Trans. S.H. Butcher. In *Critical Theory since Plato*. Ed. Hazard Adams. New York: Harcourt, Brace, Jovanovich, 1971, 48-66.

— *The Art of Rhetoric*. Trans. J.H. Freese. Loeb Classical Library. Cambridge, MA: Harvard University Press, 1926.

Aune, David E. *Prophecy in Early Christianity and the Ancient Mediterranean World*. Grand Rapids: Eerdmans, 1983.

Aurelio, Tullio. *Disclosures in den Gleichnissen Jesus*. Frankfurt: Peter Lang, 1986.

Aymer, B.C. 'A Socioreligious Revolution: A Sociological Exegesis of "Poor" and "Rich" in Luke–Acts'. Ph.D. dissertation, Boston University, 1987.

Babcock, B.A., ed. *The Reversible World*. Ithaca, NY: Cornell University Press, 1978.

Bailey, K.E. *Poet and Peasant: A Literary-Cultural Approach to the Parables in Luke*. Grand Rapids: Eerdmans, 1976.

—'The Song of Mary: Vision of a New Exodus (Luke 1.46-55)'. *Theological Review* 2 (1979), 29-35.

—*Through Peasant Eyes: More Lucan Parables*. Grand Rapids: Eerdmans, 1980.

Bajard, S. 'La Structure de la péricope de Nazareth en Lc., IV,16-30'. *Ephemerides theologicae lovanienses* 45 (1969), 165-71.

Ballard, P.H. 'Reasons for Refusing the Great Supper'. *Journal of Theological Studies* n.s. 23 (1972), 341-50.

Batey, Richard. *Jesus and the Poor*. New York: Harper and Row, 1972.

Batsdorf, I.W. *Interpreting the Beatitudes*. Philadelphia: Fortress, 1966.

Bauer, J.B. 'Wer sein Leben retten will... Mk 8,35 Parr'. *Neutestamentliche Aufsätze: Festschrift für Josef Schmid zum 70. Geburtstag*. Ed. J. Blinzer *et al*. Regensburg: Pustet, 1963, 7-10.

Bauer, W. *A Greek-English Lexicon of the New Testament and other Early Christian Literature*. 2nd edn. Trans. W.F. Arndt, W. Gingrich and F.W. Danker. Chicago: University of Chicago Press, 1979.

Beardslee, William A. *Literary Criticism of the New Testament*. Philadelphia: Fortress, 1970.

—'Parable, Proverb, and Koan'. *Semeia* 12 (1978), 151-78.

—'Saving One's Life by Losing It'. *Journal of the American Academy of Religion* 47 (1979), 57-72.

—'Uses of the Proverb in the Synoptic Gospels'. *Interpretation* 24 (1970), 61-73.

Bemile, Paul. *The Magnificat within the Context and Framework of Lukan Theology*. Frankfurt: Peter Lang, 1986.

Benko, S. 'The Magnificat: A History of the Controversy'. *Journal of Biblical Literature* 86 (1967), 263-75.

Betz, H.D. 'The Cleansing of the Ten Lepers (Luke 17.11-19)'. *Journal of Biblical Literature* 90 (1971), 314-28.

—'The Sermon on the Mount: Its Literary Genre and Function'. *Journal of Religion* 59 (1979), 285-97.

Bilezikian, G. *The Liberated Gospel: A Comparison of the Gospel of Mark and Greek Tragedy*. Grand Rapids: Baker, 1977.

Blass, F., A. Debrunner and R.W. Funk, *A Greek Grammar of the New Testament and Other Early Christian Literature*. Chicago: University of Chicago Press, 1961.

Booth, Wayne C. *The Rhetoric of Fiction*. 2nd edn. Chicago: University of Chicago Press, 1983.

Bornkamm, G. *Jesus of Nazareth*. Trans. I. and F. McLuskey with J.M. Robinson. New York: Harper and Row, 1960.

Borsch, F. H. *Many Things in Parables*. Philadelphia: Fortress, 1988.

Bossuyt, P., and J. Radermaker. *Jésus, Parole de la grace*. Vol. II. Bruxelles: Institut d'Études Théologiques, 1981.

Brawley, Robert L. *Luke–Acts and the Jews: Conflict, Apology, and Conciliation*. Society of Biblical Literature Monograph Series, 33. Atlanta: Scholars Press, 1987.

Brodie, T.L. 'Greco-Roman Imitation of Texts as a Partial Guide to Luke's Use of Sources'. *Luke–Acts: New Perspectives from the Society of Biblical Literature Seminar*. Ed. Charles Talbert. New York: Crossroad, 1984, 17-46.

—'Luke 7,36-50 as an Internalization of 2 Kings 4,1-37: A Study in Luke's Use of Rhetorical Imitation'. *Biblica* 67 (1983), 457-85.

—'Towards Unraveling Luke's Use of the Old Testament: Luke 7.11-17 as an Imitation of I Kings 17.17-24'. *New Testament Studies* 32 (1986), 247-67.

Broer, I. 'Das Gleichnis vom verlorenen Sohn und die Theologie des Lukas'. *New Testament Studies* 20 (1973/74), 453-62.

Brown, C., J. Eichler, E. Beyreuther and F. Selter. 'Possessions'. *New International Dictionary of New Testament Theology.* Vol. II. Ed. C. Brown. Grand Rapids: Zondervan, 1976, 829-47.
Brown, Raymond E. 'The Beatitudes according to St. Luke', *Bible Today* 1 (1965), 1176-80.
—*The Birth of the Messiah.* Garden City, NY: Doubleday, 1977.
—*The Gospel of John.* The Anchor Bible. Garden City, NY: Doubleday, 1966.
Bultmann, Rudolph. *History of the Synoptic Tradition.* New York: Harper and Row, 1963.
Burke, Kenneth. *A Grammar of Motives.* Berkeley: University of California Press, 1969.
—*Counter-Statement.* Berkeley: University of California Press, 1968.
—*Language as Symbolic Action: Essays on Life, Literature, and Method.* Berkeley: University of California Press, 1966.
Buth, R. 'Hebrew Poetic Tenses and the Magnificat', *Journal for the Study of the New Testament* 21 (1984), 67-83.
Cadbury, H.J. 'Four Features of Lukan Style'. *Studies in Luke–Acts.* Ed. L.E. Keck and J.L. Martyn. Philadelphia: Fortress, 1980, 87-102.
—*The Making of Luke–Acts.* New York: Macmillan, 1927.
—*The Style and Literary Method of Luke–Acts.* Harvard Theological Studies, 6. Cambridge, MA: Harvard University Press, 1920.
Caird, G.B. *Saint Luke.* Baltimore: Penguin Books, 1963.
Carlston, Charles E. 'Proverbs, Maxims, and the Historical Jesus'. *Journal of Biblical Literature* 99 (1980), 87-105.
—'Reminiscence and Redaction in Luke 15.11-32'. *Journal of Biblical Literature* 94 (1975), 368-90.
Carpenter, S.C. *Christianity according to St. Luke.* New York: Macmillan, 1919.
Cave, C.H. 'Lazarus and the Lukan Deuteronomy'. *New Testament Studies* 15 (1968/69), 319-25.
Charlesworth, J.H., ed. *The Old Testament Pseudepigrapha.* 2 vols. Garden City, NY: Doubleday, 1983, 1985.
Chatman, Seymour. *Story and Discourse: Narrative Structure in Fiction and Film.* Ithaca, NY: Cornell University Press, 1978.
Coen, L., H. Esser and C. Brown. 'Poor'. *The New International Dictionary of New Testament Theology.* Vol. II. Grand Rapids: Baker, 1976, 820-29.
Conzelmann, Hans. *The Theology of St. Luke.* Trans. George Buswell. New York: Harper and Row, 1961.
Cornford, Francis M. *The Origin of Attic Comedy.* Cambridge: Cambridge University Press, 1934.
Corrigan, Robert, ed. *Comedy. Meaning and Form.* 2nd edn. New York: Harper and Row, 1981.
Cosgrove, Charles H. 'The Divine ΔEI in Luke–Acts: Investigations into the Lukan Understanding of God's Providence'. *Novum Testamentum* 26 (1984), 168-90.
Creed, J.M. *The Gospel according to St. Luke.* London: Macmillan, 1957.
Crespy, G. 'The Parable of the Good Samaritan: An Essay in Structural Research'. *Semeia* 2 (1974), 27-50.

Crossan, J.D. *In Fragments: The Aphorisms of Jesus.* San Francisco: Harper and Row, 1983.

—*In Parables: The Challenge of the Historical Jesus.* New York: Harper and Row, 1973.

—*Sayings Parallels: A Workbook for the Jesus Tradition.* Philadelphia: Fortress, 1986.

—'Structuralist Analysis of the Parables of Jesus'. *Semeia* 1 (1974), 192-221.

—*The Dark Interval: Towards a Theology of Story.* Allen, TX: Argus Communications, 1975.

—'The Good Samaritan: Towards a Generic Definition of Parable'. *Semeia* 2 (1974), 82-112.

—'The Servant Parables of Jesus'. *Semeia* 1 (1974), 17-62.

Dahl, Nils. *Jesus in the Memory of the Early Church.* Minneapolis: Augsburg, 1976.

—'The Story of Abraham in Luke–Acts'. *Studies in Luke–Acts*, 139-58.

Danker, F.W. *Benefactor: an Epigraphic Study of a Graeco-Roman and New Testament Semantic Field.* St. Louis: Clayton, 1982.

—'Graeco-Roman Cultural Accommodation in the Christology of Luke–Acts'. *SBL 1983 Seminar Papers.* Ed. K.H. Richards. Chico, CA: Scholars Press, 1983, 391-414.

—*Jesus and the New Age according to St. Luke: A Commentary on the Third Gospel.* 1st edn. St. Louis: Clayton, 1972. 2nd edn. Philadelphia: Fortress, 1988.

—*Luke.* Proclamation Commentaries. 2nd edn. Philadelphia: Fortress, 1987.

Daube, D. 'Inheritance in Two Lukan Pericopes'. *Zeitschrift der Savigny-Stiftung für Rechtsgeschichte* 72 (1955), 327-38.

—'Shame Culture in Luke'. *Paul and Paulinism: Essays in Honour of C.K. Barrett.* Ed. Morna Hooker and S.G. Wilson, London: SPCK, 1982, 355-72.

Davis, C.T. 'The Literary Structure of Luke 1–2'. *Art and Meaning. Rhetoric in Biblical Literature.* Ed. D.J.A. Clines, D.M. Gunn and A.J. Hauser. Sheffield: JSOT Press 1982, 215-29.

Dawsey, James. *The Lukan Voice: Confusion and Irony in the Gospel of Luke.* Macon, GA: Mercer, 1986.

De Beaugrande, R., and W.U. Dressler. *Introduction to Text Linguistics.* New York: Longman, 1981.

Degenhart, H.J. *Lukas—Evangelist der Armen.* Stuttgart: Katholisches Bibelwerk, 1965.

Delobel, J. 'L'Onction par la pécheresse: La composition littéraire de Lc., VII, 36-50'. *Ephemerides theologicae lovanienses* 42 (1966), 414-75.

De Meeus, X. 'Composition de Lc., XIV et genre symposiaque'. *Ephemerides theologicae lovanienses* 37 (1961), 847-70.

Derrett, J.D.M. 'Fresh Light on Luke XVI. Dives and Lazarus and the Preceding Sayings'. *New Testament Studies* 7 (1960/61), 364-80.

—*Law in the New Testament.* London: Darton, Longman and Todd, 1970.

—'Law in the New Testament: The Parable of the Prodigal Son'. *New Testament Studies* 14 (1967/68), 56-74.

Dibelius, Martin. *From Tradition to Gospel.* Trans. B.T. Woolf. New York: Scribner's, 1934.

—*The Epistle of James*. Hermeneia New Testament Commentaries. Philadelphia: Fortress, 1976.

Diogenes Laertius. *Lives of Eminent Philosophers*. Trans. R.D. Hicks. Loeb Classical Library. New York: G.P. Putnam, 1925.

Dodd, C.H. *More New Testament Studies*. Grand Rapids: Eerdmans, 1968.

—*Parables of the Kingdom*. New York: K. Scribner's, 1961.

Doty, William. 'The Parables of Jesus, Kafka, Borges, and Others, with Structural Observations'. *Semeia* 2 (1974), 152-93.

Downey, G. 'Who Is My Neighbor? The Greek and the Roman Answer'. *Anglican Theological Review* 47 (1965), 3-15.

Drake, Larry. 'The Reversal Theme in Luke'. Ph.D. dissertation. St Louis University, 1985.

Drury, John. *The Parables of the Gospels*. New York: Crossroad, 1985.

—*Tradition and Design in Luke's Gospel*. Atlanta: John Knox, 1976.

Dupont, Jacques. *Les Béatitudes*. Vol. 1. Bruges: Abbaye de Saint-André, 1958. Vols. 2 and 3. Paris: J. Gabalda, 1969, 1973.

—'Die individuelle Eschatologie im Lukasevangelium und in der Apostelgeschichte'. *Orientierung an Jesus. Zur Theologie der Synoptiker*. Ed. Paul Hoffmann. Freiburg: Herder, 1973, 37-47.

—'Le Magnificat comme discours sur Dieu'. *Nouvelle Revue Théologique* 102 (1980), 321-43.

—'The Poor and Poverty in the Gospels and Acts'. *Gospel Poverty: Essays in Biblical Theology*. Chicago: Franciscan Herald Press, 1977, 25-52.

Easton, B.S. *The Gospel according to St Luke. A Critical and Exegetical Commentary*. New York: Scribner's, 1926.

Edwards, R.A. *A Theology of Q*. Philadelphia: Fortress, 1976.

Elliot, John H. 'Patronage and Clientism in Early Christian Society: A Short Reading Guide'. *Forum* 3/4 (1987), 39-48.

Ellis, Earle E. *Eschatology in Luke*. Facet Books. Philadelphia: Fortress, 1972.

—*The Gospel of Luke*. Rev. edn. New Century Bible Commentary. Grand Rapids: Eerdmans, 1981.

Ernst, J. *Das Evangelium nach Lukas*. Regensburg: Friedrich Pustet, 1976.

—'Gastmahlgespräche Lk 14,1-24'. *Die Kirche des Anfangs*. Ed. R. Schnackenburg, J. Ernst and J. Wanke. Freiburg: Herder, 1978, 57-78.

Esler, Philip. *Community and Gospel in Luke–Acts: The Social and Political Motivations of Lucan Theology*. Society for New Testament Studies Monograph, 57. Cambridge: Cambridge University Press, 1987.

Farris, Stephen. *The Hymns of Luke's Infancy Narratives: Their Origin, Meaning and Significance*. Sheffield: JSOT Press, 1985.

Ferguson, Everett. *Backgrounds of Early Christianity*. Grand Rapids: Eerdmans, 1987.

Feuillet, A. 'La Parabole du mauvais riche et du pauvre Lazare'. *La nouvelle revue théologique* 101 (1979), 212-23.

Finkel, A. *The Pharisees and the Teacher of Nazareth*. Leiden: Brill, 1964.

Fitzmyer, Joseph. *The Gospel according to Luke*. The Anchor Bible 28, 28A. Garden City, NY: Doubleday, 1982, 1985.

Flender, H. *St Luke, Theologian of Redemptive History*. London: SPCK, 1967.

Flusser, David. 'Blessed Are the Poor in Spirit'. *Israel Exploration Journal* 10 (1960), 1-10.
—'Some Notes to the Beatitudes (Matthew 5.3-12; Luke 6.20-26)'. *Immanuel* 8 (1978), 37-47.
Fokkelman, J.P. 'Stylistic Analysis of Isaiah 40.1-11'. *Oudtestamentische Studiën* 21 (1981), 68-90.
Ford, J. M. *My Enemy is My Guest*. Maryknoll, NY: Orbis, 1984.
Franklin, E. *Christ the Lord: A Study in the Purpose and Theology of Luke–Acts*. Philadelphia: Westminster, 1975.
Frankemölle, H. 'Die Makarismen (Mt 5,1-12; Lk 6,20-23). Motiv und Umfang der redaktionellen Komposition'. *Biblische Zeitschrift* 15 (1971), 52-75.
Funk, Robert W. *New Gospel Parallels*. 2 vols. Philadelphia: Fortress, 1985.
—*Language, Hermeneutics, and the Word of God*. New York: Harper and Row, 1966.
—*Parables and Presence: Forms of the New Testament Tradition*. Philadelphia: Fortress, 1982.
—'Structure in the Narative Parables of Jesus'. *Semeia* 2 (1974), 51-73.
—'The Good Samaritan as Metaphor'. *Semeia* 2 (1974), 74-81.
George, A. *Études sur l'oeuvre de Luc*. Paris: Gabalda, 1978.
Giblin, C.H. 'Structural and Theological Considerations on Luke 15'. *Catholic Biblical Quarterly* 24 (1962), 15-31.
Gilmore, David D., ed. *Honor and Shame and the Unity of the Mediterranean*. Special Publication of the American Anthropological Association, 22. Washington, DC: American Anthropological Association, 1987.
Glombitza, O. 'Das grosse Abendmahl Lukas 14.12-24'. *Novum Testamentum* 11 (1969), 10-16.
—'Der reiche Mann und der arme Lazarus Luk. xvi 19-31'. *Novum Testamentum* 12 (1970), 166-180.
Godet, F. *A Commentary on the Gospel of St Luke*. Trans. E.W. Shalders and M.D. Cusin. New York: I.K. Funk, 1881.
Goldberg, S.M. *The Making of Menander's Comedy*. Berkeley: University of California Press, 1980.
Goulder, M.D., and M.A. Sanders. 'St. Luke's Genesis'. *Journal of Theology Studies* 8 (1957), 12-30.
Gowler, David B. 'Characterization in Luke: A Socio-Narratological Approach'. *Biblical Theological Bulletin* 19 (1989), 54-62.
Grobel, K. '... Whose Name was Neves'. *New Testament Studies* 10 (1963/64), 373-82.
Grundmann, W. *Das Evangelium nach Lukas*. Berlin: Evangelische Verlagsanstalt, 1963.
Gryglewicz, F. 'Die Herkunft der Hymnen des Kindheitsevangeliums des Lukas'. *New Testament Studies* 21 (1975), 265-73.
Guelich, Robert. 'The Matthean Beatitudes: "Entrance Requirements" or Eschatological Blessing?' *Journal of Biblical Literature* 95 (1976), 415-34.
—*The Sermon on the Mount*. Waco: Word Books, 1982.
Hamel, Edouard. 'Le Magnificat et le renversement des situations'. *Gregorianum* 60 (1979), 55-84.

Hanson, Paul D. *The Dawn of Apocalyptic*. Philadelphia: Fortress, 1979.

Herodotus. *The History*. Trans. David Grene. Chicago: University of Chicago Press, 1987.

Hesiod. *The Homeric Hymns and Homerica*. Trans. H.G. Evelyn-White. Loeb Classical Library. Cambridge, MA: Harvard University Press, 1943.

Hesla, David H. 'Greek and Christian Tragedy: Notes Toward a Theology of Literary History'. *Art / Literature / Religion / Life on the Borders*. Ed. Robert Detweiler. Journal of American Academy of Religion Thematic Studies, 49/2. Chico, CA: Scholars Press, 1983, 71-87.

Hill, D. 'The Rejection of Jesus at Nazareth (Lk. 4.16-30)'. *Novum Testamentum* 13 (1971), 161-80.

Hillyer, N. 'Woe'. *New International Dictionary of New Testament Theology*. Vol. 3. Ed. C. Brown. Grand Rapids: Zondervan, 1978, 1051-54.

Hock, Ronald R. 'Lazarus and Micyllus, Greco-Roman Backgrounds to Luke 19.19-31'. *Journal of Biblical Literature* 106 (1987), 447-63.

Horn, R. *Glaube und Handeln in der Theologie des Lukas*. Göttingen: Vandenhoeck und Ruprecht, 1983.

Houlden, J.L. 'The Purpose of Luke'. *Journal for the Study of the New Testament* 21 (1984), 53-65.

Hoyt, Thomas. 'The Poor in Luke–Acts'. Ph.D. dissertation, Duke University, 1975.

Janzen, W. *Mourning Cry and Woe Oracle*. Berlin: Walter de Gruyter, 1972.

Jeremias, J. *Die Sprache des Lukasevangeliums*. Göttingen: Vandenhoeck und Ruprecht, 1980.

—*Jerusalem in the Time of Jesus*. Philadelphia: Fortress, 1969.

—*New Testament Theology*. New York: Scribner's, 1971.

—*The Parables of Jesus*. New York: Scribner's, 1963.

—*The Sermon on the Mount*. Facet Books. Philadelphia: Fortress, 1963.

—'Tradition und Redaction in Lukas 15'. *Zeitschrift für die neutestamentliche Wissenschaft* 62 (1971), 172-89.

Jervell, J. *Luke and the People of God: A New Look at Luke–Acts*. Minneapolis: Augsburg, 1972.

Johnson, Luke T. *Luke–Acts: A Story of Prophet and People*. Chicago: Franciscan Herald Press, 1981.

—*The Literary Function of Possessions in Luke–Acts*. SBL Dissertation Series, 39. Missoula, MT: Scholars Press, 1977.

Jones, Douglas. 'The Background and Character of the Lukan Psalms'. *Journal of Theological Studies* n.s. 19 (1968), 19-50.

Juel, Donald. *Luke–Acts: The Promise of History*. Atlanta: John Knox, 1983.

Jülicher, A., *Die Gleichnisreden Jesu*. Tübingen: Mohr, 1910.

Karris, R.J. 'Poor and Rich: The Lukan Sitz im Leben'. *Perspectives on Luke–Acts*. Ed. Charles Talbert. Danville, PA: Association of Baptist Professors of Religion, 1978.

Käsemann, Ernst. *New Testament Questions of Today*. Trans. W.J. Montague and W.F. Bunge. Philadelphia: Fortress, 1969.

Keck, Leander E. 'Jesus' Entrance upon his Mission'. *Review and Expositor* 64 (1967), 465-83.

—'The Poor among the Saints in the New Testament'. *Zeitschrift für die neutestamentliche Wissenschaft* 56 (1965), 100-29.

Kennedy, George. *New Testament Interpretation through Rhetorical Criticism*. Chapel Hill, NC: University of North Carolina Press, 1984.

Kijanto, Iiro. 'Fortuna'. *Aufstieg und Niedergang der römischen Welt*, 17.1 Ed. Wolfgang Haase. New York: Walter de Gruyter, 1981, 502-58.

Kistemaker, S.J. 'The Structure of Luke's Gospel'. *Journal of the Evangelical Theological Society* 25 (1982), 33-39.

Kittel, G., G. Friedrich and R. Pitkin, eds. *Theological Dictionary of the New Testament*. 10 vols. Trans. G.W. Bromiley. Grand Rapids: Eerdmans, 1964-76.

S.v. 'δικαιόω', by G. Schrenk.
S.v. 'κάμηλος', by O. Michel.
S.v. 'κόλπος', by R. Meyer.
S.v. 'μακάριος', by F. Hauck and G. Bertram.
S.v. 'μετανοέω', by J. Behm.
S.v. 'ὁ υἱὸς τοῦ ἀνθρώπου', by C. Colpe.
S.v. 'ὀλίγος', by H. Seesemann.
S.v. 'παραιτέομαι', by G. Stählin.
S.v. 'πλοῦτος', by F. Hauck and W. Kasch.
S.v. 'πτωχός', by E. Bammel.
S.v. 'σώζω', by E. Schweizer and G. Fohrer.
S.v. 'ταπεινόω', by W. Grundmann.
S.v. 'τύπτω', by G. Stählin.
S.v. 'ὑπερήφανος', by G. Bertram.
S.v. 'ὕψος', by G. Bertram.

Klein, P. 'Die lukanischen Weherufe Lk 6.24-26'. *Zeitschrift für die neutestamentliche Wissenschaft* 71 (1980), 150-59.

Klostermann, E. *Das Lukasevangelium*. Tübingen: Mohr, 1929.

Koch, K. *The Growth of the Biblical Tradition*. Trans. S.M. Cupitt. New York: Scribner's, 1969.

Kodell, J. 'Luke's Gospel in a Nutshell (Lk 4.16-30)'. *Biblical Theology Bulletin* 13 (1983), 16-18.

Kraybill, Donald B. 'Possessions in Luke–Acts: A Sociological Perspective'. *Perspectives in Religious Studies* 10 (1983), 215-39.

Lagrange, M.-J. *Evangile selon Saint Luc*. Paris: J. Gabalda, 1948.

Lambrecht, J. *Once More Astonished*. New York: Crossroad, 1981.

Lattimore, R., trans. *Euripides III: Four Tragedies*. Chicago: University of Chicago Press, 1958.

Laurentin, Réne. *Stucture et Théologie de Luc I–II*. Paris: J. Gabalda, 1957.

—'Traces d'allusions étymologiques in Luc 1–2 (I)'. *Biblica* 37 (1956), 435-56.

—'Traces d'allusions étymologiques in Luc 1–2 (II)'. *Biblica* 38 (1957) 1-23.

LaVerdiere, E. *Luke*. Wilmington, DE: Michael Glazier, 1980.

Leivestad, R. 'ΤΑΠΕΙΝΟΣ—ΤΑΠΕΙΝΟΦΡΩΝ'. *Novum Testamentum* 8 (1966), 36-47.

Lever, Katherine. *The Art of Greek Comedy*. London: Methuen, 1956.

Linnemann, E. *Parables of Jesus*. London: SPCK, 1966.

Linton, O. 'Coordinated Sayings and Parables in the Synoptic Gospels: Analysis versus Theories'. *New Testament Studies* 26 (1980), 139-63.
Louw, J. 'A Semiotic Approach to Discourse Analysis with Reference to Translation Theory'. *The Bible Translator* 36 (1985), 101-107.
Lucas, F.L. 'The Reversal of Aristotle'. *Classical Review* 37 (1923), 98-104.
Mack, Burton L., and Vernon K. Robbins. *Patterns of Persuasion in the Gospels*. Sonoma, CA: Polebridge, 1989.
Macmullen, Ramsay. *Roman Social Relations: 50 B.C. to A.D. 284*. New Haven: Yale University Press, 1974.
Maddox, R. 'The Function of the Son of Man according to the Synoptic Gospels'. *New Testament Studies* 15 (1968/69), 45-74.
—*The Purpose of Luke–Acts*. Göttingen: Vandenhoeck und Ruprecht, 1982.
Malina, Bruce J. 'Interpreting the Bible with Anthropology: The Case of the Rich and Poor'. *Listening* 21 (1986), 148-59.
—*The New Testament World: Insights from Cultural Anthropology*. Atlanta: John Knox, 1981.
—'Wealth and Poverty in the New Testament and Its World'. *Interpretation* 41 (1987), 354-67.
Marshall, I.H. *The Gospel of Luke: A Commentary on the Greek Text*. New International Greek Commentary. Grand Rapids: Eerdmans, 1978.
—*Luke: Historian and Theologian*. Grand Rapids: Eerdmans, 1971.
Manson, T.W. *The Sayings of Jesus*. London: SCM, 1957.
Martin, Luther. *Hellenistic Religions: An Introduction*. New York: Oxford University Press, 1987.
—'The Rule of Tyche and Hellenistic Religion'. *SBL 1976 Seminar Papers*. Ed. George MacRae. Missoula, MT: Scholars Press, 1976, 453-59.
Mattill, A.J. *Luke and the Last Things: A Perspective for the Understanding of Lukan Thought*. Dillsboro, NC: Western North Carolina Press, 1979.
Meaders, Gary T. 'The "Poor" in the Beatitudes of Matthew and Luke'. *Grace Theological Journal* 6 (1985), 305-14.
Meynet, R. *Quelle est donc cette Parole?* Paris: Cerf, 1979.
Minear, Paul. 'Luke's Use of the Birth Stories'. *Studies in Luke–Acts*, 111-30.
—'The Needle's Eye: A Study in Form Criticism'. *Journal of Biblical Literature* 61 (1942), 157-69.
—*To Heal and To Reveal: The Prophetic Vocation according to Luke*. New York: Seabury, 1976.
Morris, Leon. *Gospel according to St. Luke*. Grand Rapids: Eerdmans, 1974.
Moulton, J.H., and G. Milligan. *The Vocabulary of the Greek New Testament Illustrated from the Papyri and Other Non-Literary Sources*. Grand Rapids: Eerdmans, 1930.
Moulton, J.R., W.F. Howard and N. Turner. *Grammar of New Testament Greek*. 4 vols. Edinburgh: T. & T. Clark, 1963, 1976.
Moulton, W.F., A.S. Geden and H.K. Moulton. *Concordance to the Greek New Testament*. 5th edn. Edinburgh: T. & T. Clark, 1978.
Moxnes, Halvor. *The Economy of the Kingdom: Social Conflict and Economic Relations in Luke's Gospel*. Philadelphia: Fortress, 1988.
Murray, G. *Five Stages of Religion*. New York: Columbia University Press, 1925.

Navone, J. *Themes of St Luke*. Rome: Gregorian University Press, 1970.

Nickelsburg, G.W.E. 'Riches, the Rich and God's Judgment in I Enoch 92–105 and the Gospel According to Luke'. *New Testament Studies* 25 (1978), 325-44.

—'The Apocalyptic Message of I Enoch 92–105'. *Catholic Biblical Quarterly* 39 (1977), 309-28.

Nilsson, M.P. *Geschichte der Griechischen Religion*. Vol. 2. Munich: C.H. Beck', 1961.

Noel, T. M. 'Parables in Context: Developing a Narrative-Critical Approach to Parables in Luke'. Ph.D. dissertation. The Southern Baptist Seminary, 1986.

Oakman, Douglas E. 'The Buying Power of Two Denarii: A Commentary on Luke 10:35'. *Forum* 3/4 (1987), 33-38.

O'Hanlon, 'The Story of Zacchaeus and the Lukan Ethic'. *Journal for the Study of the New Testament* 12 (1981), 2-26.

Oliver, H.H. 'The Lucan Birth Stories and the Purpose of Luke–Acts'. *New Testament Studies* (1963/64), 202-36.

O'Rourke, J.J. 'Some Notes on Luke xv. 11-32'. *New Testament Studies* 18 (1971/72), 431-33.

O'Toole, R.F. 'Luke's Position on Politics and Society in Luke–Acts'. *Political Issues in Luke–Acts*. Ed. R.J. Cassidy and P.J. Scharper. Maryknoll, NY: Orbis, 1983, 1-17.

—*The Unity of Luke's Theology*. Wilmington, DE: Michael Glazier, 1984.

Pax, E. 'Der Reiche und der arme Lazarus: Eine Milieustudie'. *Studii biblici franciscani liber annuus* 25 (1975), 254-68.

Percy, E. *Die Botschaft Jesus*. Lund: Gleerup, 1953.

Perdue, Leo G. 'Wisdom Sayings of Jesus'. *Forum* 2 (1986), 3-35.

—and John Gammie. 'Paraenesis: Act and Form'. *Semeia* 50 (1990).

Perkins, Pheme. *Hearing the Parables of Jesus*. Ramsay, NY: Paulist, 1981.

Perpich, Sandra Wachman. *A Hermeneutic Critique of Structuralist Exegesis, with Specific Reference to Lk 10.29-37*. Lanham, MD: University Press of America, 1984.

Perrin, Norman. *Jesus and the Language of the Kingdom: Symbol and Metaphor in New Testament Interpretation*. Philadelphia: Fortress, 1974.

—*Rediscovering the Teaching of Jesus*. New York: Harper and Row, 1976.

Pilgrim, Walter. *Good News to the Poor: Wealth and Poverty in Luke–Acts*. Minneapolis: Augsburg, 1981.

Pliny. *Natural History*. Trans. H. Rackham. Loeb Classical Library. Cambridge, MA: Harvard University Press, 1938.

Plummer, Alfred. *The Gospel According to St Luke*. New York: Scribner's, 1902.

Plutarch. *Moralia*. Vol. II. Trans. F.C. Babbitt. Loeb Classical Library. New York: G.P. Putnam, 1928.

Polybius. *The Histories*. Vol. I. Trans. W.R. Paton. Loeb Classical Library. Cambridge, MA: Harvard University Press, 1921.

Price, J. 'Luke 15.11-32'. *Interpretation* 31 (1977), 64-69.

Ravens, D.A.S. 'The Setting of Luke's Account of the Anointing: Luke 7.2–8.3'. *New Testament Studies* 34 (1988), 282-92.

Rengstorf, K.H. *Die Re-Investiture des verlorenen Sohnes in der Gleichniserzählung Jesu: Luk. 15,11-32*. Köln: Westdeutscher Verlag, 1967.
Resseguie, James. 'Point of View in the Central Section of Luke (9.51–19.44)'. *Journal of the Evangelical Theological Society* 25 (1982), 41-47.
Richard, E. 'Luke—Writer, Theologian, Historian: Research and Orientation of the 1970's'. *Biblical Theology Bulletin* 13 (1983), 2-15.
Ricoeur, Paul. 'Biblical Hermeneutics'. *Semeia* 5 (1975), 29-148.
Robbins, Vernon K. *Ancient Quotes & Anecdotes: From Crib to Crypt*. Sonoma, CA: Polebridge, 1989.
—*Jesus the Teacher: A Social-Rhetorical Interpretation of Mark*. Philadelphia: Fortress, 1984.
—'Picking Up the Fragments: From Crossan's Analysis to Rhetorical Analysis'. *Forum* 1/2 (1985), 31-64.
—'Pragmatic Relations as a Criterion for Authentic Sayings'. *Forum* 1/3 (1985), 31-64.
—'Pronouncement Stories and Jesus' Blessing of the Children: A Rhetorical Approach'. *Semeia* 29 (1983), 43-74.
—'Summons and Outline to Mark: The Three Step Progression'. *Novum Testamentum* 23 (1981), 97-114.
—'The Woman who Touched Jesus' Garment: Socio-Rhetorical Analysis of the Synoptic Accounts'. *New Testament Studies* 33 (1987), 502-15.
Sanders, J.A. 'Isaiah in Luke'. *Interpretation* 38 (1982), 144-56.
—'Luke's Great Banquet Parable'. *Essays in Old Testament Ethics*. Festschrift for J. Philip Hyatt. Ed. J.L. Crenshaw and J.T. Willis. New York: KTAV, 1974, 247-71.
Sanders, J.T. *The Jews in Luke–Acts*. Philadelphia: Fortress, 1987.
—'The Pharisees in Luke–Acts'. *The Living Text: Essays in Honor of Ernest W. Saunders*. Ed. Dennis E. Groh and Robert Jewett. Lanham, MD: University Press of America, 1985, 141-88.
—'The Salvation of the Jews in Luke–Acts'. *Luke–Acts: New Perspectives from the Society of Biblical Literature Seminar*, 104-28.
—'Tradition and Redaction in Luke xv. 11-32'. *New Testament Studies* 15 (1968/69), 433-38.
Schmidt, P. 'Maria und das Magnificat Marias im Heilshandeln Gottes im alten and neuen Gottesvolk'. *Catholica* 29 (1975), 230-46.
Schnackenburg, R. 'Das Magnificat, seine Spiritualität und Theologie'. *Geist und Leben* 38 (1965), 342-57.
Schneider, G. *Das Evangelium nach Lukas*. 2 vols. Gütersloh: Mohn, 1977.
Schnider, F., and W. Stenger. 'Die offene Tür und die unüberschreitbare Kluft'. *New Testament Studies* 25 (1978/79), 273-83.
Schoonheim, P.L. 'Der alttestamentliche Boden der Vokabel ὑπερήφανος Luke I,51'. *Novum Testamentum* 8 (1966), 235-46.
Schottroff, Luise. 'Das Gleichnis vom verlorenen Sohn'. *Zeitschrift für Theologie und Kirche* 68 (1971), 27-52.
—'Das Magnificat und die älteste Tradition über Jesus von Nazareth'. *Evangelische Theologie* 38 (1978), 298-313.

The Last Shall Be First

—and Wolfgang Stegemann. *Jesus von Nazareth: Hoffnung der Armen*. Stuttgart: Kohlhammer, 1978.

Schürmann, H. *Das Lukasevangelium, Erster Teil, Kommentar zu Kap 1,1–9,50*. Freiburg: Herder, 1969.

—*Traditionsgeschichtliche Untersuchungen zu den synoptischen Evangelien*. Düsseldorf: Patmos, 1968.

Schweizer, Eduard. 'Formgeschichtliches zu den Seligpreisungen Jesu'. *New Testament Studies* 19 (1970/71), 121-26.

—*Luke: A Challenge to Present Theology*. Atlanta: John Knox, 1982.

—*The Good News according to Luke*. Trans. David Green. Atlanta: John Knox, 1984.

Scott, Bernard B. *Jesus, Symbol-Maker for the Kingdom*. Philadelphia: Fortress, 1981.

Seccombe, David. *Possessions and the Poor in Luke–Acts*. Studien zum Neuen Testament und seiner Umwelt. Linz: Fuchs, 1972.

Sloan, R.B. *The Favorable Year of the Lord*. Austin, TX: Schola, 1977.

Smith, Dennis. 'Table Fellowship as a Literary Motif in the Gospel of Luke'. *Journal of Biblical Literature* 106 (1987), 613-38.

Steele, E. Springs. 'Jesus' Table-Fellowship with Pharisees: An Editorial Analysis of Luke 7:36-50, 11:37-54, 14:1-24'. Ph.D. dissertation. Notre Dame, 1981.

—'Luke 11:37-54—A Modified Hellenistic Symposium?' *Journal of Biblical Literature* 103 (1984), 379-94.

Strack, H.L., and P. Billerbeck. *Kommentar zum Neuen Testament aus Talmud und Midrasch*. 6 vols. Munich: C.H. Beck, 1924.

Strecker, G. 'Die Makarismen der Bergpredigt'. *New Testament Studies* 17 (1970/71), 255-75.

Talbert, Charles H. *Literary Patterns, Theological Themes and the Genre of Luke–Acts*. Missoula, MT: Scholars Press, 1974.

—'Promise and Fulfillment in Lucan Theology'. *Luke–Acts: New Perspectives from the Society of Biblical Literature Seminar*, 91-103.

—*Reading Luke: A Literary and Theological Commentary on the Third Gospel*. New York: Crossroad, 1982.

—'Shifting Sands: The Recent Study of the Gospel of Luke'. *Interpretation* 30 (1976), 381-95.

—'The Redaction Critical Quest for Luke the Theologian'. *Jesus and Man's Hope*. Ed. David G. Buttrick Vol. 1. Pittsburgh: Pittsburgh Theological Seminary, 1970, 171-222.

Tam, D.S. 'The Literary and Theological Unity between Lk 1–2 and Lk 3–Acts 28'. Ph.D. dissertation. Duke University, 1978.

Tannehill, Robert C. 'Attitudinal Shift in Synoptic Pronouncement Stories'. *Orientation by Disorientation: Studies in Literary Criticism Presented in Honor of William A. Beardslee*. Ed. R.A. Spencer. Pittsburgh: Pickwick, 1980, 183-97.

—'Introduction: The Pronouncement Story and Its Types'. *Semeia* 20 (1981), 1-13.

—'Israel in Luke-Acts: A Tragic Story'. *Journal of Biblical Literature* 104 (1985), 69-85.

—'Synoptic Pronouncement Stories: Form and Function'. *SBL 1980 Seminar Papers*. Ed. P. Achtemeier. Chico, CA: Scholars Press, 51-57.

—'The Magnificat as Poem'. *Journal of Biblical Literature* 93 (1974), 263-75.

—'The Mission of Jesus according to Luke iv 16-30'. *Jesus in Nazareth*. Ed. Walther Eltester. Berlin: Walter de Gruyter, 1972, 51-75.

—*The Narrative Unity of Luke–Acts: A Literary Interpretation*. Vol. 1. *The Gospel according to Luke*. Philadelphia: Fortress, 1986.

—*The Sword of His Mouth*. Missoula, MT: Scholars Press, 1975.

—'Varieties of Synoptic Pronouncement Stories'. *Semeia* 20 (1981), 101-19.

Tatum, W.B. 'The Epoch of Israel: Luke I–II and the Theological Plan of Luke–Acts'. *New Testament Studies* 13 (1966/67), 184-95.

Theissen, G. *Sociology of Early Palestinian Christianity*. Trans. John Bowden. Philadelphia: Fortress, 1978.

—*The Miracle Stories of the Early Christian Tradition*. Philadelphia: Fortress, 1983.

Tiede, David. *Prophecy and History in Luke–Acts*. Philadelphia: Fortress, 1980.

Tolbert, M.A. *Perspectives on the Parables: An Approach to Multiple Interpretations*. Philadelphia: Fortress, 1979.

Toynbee, Arnold. *A Study of History*. Vol. IV. London: Oxford University Press, 1939.

Tuckett, C.M. 'Luke 4,16-30, Isaiah and Q'. *Logia: The Sayings of Jesus*. Ed. J. Delobel. Leuven: Leuven University Press, 1982, 343-54.

Via, Dan O. *Kerygma and Comedy in the New Testament*. Philadelphia: Fortress, 1971.

—*The Parables: Their Literary and Existential Dimension*. Philadelphia: Fortress, 1967.

Vogels, W. 'Le Magnificat, Marie et Israël'. *Église et Théologie* 6 (1975), 279-96.

Wilder, Amos. *Early Christian Rhetoric: The Language of the Gospel*. 2nd edn. Cambridge, MA: Harvard University Press, 1971.

—'The Parable of the Sower: Naivete and Method'. *Semeia* 2 (1974), 134-51.

Williams, James G. *Those Who Ponder Proverbs: Aphoristic Thinking and Biblical Literature*. Sheffield: Almond, 1981.

Wilson, S.G. 'Lukan Eschatology'. *New Testament Studies* 16 (1969/70), 330-47.

Wimsatt, W.K., and C. Brooks. *Literary Criticism*. New York: Vintage Books, 1957.

Winandy, J. 'La Prophétie de Syméon (Lc, ii,34-35)'. *Revue biblique* 72 (1965), 321-51.

Winter, Paul. 'Magnificat and Benedictus—Maccabaean Psalms?' *Bulletin of the John Rylands Library* 37 (1954), 328-47.

—'The Main Literary Problem of the Lucan Infancy Story'. *Anglican Theological Review* 40 (1958), 257-66.

Wrege, H.-T. *Die Überlieferungsgeschichte der Bergpredigt*. Tübingen: Mohr, 1968.

Xenophon. *Hellenica, Books VI & VII; Anabasis, Books I-III*. Trans. C.L. Brownson. Loeb Classical Library. New York: G.P. Putnam, 1932.

Yoder, J.H. *The Politics of Jesus*. Grand Rapids: Eerdmans, 1972.

Zerwick, M. *Biblical Greek*. Rome: Pontifical Biblical Institute, 1963.

Ziesler, 'Luke and the Pharisees'. *New Testament Studies* 25 (1979), 146-57.

Zmijewski, J. *Die Eschatologiereden des Lukas-Evangeliums*. Bonn: Peter Hanstein, 1972.

INDEXES

INDEX OF BIBLICAL REFERENCES

OLD TESTAMENT

JOURNAL FOR THE STUDY OF THE NEW TESTAMENT

Supplement Series

DATE DUE